HOLY HUMANITY

HOLY HUMANITY
We Are All Made of God Stuff

by James L. Foster

iv

Published in the United States by
James L. Foster
Institutes for Christian Spirituality,
204 Busbee Road, Knoxville, Tennessee 37920
www.christianspirituality.org

First printing, 2014

Ordering Information:
For Print editions contact Create Space, www.CreateSpace.com
For E-book or print editions, contact, www.Amazon.com

For details, contact the publisher at the address above.

Library of Congress Cataloging-in-Publications Data

Foster, James L.
Holy Humanity: We Are All Made of God Stuff
James L. Foster.
2013
Includes bibliography and indices.
ISBN: 13-978-1493626335
ISBN: 10-1493626337
LCCN: 2013922940
1. Religion and science. 2. Spirituality 3. Theology

First Edition: January 2014

CREDITS

Editor, **FairWeather Editors**
Oak Ridge, Tennessee

Cover designer and technical advisor, Ralph Hubbard
Computer Solutions of Tennessee
Clinton, Tennessee

Print-on-demand distributor
Create Space

E-book distributor
Amazon

The cover art is the hands portion of Michelangelo's "Creation of Adam" painting on the ceiling of the Sistine Chapel in Rome. This image of the painting was provided courtesy of the online http://www.michelangelo-gallery.org/.

This book is dedicated to Sandy, my wife and spiritual companion for almost 60 years.
It is she who taught me Agápe love.

HOLY HUMANITY
CONTENTS

ADDENDA

God
Creator of worlds, Designer of universes,
Artist of nature, and cosmic Potter!
Great Spirit of evolution, Nurturer of the seeds of Life
Sharer of visions and sacred Inspirer!

Humankind
Eternal, transcendent, luminous and living!
Purveyors of truth and Bringers of hope!
Benefactors of earth and willing partners
In union with God and with one another.

God's Spirit
Beyond us, within us and as us,
Filling us with Life and Love and Light!
Embodied Presence, divine Lovers
Making lives sacred, souls full and infinite!

James L. Foster

PREFACE

This is a book I am compelled to write even though I confess to being somewhat intimidated by the subject. I was already working on two other books—a new one on the Apostle Paul and a rewrite of an earlier manuscript on *Agápe* Love. Whatever you choose to call it—serendipity or the Spirit's leading—I used the phrase "holy humanity" in a conversation with a friend, who then challenged me to write a book on the subject. It has not been the struggle I expected. Even the "bottom line" phrase with which I start—"We are all made of God stuff"—came to me in a flash. From then on the text has flowed relatively seamlessly in what seems to be a sort of subliminal stream of consciousness. My *modus operandi* has been to immerse myself first in weeks-long study and reflection on whatever aspect of the "God stuff" is coming up next, and then I write without notes or detailed outline about that particular aspect until I have said all I have to say. Lastly, I go back to my source materials and insert supportive or clarifying material into my text from other authors who have addressed the same particular issue I am writing about at the time. Years from now, I will probably find myself rewriting or wanting to rewrite portions of the book. In the meantime, it has been an exciting journey in the creation of what I hope will be an instrument for helping to rescue a Church that I believe has lost its way.

Personal Awakening

"Holy humanity"—just so you can have a feel for where I have been and what has brought me to this time and place in which I believe I might have something to say on "holy humanity," I would like to share with you some of my personal spiritual journey. When I was sixteen, I became a Christian in a community spring revival in my hometown. I was a junior in high school and though I had participated in a main line denominational church throughout my childhood, I had zero interest in spiritual matters. That changed dramatically at that first-time meeting with God in Christ. I was apparently a quick under-study and within two or three weeks was sharing my story extemporaneously in school assemblies and on local radio. I learned very early that I could depend on the Holy Spirit to supply the words I needed (when I needed them, and not before). I suspect my audiences were as mystified as I was, especially since they knew me well in my small hometown and correspondingly small high school. They knew, however, that they had *never* known the young man who was speaking to them now.

I left for college in the fall of 1954 to begin a five year course of study in architecture. There, in addition to my studies; I continued teaching Bible Study groups, students and adults, all the time knowing that I often knew less than they did. However it happened, they were fed by my (the Spirit's?) teaching and I continued to get more invitations to teach than I could accommodate. I left my architectural studies after that first term with plans to study for ministry.

Moving on—through college and two seminaries and a student pastorate, I learned to think critically and to appreciate the writings of both modern theologians and ancient mystics. I also received a good working knowledge of *Koine* Greek, the common Greek of the first and second centuries (also known as "biblical" Greek as it was the language of the New Testament writers). If I had had the financial resources to do so, I would have pursued a doctorate in theology. Academia for me was heaven on earth.

From Academia to Real Life

Following a student pastorate in a small Kansas town and a brief sojourn as a district executive with the Boy Scouts of America, I received a call to be an associate pastor in a large Southern Baptist Church in Virginia. Somewhere along the way, my halo had apparently fallen off. After four years of ministry in this church, nothing was happening. Nobody that I had ministered to was any better off because of my ministry. Going into my fifth year as an associate pastor, I was ready to give it up, counting myself a failure in ministry. I had begun to explore other possible vocations, when, staying up late one evening, aimlessly flipping through my Bible, I came upon a passage in Paul's Letter to the Galatians. I read, "The Spirit produces love, joy, peace, patience, kindness, generosity, faithfulness, gentleness, and self-control." (Galatians 5:22) I dropped the Bible in my lap and in a prayer of despair cried "Lord, the Spirit has not produced any of these qualities in my life! I'm losing ground, not gaining. I have less love, not more; no joy or peace, little patience..." I then flipped back in my Bible to the gospels and my eyes alit on *Luke 11, verses 11 and 12:*[1] "If a son shall ask bread of any of you who is a father, will he give him a stone? Or, if he asks for a fish, will he for a fish give him a serpent? Or if he shall ask for an egg, will he offer him a scorpion? If you then, being evil know how to give good gifts to your children, how much more shall the heavenly Father give the Holy Spirit to them who ask him?" (KJV) I prayed again, "Lord, if this is where I've missed the boat the last 20 years, then I'm asking you for your Spirit right now." There was no thunder or lightning, but an incredible peace settled upon me such as I had never known. And I began to pray again, this time in tongues. Even though I did not believe in speaking in tongues, I somehow knew it was right, and more, a gift from God. And, yes, my first prayer was answered, too, as the Spirit began to fill me with the love and joy and peace I longed for. That was a Saturday evening.

The fireworks held off until the next day when I filled in for the absent teacher of the 9th grade girls' Sunday school class. I did not teach the prescribed lesson, and I never remembered what I did say, but whatever it was turned the lives of a dozen junior high girls upside down. By the next Sunday, the Spirit, like a flame, had spread to the entire junior high department—about 90 young people—and by the next Sunday had spread to virtually the whole 1,500 member

1 On this occasion years ago, I was probably reading the Revised Standard Version of the Bible—the RSV. It translated the Greek term *porneros* with the English word "evil." That was the favored translation of that day, though biblical scholars of this era may well choose another term such as "derelict" or "sinners." At that particular time, I was not focused on the nuances of language and translation but rather on the derelict state of my ministry.

church. Thus began a spontaneous, totally unprogrammed, four-month charismatic revival in this formerly staid and proper Southern Baptist church. First Baptist had been resurrected by the Spirit of God. I resigned my Associate Pastor position seven months later to begin, with my wife, Sandy, and our three children, a thirteen year counseling and retreat ministry in the Blue Ridge Mountains of Virginia. Years later—in 1985—I had more seminary under my belt and a Masters degree in Christology. But infinitely more important, I had a new spiritual orientation which was to change the way I approached everything I did in the years to come. I would in time realize that in my surrender to the Spirit of God, on that fateful Saturday evening years before, I had crossed the line from what had become a knowledge based faith to an experientially based faith where experience sits in judgment of rationality. (See discussion of *The Three Fold Path* in chapter two, "The Mystical Experience.") Subsequent experiences, some knowledge based, others experiential, have only deepened the conviction that we are each one called to walk a path in which "angels fear to tread," a sometimes perilous path leading inevitably to continuing evolutionary change.

A New Orientation

When I began my studies in Christology, there were two questions I wanted to address: First, who, really, is Jesus Christ? That question I hoped to address academically. And second, who am I? I reasoned that if I was ever to have a really close relationship with Jesus, I needed to know both parties in the relationship. The second question I planned to take on as a personal quest parallel to my academic study. In my Masters thesis I addressed both questions by undertaking an exhaustive study of one phrase in the Apostle Paul's Letter to the Philippians "Let this mind be in you, which was also in Christ Jesus." (2:5 KJV) One hundred twenty pages later I was beginning to get an inkling of the answers to both my questions. Though I had not consciously formulated the phrase "holy humanity" prior to my conversation with my friend in 2011, I have no doubt that the seed for it was planted years before in my exposition of Philippians 2:5.

xviii

Continuing the Journey in Community

I have not written *Holy Humanity* alone. My wife, Sandy, a chaplain with a Masters of Arts degree in Church ministries, who also has excellent editing skills, has kept me on the straight and narrow way grammatically and otherwise. I have had a number of readers who have served as "devil's advocates" by making me defend and clarify some of my most outrageous conclusions. These are Michele Foulk, who has faithfully met every two weeks with Sandy and me to discuss the theological dimensions of my writing; retired UCC pastor John Lackey has likewise met with me every two weeks to discuss one or another of the themes I address; John Wilkins, Presbyterian elder and lay theologian has provided helpful historical-critical insights; Marcia Free, an ordained UCC minister, provided very valuable editorial and theological and linguistic advice; and the friend who initially challenged me to write a book about holy humanity, Ann Hake, has continued to critique each chapter as I could get it to her. Tony Bartlett, theologian and author, has favored me with an excellent review (posted on Amazon) and on www.ChristianSpirituality.org. I am also grateful to Victoria Medaglia for her professional assistance in getting the manuscript into the required formats for publishing, and to Ralph Hubbard for his work on the cover and the formatting for the E-book editions. Beyond these, I have asked for and received feedback from many, many others concerning some of the ideas I present, including the "Issues Class" and the adult Bible Study class of Church of the Savior, UCC, in Knoxville, Tennessee. Most of these have seemed appreciative; a few think I'm nuts. For all these I am eternally grateful.

First and finally, my heart-felt thanks to the one I call the Holy Spirit for opening my heart and mind to this "God stuff" in *Holy Humanity*. The Spirit has made me, I think, a better person—and certainly a better informed person through the writing of *Holy Humanity*. I devoutly hope that the Holy Spirit will join me and my very supportive church community in our future literary endeavors, as well.

–James L. (Jim) Foster, 2013

1

Introduction

WE ARE ALL MADE OF GOD STUFF

Faith and love are apt to be spasmodic in the best minds.
[Humans] live on the brink of mysteries and harmonies into which
They never enter, and with their hand on the door latch,
They die outside.
—Ralph Waldo Emerson

"For all who are led by the Spirit of God are children of God.
For you did not receive a spirit of slavery to fall back into fear.
But you have received a spirit of adoption
When we cry, "Abba! Father!" it is that very Spirit bearing witness
with our spirit
That we are children of God."

—Romans 8:14-15 (NRSV)

"I celebrate myself,
And what I assume you shall assume
For every atom belonging to me as good belongs to you."

—Walt Whitman, *Leaves of Grass*

We are all made of God stuff

We are all made of God stuff. That is the bottom line. All the following is just the details that support this observation. Writing from a Christian context, I will begin with the biblical support and then move on to other material evidence supportive of the biblical findings. This approach by no means implies that the application of the above thesis includes only those of like Christian persuasion. Indeed, it is this author's conviction that it applies to every human being regardless of his or her religious inclinations, or even if they have no religious inclinations at all.

So, what does it mean to be human? Not many people have a good answer for this. Most of us have, I think, concluded that being human consists of being born and being nurtured and trained to take on some specific job (or jobs) in life, marrying, procreating, retiring, and dying. Some would add eternal life or some other ill-defined heavenly existence to the mix. Others would add eternal damnation for those who do not measure up to their own or others' self-righteous standards. Still others foresee a rebirth, a reincarnation, endlessly going through a continuing succession of multiple lives, presumably until they get it right. But for many people—perhaps most—human life is, as Henry David Thoreau observed, an experience of "quiet desperation." (*Walden*, 1854) or as Siddhartha Gautama, the Buddha. said, "There is suffering in the world." As a general rule, people never satisfactorily answer the question "what does it mean to be human?" They never discover who they are or why they exist. They have no reason for being, except, perhaps, to bring others into existence to experience the same sense of desperation.

The Biblical Witness

In spite of our pervasive low opinion of ourselves, the Psalmist exclaims that we are wonderfully made (Psalm 139:14), even that we are created "a little less than God" (Psalm 8:5). Does the Psalmist know something we don't know? Surely gods do not live lives of quiet desperation!

Yet the author of Genesis states unequivocally, "So God created humankind (Hebrew, *adham* transliterated Adam) in his [own] image, in the image of God they were created, male and female they were created...and, indeed, it was very good" (Genesis 1:27 & 31, NRSV, adapted). So what does it mean to be created in God's image? It certainly could not have been a physical one. The mapping of our genome has demonstrated that our physical variations as a human race are virtually infinite. Each one of us is a unique creation.

Perhaps it is *Creator* God we image. That would mean that we are co-creators with God. The human biological reproductive process would certainly appear to be a kind of co-creation. At the very least we are key participants in the creative process. The problem with this thesis, however is that other species participate in the creative process in much the same way, so would that mean that bears and bats, dogs and dingoes and cats and caterpillars, too, are created in God's image? As complex as the procreative processes are, somehow they do not quite measure up to whatever may be meant by the *Imago Dei*, (theologians' Latin jargon meaning "image of God.") Bonaventure, for example, was a 13th century Catholic theologian who believed that the image of God in man is that which leads man to the concept of the Trinity as an example of humankind's trinity of powers, whatever *that* means. Perhaps it is a reference to the common belief that reality comes in threes—e.g. fire, water, air; male, female, child; and, in the biology of our bone cells— osteoblasts, osteocytes and osteoclasts (creating, saving and death into new life—a complete cycling of the cells in our bones every seven years). This trinity is expressed in Christianity as Father, Son, Holy Spirit. This same trinitarian formulation is found again in Hinduism as Brahma (Creator), Vishnu (maintainer/Savior) and Shiva (as in death into new life, Holy Spirit—born again). If, indeed, it was the Creator's plan for each triplet to in some way represent positive, negative and balance or resolution, it was inculcated early on into the very fabric of our biological and theological development. Thus, as created biological beings we mirror the Creator.

To be honest, it is sometimes difficult to see any semblance of God at all in some of our fellow human beings—or even in ourselves. But then it may be that we are simply a work in progress. The Apostle Paul, in his second letter to the church in Corinth, makes this astonishing observation: "Now the Lord is the Spirit, and where the Spirit of the Lord is, there is freedom. And we all, with unveiled face [with nothing hidden], reflecting as in a mirror the glory [demonstrated presence] of the Lord [the free Spirit], are being changed [orig. Greek, *metamorphoumetha,* metamorphosed] from glory to glory [orig. Greek, *doxa,* from one demonstration of his presence to another], even as by the Spirit, who is the Lord." (II Corinthians 3:17-18, author's translation, with interpretations in brackets). It is readily apparent that Paul is here speaking of the Image of God being progressively revealed in us, as we are dramatically metamorphosed (think caterpillar to butterfly and crawling to flying) into Spirit beings who are radically free. According to Paul, we are undergoing a *spiritual* transformation. The "God stuff" of which we are made, and still being made, is Spirit, and we have yet to see in ourselves the finished product.

This understanding is echoed in Paul's first letter to the Corinthian church: "For now we see in a mirror dimly, but then we will see face to face. Now I know in part; then I will know fully, even as I have been fully known. And now faith, hope, and love abide, these three; and the greatest of these is love [*agápe,* unconditional love]. (I Corinthians 13:12-13, NRSV)

One further biblical text is worthy of note. The attribution of the two letters of Peter in the New Testament to Simon Peter, a disciple and close companion of Jesus, is generally accepted by biblical scholars. In the introduction to his second letter, Peter makes this astounding observation: "His [God's] divine power has given us everything needed for life and godliness, through the knowledge of him who called us by his own glory and goodness. Thus, he has given us, through these things his precious and very great promises, so that through them you may escape from the corruption that is in the world because of lust, *and become participants of the divine nature"*. (II Peter 1:3-4, NRSV, italics added)

I do not think it is too great a leap, taking Paul's and Peter's concepts together, that the Spirit into which we are being transformed, is the Spirit of *agápe* love, the same unconditional love with which God loves us. *God is changing us from self-centered egotists to other-centered lovers.* When this process is complete, wars will cease, peace will prevail, and our world will become the Eden God intended from the beginning.

The Witness of Anthropology

Now we change perspective, asking the question "Who are we?" from the context of our prehistoric past. As is common in Western cultures, I confess to a predisposition to think of science and scientists as more to be trusted than religion and religionists. Although scientific method has appeared to me to be less fraught with personal investment in particular results than is the case with theological discourse, it has also been shown that scientists are not immune to the problem of personal investment, particularly when scientific careers may rise or fall depending on which sacred cows one supports. (see Stephen J. Gould, *The Mismeasure of Man,* second edition, 1996[1]) However, when it comes to anthropology, I have tended to buy into the evolutionary theory of human development as opposed to Creationism. I followed Darwin and the Leakey family as opposed to Archbishop James Ussher, who dated

---

1   The *Mismeasure of Man* is a book by Harvard evolutionary biologist, paleontologist and science historian Stephen Jay Gould, first published in 1981. It is both a history and a critique of the statistical methods and cultural motivations underlying biological determinism, the belief that "social and economic differences between human groups— primarily races, classes, and sexes—arise from inherited, inborn distinctions, and that society, in this sense, is an accurate reflection of biology." (Stephen Gould, 1996, p. 52) Gould refutes biological determinism and shows the cultural bias and mistakes made by the scientists of that day.

the creation of the world to 4004 BC, a conclusion which has for me been convincingly and totally discredited by the scientific method.

But the idea of the evolution of humans has always had for me one small problem. I could never find a place for the development or even the presence of the spiritual aspect of human identity in the evolutionary scheme. I would occasionally take the problem off the shelf and ponder it, only to put it back on the shelf unresolved. That was before I discovered a long forgotten report from the anthropologist, Hans Reck, a contemporary of Louis Leakey, working in the same region of Africa and in the same geologic strata. Reck found a fully modern *Homo sapiens* skeleton, dated about 1.6 million years old, a supposed contemporary of Java man and Peking man[2] (as reported in *Nature*, vol. 128, October 24, 1931, p. 724); confirmed more recently in *Nature* (vol. 404, March 30, 2000); more recently still, on August 31, 2011 the findings of Hans Reck and his conclusions were corroborated on the PBS Nova program, *Becoming Human,* which reported on a comparative study of modern and Neanderthal DNA. Neanderthals date from c. 30,000 to 150,000 years ago and had been thought to be the immediate ancestors of modern humans. The report concluded that "modern [hu]man was not, in fact, descended from Neanderthals." This was confirmed again on the January 2013 PBS Nova program *Decoding Neanderthals. Homo sapiens*, modern humans, according to recent DNA analysis, were contemporaries, not descendents, of the Neanderthals. In a word, *modern humans do not fit into the evolutionary scheme either in terms of sequence or in terms of evolutionary change.* Humankind has basically remained unchanged physically for perhaps 1,500,000 years (or more according to the first Nova report cited above), and have lived contemporaneously with those who were assumed to be our evolutionary predecessors.

---

2 The dating and significance of both Java man, discovered by Eugene Dubois in 1893, and Peking man, discovered by Swedish geologist Johan Gunnar Andersson and American paleontologist Walter W. Granger in 1929, have been challenged and the fossil age claims rejected by many paleontologists, some even calling the fossils a hoax.

Citing significant differences between human DNA and the DNA of other primates, Gregg Braden[3] opines that "there is a growing body of evidence suggesting that, as *Homo sapiens*, we evolved not from but parallel to other species. Rather than being part of a tidy linear progression descending directly from earlier forms of primates, this theory takes the approach that we developed along with earlier primates in a sort of parallel evolution." (*Braden 2004*, p. 31) Such a "parallel evolution" would not be a physiological one, at least as far as the fossil evidence indicates, but more likely the intellectual and spiritual one which we can still witness taking place.

Carl Jung has opined that "...man must continue to resemble a hermit who knows that in respect of comparative anatomy he has affinities with the anthropoids but, to judge by appearances, is extraordinarily different from his cousins in respect of his psyche [Greek root, "soul"]. It is just in this most important characteristic of his species that he cannot know himself and therefore remains a mystery to himself... Our psyche, which is primarily responsible for all the historical changes wrought by the hand of man on the face of this planet, remains an insoluble puzzle and an incomprehensible wonder, an object of abiding perplexity..." (Jung, *The Undiscovered Self,* 1958, p. 56).

When we take human beings out of the evolutionary lineage, then the possibility arises that the Creator has indeed done something unique when she created men and women in Her image. The presence of the divine Spirit in us, of soul, is not something that was accomplished at some unidentified stage in an evolutionary process. It is reasonable to suppose that God's Spirit has been there from the beginning of our creation, and, further, that the creationist theory in this instance got it right and the scientists, until recently, got it wrong. (This does not mean that we should start teaching religion in our public schools—only that evolutionary theory should be taught

---

3   Gregg Braden is a scientist, visionary, and scholar whose quest is to build bridges between science and ancient wisdom traditions. He is the author of several books exploring the confluence of wisdom traditions and quantum theory and is a participant in Deepak Chopra's Evolutionary Leadership think tank. His work has been featured in media specials on the History Channel, the Discovery Channel, National Geographic, ABC and NBC. See Bibliography reference for his book *The God Code.*

as just that—theory—and theory that is only partially amenable to dissection by empirical scientific method. Science and religion, however, do not need to be cast as polar opposites, but rather as mutual endeavors to ascertain truth, an undertaking requiring humility, cooperation, and mutual respect.)

The Witness of Modern Biology

In the past few decades, humankind has experienced a revolution in biological science. The area in which this is most evident and which holds perhaps the greatest promise is the discovery and mapping of the human genome. I would propose that it is not mere happenstance that the chemical elements of our DNA, the "dust" out of which we were created (according to the biblical account of creation) is a sign of the divine meaning of our existence.

Anthony Bartlett, author and Gerardian theologian, has this to say about the relevance of signs for modern humanity. He observes that "the world of electronic communication has become another 'real' layer of reality shaping people's lives and destiny." Furthermore,

> "...this intense world of signs is just the latest complex mode of the universal human capacity for symbol making ...human beings have always existed within some kind of sign system, within a visual and verbal world order. This could easily be humanity's distinctive defining feature. Today the symbolic order has reached a level of extraordinary development and depth, but it has always in one way or another been proper to human beings... Philosophers recognize this, that it is impossible in fact to separate the thing from the sign. They have become more and more resigned to not being able to do so. And many of them are not just resigned. They see this as the distinctive quality of human existence. *To be inside a sign is to be human.*" (Bartlett 2011, p. 34, emphasis added)

It is so distinctive, in fact, that it was written into our DNA at the very beginning of our existence. Gregg Braden has summarized his findings supporting this view as follows:

> "The basic elements of DNA—hydrogen, nitrogen, oxygen, and carbon—translate directly to key letters of the Hebrew and Arabic alphabets.
>
> In these languages, our genetic code spells the ancient name of God. The same name lives within all humans, regardless of their beliefs, actions, lifestyle, religion, or heritage.
>
> This relationship was described in sacred texts, such as the Hebrew *Sepher Yetzirah*,[4] at least one thousand years before modern science verified such connections." (Braden 2004, p. xvi)

In a world of signs which define our existence, perhaps we should take more seriously those creation accounts such as Genesis, in which God *speaks* the universe into existence, as well as the first words of the Gospel of John which says "In the beginning was the Word, and the Word was with God, and the Word was God..." (Gospel of John 1:1, NRSV) It may not be too much of a stretch to assert that apart from a sign a thing does not exist, that signs are the basis of creation, and that *as co-creators, we participate in sign-making.* If we can speak it, we can create it!

The Witness of Language[5]

Hebrew is classified as a Semitic (or Shemitic, from Shem, the son of Noah) language. Most of the Hebrew Bible is written in Classical Hebrew, and much of its present form is specifically the dialect of biblical Hebrew that scholars believe flourished around the 6th century BCE, around the time of the Babylonian exile. For this

---

4   The *Sepher Yetzirah* (the Book of Creation) is one of a plethora of ancient creation accounts, this particular one coming out of the Jewish Kabbalah tradition.

5   I am indebted to Gregg Braden, who in Chapter 5 of *The God Code* presents much of the material in this section in considerably more detail. This is a condensed version of his insights along with additional observations of my own.

reason, Hebrew has been referred to by Jews as *Leshon HaKodesh* (לשון הקודש), "The Holy Language," since ancient times. A three thousand year old pottery shard bearing five lines of faded characters is the earliest verification of the age of the Hebrew language. It is certainly old, but a "holy language?" Consider the evidence. Early biblical Hebrew has an alphabet of twenty-two characters, not counting six additional characters added later. Each letter, in addition to having its own unique pronunciation, is also assigned a numerical value. (This is not unique to Hebrew, being true of most, if not all languages) Vowels were not added until later so do not appear initially as part of the Hebrew alphabet.

The *Sepher Yetzirah* (cited above) observes that "it is from the letters themselves that God 'depicted all that was formed and all that would be formed.'" According to Braden, scholars have historically viewed this statement "as a metaphor symbolizing the power of God as the source of creation." The evidence points to the high probability that the symbols themselves were the instruments of creation, indelibly imprinted in our DNA. The following chart shows the letters of the Hebrew alphabet and their numerical values:

Letter	Serif	Sound	Numeric Value
Alef	א	Silent	1
Bet/Vet	ב	B/V	2
Gimel	ג	G	3
Dalet	ד	D	4
He	ה	H	5
Vav	ו	V	6
Zayin	ז	Z	7
Chet	ח	Ch	8
Tet	ט	T	9
Yod	י	Y	10
Kaf	כ	Kh/K	20

Lamed	ל	L	30
Mem	מ	M	40
nuN	נ	N	50
Samekh	ס	S	60
Ayin	ע	Gutteral	70
Peh	פ	F/P	80
Tzadi	צ	Tz	90
Qof	ק	K	100
Resh	ר	R	200
Shin	ש	S/Sh	300
Tav	ת	T	400

Now we must shift our focus to a few interesting details of the above alphabet. The most common name for God in the Hebrew scriptures (also referred to as the *Old Testament*) is, in its transliterated form, YAHWEH (the W is written as a V in Hebrew, which has no W as such in its alphabet, thus is actually spelled, without the English vowels, YHVH,) *"Scholars of the Kabbalah state that the letters of God; YHV are actually derived from, and correspond to, the three Mother Letters (AMSh)."* (Braden, referring to commentary on the *Sepher Yetzirah* and the letters of the world of chaos, the time before time and order). Thus in the subsequent era, the world of order, the letters change, *but the numerical values do not.* YHV and AMSh are equal with the latter's values prevailing. "They represent the same force manifested in different realms with total numeric values of 1, 5, and 6."

For the ancients, the observable "stuff" of which the universe was made was Fire, Air, Water, and Earth or the equivalent, in modern chemistry, of Hydrogen, Nitrogen, Oxygen and Carbon. The atomic mass of the first three of these particular elements (the gases) total 1, 5, and 6. (The mass numbers are obtained by adding the whole numbers to the left of the decimal in the same manner in which the Hebrew letter values were manipulated.) Of course, as these are all gases, there is the need for a non-gaseous element to bond them all together, something solid. For the ancients this was earth, the equivalent of carbon with an atomic mass of 12, the total of $1 + 5 + 6$. These are the only elements for which this combination is possible. The process of getting to this point is tedious but the result is stunning! A comparison of the numerical values of the Hebrew letters which make up the name of God, YHVH finds it to be the numerical equivalent of the atomic mass of four basic chemical building blocks, the stuff of which we are made.

But it gets even more outrageous. The four DNA bases which make up our genetic code are thymine, cytosine, adenine and guanine. The chemical components of each one of these are hydrogen, nitrogen, oxygen and carbon. *All life, of whatever description, is made from these four elements*, four elements which all bear the imprint of Yahweh. In a word, *we carry the imprint of God on every cell in our bodies.*

And so we have come full circle, from the biblical witness to the witness of anthropology and biology to the witness of the Hebrew language from the perspective of the *Sepher Yetzirah* (the Book of Creation). A remaining question is whether our human experience supports our other witnesses. I believe it does, though many of us have been blind to it.

The Witness of Human Experience

At the Council of Chalcedon, in 451 C.E., the early Church fathers, or at least a majority of them, concluded that Jesus was fully God and fully human (though without sin), thereby setting up a paradox wherein the totally righteous God is paired with totally depraved, sinful humanity. (The latter was, incidentally, never so thoroughly demonstrated as in the First Council of Nicaea in 325 C.E., where the council itself was the scene of mayhem and murder.) I question the implication that the Chalcedonian statement was a paradox. I would suggest that to be *fully* God and *fully* human is instead *synonymous*—that to be fully one is to be fully the other. The problem is that we have never known what it is to be *fully human*.

We have assumed that our sin is an indication of our humanity. If on occasion we blow it, we say "that's only human." No! I shout it from the rooftops! That is less than human—even sub-human! God did not create sinners. God created saints. To be sure, we are saints who sin, but nevertheless, saints. Our *identity* is saints—literally, holy ones, separated *to* God, not *from* God. We are saints because that is what God created us to be. That is who we *are*. God's autograph is on our every cell! So why do we not act like saints?

Perhaps an analogy will be helpful. If a bird thinks it is a fish, it will neither fly very well nor swim very well. But if a bird knows it is a bird, it will likely fly very well indeed. Likewise, if a saint thinks he or she is a sinner, then s/he will not likely "saint" very well. But if she knows she is a saint, she may "saint" very well indeed. Identity is the key. Do not be blinded by your sin, or by a world constantly telling you the error of your ways. God will take care of that in due course. But know that you were created a saint, a holy one. In time you will find yourself living the role and having the peace that comes from both knowing who you are and living it.

In the chapters that follow we will be looking at various options for the spiritual journey: the mystical experience (all spiritual experience is shrouded in mystery), God's dream for creation, what it means to be a co-creator with God and what it means to be made of God stuff, God's and our work of reconciling heaven and earth, the meaning of soul, and a final look at who or what God is. I hope to entice you to consciously undertake your own spiritual journey (or to shed light on the journey you are already on) to the ends that:

> Love will no longer be a struggle—you will be Love, *agápe* Love.

> You will no longer need to seek Peace—you will embody Peace.

> You will no longer seek to understand yourself—you will understand yourself fully, even as you are fully understood by God who made you of God stuff in the first place.

These are my goals both as presenter and as participant in the journey. Will you join me on the journey?

Chapter 1

THE JOURNEY

"Stand at the crossroads, and look, and ask for the ancient paths,
Where the good way lies; and walk in it..."

—Jeremiah 6:16 NRSV

"...the path of the righteous is like the light of dawn,
Which shines brighter and brighter until full day."

—Proverbs 4:18 (NRSV)

"The Godward journey is a journey on which every individual is
launched, all unknowingly, at birth."

Christopher Bryant

"The longest journey is the journey inward."

Dag Hammarskjöld

The Journey Back to the Heart of the Creator

Every human being is on a journey. It is a journey that started in the heart of the Creator—called by many names, including God, Allah, Great Spirit, Yahweh, Brahma, and Aten—long before recorded human history began. It can be thought of as a journey with many paths or as one river with many wells, but each human's journey has two aspects in common with all the others. Our journeys have a common origin and a common destination—the Creator. And on our varying paths we all become co-Creators, participating in the work of the prime Creator. Many times we lose our way, are derailed, only to be wooed back to our chosen path by the Creator who set us on our particular path in the first place.

Diarmuid O'Murchu is a Roman Catholic priest and social psychologist residing in England. (Some of his books, *Quantum Theology*, 1998; *Evolutionary Faith,* 2002; and *Ancestral Grace,* 2008, are listed in the Bibliography at the end of this book.) He has listed twelve fundamentally *flawed* cultural assumptions which have derailed whole generations of human evolution for thousands of years (O'Murchu 2008, p. 12). These assumptions are:

1. *Man is the measure of all things (anthropocentrism).*
2. *Humans are the most highly evolved creatures in the whole of creation.*
3. *Humans alone possess developed intelligence.*
4. *Humans alone can make rational, moral decisions.*
5. *To make those decisions intelligently, we use only information we can verify objectively and quantitatively.*
6. *Objective knowledge requires us to take seriously things that have happened closer to our time rather than those of the distant past. Mythology is mere myth and of little use to rational human beings.*
7. *Imagination, intuition, feelings, and emotions are suspect, difficult to control, and not to be taken seriously. Cherish hard science and dogmatic religion rather than artistic expression.*

8. *The earth, and all of creation, is an object for human use and benefit.*
9. *To master creation and manage human affairs in a rational way we need hierarchical structures of governance.*
10. *Religion, based on a sky-God, hierarchically ruling over all human hierarchies, is our ultimate referent point.*
11. *Creation is fundamentally flawed, but concerted human effort can mold it into something reasonably good.*
12. *Those who work hard will be rewarded either in this life or in the next.*

O'Murchu goes on to say, "These are among the leading assumptions of our dominant patriarchal culture, one that has thrived since the agricultural revolution of about ten thousand years ago. It is an evolutionary cycle that has largely run its course and... is now entering its wave of decline and disintegration. It has had its moments of glory, but for the greater part it has been something of a dark age for humanity, and darker still for the surrounding creation because of dysfunctional human interference" (ibid., p. 13).

On the other hand, Matthew Fox, in chapter one of his 2002 book, *Creativity,* dwells at some length on our false perceptions of our collective selves. He argues that for the vast majority of our time on earth, we have not been consumers, nor addicts, nor passive couch potatoes, nor boring, nor cogs in a machine. On the latter point he muses that "Maybe this is why dysfunctional relationships have so swollen in numbers during this industrial age *from which we are emerging* with our souls barely intact. Indeed, emerging with not having a clue what "soul" even means anymore." (Fox 2002, p. 23, emphasis added)

Perhaps the glimmer of light on the horizon, at this point, is the observation that the former cycle has "run its course." The good news is that, two thousand years after Jesus, humankind now has the option of going with the evolutionary tide, rather than swimming against the current. The turning point was the first century life and death of Jesus of Nazareth, as he first demonstrated who we can become and then invited us to join him on the journey.

The Starting Point

It is one thing to acknowledge our God-given identity—quite another to assimilate it and live out of it. Most Western Christians have lived so long with the mistaken identity taught by the church— an identity imposed on the followers of Jesus from the earliest days of the Christian religion by a church hierarchy committed to patriarchy and dualistic Greek philosophy—that we have had no clue that the teachings of Jesus were being subverted. Consequently, we have had a nearly two thousand year history of struggle to deduce who we are and to make sense of the teachings of Jesus as contradicted by the Church. This revised gospel, promulgated by the Church fathers and, to a lesser extent, even by the Apostle Paul, promoted self-centered individualism as opposed to relational equality; dualism as opposed to unification; violent confrontation as opposed to openness and vulnerability; arrogance as opposed to humility; and male domination as opposed to equality in gender relationships. The early Church fathers, for their own political reasons, redefined Jesus' teaching about sin from "missing the mark" to sin as failure to adhere to cultural and Church imposed rules. The truth that Jesus said was supposed to set us free was instead reinterpreted so as to put us in shackles of conformity and injustice. These are just a few of the departures from the teaching and example of Jesus who never envisioned a new religion in the first place. Had he not left the earthly scene when he did he would surely have been aghast at what the early Christian leaders did with his teachings.

In as much as the early Church Fathers, imbued with a greed for power, were the ones who chose the "holy" writings that were to be included in the "authoritative Christian scriptures," their misconstrual of the teachings of Jesus has continued to plague those who sincerely want to follow Jesus. In our quest for the new identity promised by Jesus we have received such mixed signals that few have been able to find their way, and many have given up trying altogether.

The Apostle Paul is credited by many biblical historians as being the founder of the Christian Church. It was certainly his organizational genius, passionate preaching and persistent leadership that firmly established the first few Christian congregations, including the Church in Rome, which is arguably the predecessor of the modern Catholic Church establishment. But Paul had never met Jesus (unless we count the Damascus Road mystical meeting). He certainly never had any extended conversations with him. He was entirely dependent on secondhand reports on what Jesus taught— reports which did not always agree with each other and which had typically been embellished over the years. The gospels had not been written, though Paul may have had access to some of Jesus' more memorable sayings. But whatever actually did happen on the road to Damascus, it was sufficient to change him from a feared persecutor of Christians to a vigorous promoter of the Way (the original designation of those who were followers of Jesus' teachings).

What Paul did have was Roman citizenship, a good education— probably in Greek philosophy—and a keen ability to communicate, both orally and in writing. These together with an apparently scant grasp of Jesus' teaching and worldview, were a potent preparation for founding a church that embodied a little of Jesus and a lot of Greek philosophy. Eventually, the Gospels would be written, and our understanding of Jesus would be enlarged. By then Paul's doctrine had already permeated the early Church so thoroughly that only the most perceptive—and educated—of souls noticed the inconsistencies. Patriarchy and Greek dualism were already enshrined in the doctrine of the Church. And so it has continued to the present day.

Paul lived in a world of violence. He knew humankind at its worst. Violence was everywhere, even in the Church. Jesus was only the first historically validated, but not the last, to die for *shalom* (peace). The early Church leaders often settled their differences by physically attacking and sometimes murdering those with whom they disagreed. They knew little about negotiation and nothing at all about conflict resolution. In such a violent culture, it had to be quite obvious to Paul that men and women were at heart sinners in need of redemption. His prescription was "repent and be saved." Personal transformation was the only hope for the struggling followers of the Way. So far as Paul was concerned, we were all living in depravity. Sin, defined by Paul as immorality, was our hallmark, our identity.

It is in large part due to Paul's writing and teaching that our need for "salvation from sin"—defined primarily as immorality and depravity—is writ large in evangelical Christian theology, as is our pre-Christian identity as "sinners." Even after our "salvation" we are still "sinners saved by grace." "Sinner" continues to be our primary identity, although Paul expresses some ambiguity on this point.

In justice to Paul, he did have a mystical bent which was one of his saving graces. It is evidenced in his letters to the churches in which he often spoke of Christ as foundational for our faith. It is interesting, however, that he rarely used the given name "Jesus" except in combination with "Lord" and/or "Christ". Of the two instances in those letters generally acknowledged by biblical scholars to be genuinely from Paul's hand, where "Jesus" is used by itself, one is a quote from an early hymn of the church (Philippians 2:10). Thus, it is certainly implicit in Paul's writing that his relationship was with the risen Christ rather than with the human Jesus, a connection borne out by his Damascus road experience.

Paul's spiritual connection was also implicit in his first letter to the Corinthian church where, speaking of their spiritual immaturity, he says:

> "And so, brothers and sisters, I could not speak to you as spiritual people, but rather as people of the flesh, as infants in Christ. I fed you with milk, not solid food, for you were not ready for solid food. Even now you are still not ready, for you are still of the flesh." (I Corinthians 3:1-2, NRSV)

Paul continued the diet of milk in his writings to the Corinthians and to his other churches, with only brief allusions to deeper truths which he had apparently learned from "Christ Jesus." Two of these allusions will illustrate the point, the first from the same letter to the Corinthians.

"Paul, called to be an apostle of Christ Jesus by the will of God ... to the church of God in Corinth, to those sanctified in Christ Jesus, *called to be saints [holy people]* together with all those everywhere who call on the name of our Lord Jesus Christ, their Lord and ours." (I Corinthians 1:1-2, NRSV)

Contrary to their (and our) practice and belief, Paul knew the recipients of his letter to be holy people, or at least holy people in training, not sinners. This was in spite of the fact that he spends much of the rest of the letter castigating them for their immoral and violent behavior. He addressed them for who they were, a people created by God in His/Her own image. "Saints" is who they were and their bad behavior did not change that. What had changed was their relationship through Christ to God, regardless of their behavior, good or bad.

This latter identification as "saints" has somehow escaped notice by the modern evangelical church, perhaps because of the equation of "sin" with various degrees of bad behavior, as culturally defined. But this definition of sin is not the meaning of the Greek term *hamartia,* the term used by Jesus, Paul and other New Testament writers. The root meaning of *hamartia* in the original Greek used by all the New Testament writers is "to miss the mark" or "to separate that which should not be separated." To live as though God does not exist or does not matter, thus separating one's self from God, is *hamartia.* To attribute to Satan the miracles of God is to miss the mark, *hamartia.* Jesus drank wine, engaged in revelry, was the dinner guest of sinners, and occasionally lost his temper. He neither missed the mark nor separated himself from God, but nevertheless he created a problem for religious fundamentalists who equate such "misbehaviors" with sin. Jesus reveled in life and relationships and radical freedom and this is what he offers those who choose to accept his way. We may be misguided—yes; incomplete, a work in progress, surely. But separated from the God who created us and who loves Her creation unconditionally and passionately? Never! We make mistakes, sometimes serious mistakes, but God's love, *agápe,* never falters. In our confusion, we may try to run from God, but we cannot elude Her.[6] We may even openly rebel against God, but even this will not change God's love for us. Unconditional love is something we find incomprehensible. Human loves are but a faint shadow of the love of God. Even when we earnestly attempt to emulate God's love in our human relationships we often find ourselves unable to sustain it. Therefore, it is hardly reasonable to measure God's love by our inadequacies. We woefully underestimate God and often have not an inkling of who God is or what Her end game is. As humans we have severely limited vision and understanding of what God is up to. For example, we have to think in terms of time and space while for God these are merely meaningless human constructs. Before time and space existed, God was.

Whether we believe the evolution of humans started with chimpanzees or was a special *Homo sapiens* creation—either can take us back millions of years—God was there and was instrumental in our beginning. There was never a time when God was not. Nor was there ever a time when God did not know what She was doing and what the end result would be. But typically, neither our nor Paul's theology seriously considers the ramifications of this long prehistoric era. In this scenario the two thousand years since Jesus Christ are but a miniscule speck on the time-line of creation. Likewise, in terms of space, our whole earth is only one of not billions, but billions of billions—an infinity of planets. (As of this writing, astronomers have, since 2009, confirmed the existence of 2,740 planets the size of earth in our galaxy alone. Extrapolating to the two hundred billion stars estimated to be in the Milky Way the number of potential earth-like planets is an amazing seventeen billion, dramatically increasing the odds that extraterrestrial life really exists.) In this context, we can only echo the psalmist's query, "What are human beings that you are mindful of them, or mortals that you care for them?" (Psalm 8:4, NRSV) Of one thing we can be

---

6   I have chosen to break with the traditional use of the male pronoun in reference to God. The writer of the fourth Gospel spoke truth, I believe, when he or she said "God is a spirit, and they that worship him must worship him in spirit and in truth." (John 4:24, KJV) I also believe the feminine pronoun is a more appropriate way of speaking about the Creator. I realize that to use any gendered pronoun is inadequate, but the English language alternatives otherwise are so cumbersome as to be distracting.

certain. God's grace and creative genius did not begin with Jesus or Christianity. It was there in the beginning. The incarnation of Jesus was certainly a turning point in human history, but God did not wait for the appearance of Jesus on the earthly scene to begin loving his creation. God's love is eternal and eternity goes both backward and forward and is continuing its expansion infinitely.

This leads me to the other allusion to the depth of understanding that Paul chose not to elaborate upon in his second letter to the Corinthians: "...all of us, with unveiled faces, seeing the glory of the Lord as though reflected in a mirror, *are being transformed [metamorphosed] into the same image from one degree of glory [manifest presence] to another*, for this comes from the Lord, the Spirit." (II Corinthians 3:17-18, NRSV, italics and bracketed interpretations added)

This message was and is revolutionary. But we still have not gotten it. Blinded by church teaching, and likewise blind to the implications of Paul's mystical allusions and the teachings of Jesus about the Kingdom of God, we continue in darkness, impoverished beyond imagination by our lack of understanding of who we are. But the dark ages of the past are receding. This is where we are today. *This is the starting point for our spiritual journeys.*

What Did Jesus Have to Say about Who We Are and Where We Are Headed?

When we endeavor to sort out what Jesus really said about anything from the words put into his mouth by others, we are inevitably faced with an enormous task fraught with uncertainty and the possibility of error. However, the alternative to undertaking this task is to accept at face value the claims of the early Church fathers to self-serving inerrancy—meaning that they received many early "gospels" purporting to be accurate reports on the life and teachings of Jesus, some with pseudonymous claims to authorship attached, and many with no author's name attached at all. Some were fictional accounts. It is probably safe to say that all the accounts were written not as histories, but with particular agendas, depending on who was doing the writing and for whom their writing was intended. For example, the Gospel of Matthew (whose name was not on the earliest copies available to us today) was written for the obvious purpose of convincing literate Jewish readers that Jesus was the long-awaited Messiah. To this end the author included stories of the miraculous conception of Jesus, many stories of miracles he performed, genealogical information supposedly showing Jesus to be descended from King David, biblical prophecies claimed to refer to him, and many accounts of purported miracles that he performed—all to persuade a skeptical Jewish audience that their religious leaders had had the Messiah—the one person who could have delivered the nation from Roman occupation—crucified. This author's anonymous "gospel" was so heavily biased that the task of separating fact from fiction is daunting. For the Church Fathers to then assign to it the name of one of Jesus' disciples, "Matthew" as author, only serves to muddy the waters further. It further begs the question, what else did they add or alter? And, what was *their* agenda?

Jewish expectation was that the Messiah would be a descendant of David. Two further, and flagrant, examples of gospel fiction meant to justify the claim that Jesus was the promised Messiah are in the genealogies of Jesus given by both the Gospel of Matthew and the Gospel of Luke. In each gospel (Matthew 1:1-17 and Luke 3:23-38) the lineage of Jesus is traced from King David to Joseph. Jesus' lineage in each instance is the paternal lineage through Joseph, but the infancy narrative in each gospel clearly states that Jesus was born of a virgin, Mary, who, having been impregnated by the Holy Spirit (Matthew 1:18 and Luke 1:34-35) gave birth miraculously to the promised Messiah of Israel. According to this scenario Joseph had nothing to do with Mary's pregnancy. So why trace Jesus' lineage through Joseph? Perhaps it was an attempt by somebody (not necessarily the authors, who are unknown to us in any event) to "have their cake and eat it, too." But how could he be God's son if he had a human father? Indeed the clumsy placement of the genealogy in Luke in the middle of the story of Jesus' baptism certainly appears to be an interpolation into an earlier text of the gospel no longer in existence.

Why does this matter? I subscribe to the following principles as applied to biblical interpretation: 1) The search for truth is of paramount importance, eclipsing all other concerns such as the defense of tradition, the adherence to "revealed" religious precepts, and obedience to assumed religious authority, including biblical "authority." 2) Truth is consistent with facts, even though the interpretation of facts leaves room for differing opinions as to their relevance. Different opinions may persist, but the primary aim must always be to establish what is true. Any literal interpretation that flies in the face of the *established* facts cannot be true. 3) Until such time as the facts of a particular situation are determined, it is incumbent on all participants to exercise humility by acknowledging the possibility of error. 4) Anything other than truth is error and cannot be the basis for faith or religion or life decisions. Until truth consistent with facts is reasonably determined, our faith and religious convictions are at best contingent on further understanding. (Truth may be conveyed by mythological stories as long as the stories are recognized as just that—mythological.) (5) The Holy Spirit can lead us to truth, but given our notorious proclivity as human beings to subvert revealed "truth" to our own devious ends, claims of revealed truth must still be treated as provisional until rigorously validated as consistent with known facts.

So What Can We Really Know about Jesus?

He really existed. Contrary to the claims of some modern writers, there is more first and second century documentation about Jesus, both biblical and non-biblical writing, than there is about any of his contemporaries. With such a variety of disparate sources attesting to his being, activities, and teaching, the claims that Jesus is wholly fictional are hardly credible. Further, he was a human being, and apparently never claimed to be God. If he had done so, we can be sure that claim would have been noted by the biblical writers. In addition, the church doctrine that he was God incarnate was hotly debated by the Church Fathers right up to the Council of Chalcedon in 451 CE and beyond. *Jesus was one like us.* His preferred self-designation was "son of man" meaning, I think, human being. A lot of ink has been spilled through the past two thousand years, trying to make something more of that simple phrase. Are we embarrassed that this Jesus to whom so many millions of us have sworn allegiance may not have been perfect, that he may have had doubts, that he may not have been totally cool and in control at all times?

It has taken biblical scholars almost two millennia to come to grips with the fact that the Gospel accounts of the life and ministry of Jesus are an incredible mix of myth and history. The person thought to be the first to raise the issue, Hermann Samuel Reimarus (December 22, 1694–March 1, 1768) was a German philosopher and writer who denied the supernatural origin of Christianity and is credited by some with initiating historians' investigation of the historical Jesus. He was the first scholar known to have applied historical-critical methodology to the biblical accounts of Jesus. He was followed a century later, by Albert Schweitzer (January 14, 1875–September 4, 1965), who was a German and then French theologian, organist, philosopher, physician, and medical missionary. Schweitzer, a Lutheran, challenged both the secular view of Jesus as depicted by historical-critical methodology current at his time in certain academic circles, as well as the traditional Christian view. Schweitzer's book, *The Quest of the Historical Jesus* (first German edition, 1906) propelled the modern day efforts to separate that which can be historically known about Jesus from the fantastical legends that were perpetuated about him by the early Church. Today the "Quest" continues and in the last couple of decades has made huge strides towards accomplishing that goal.

Jesus was an itinerant religious teacher and, perhaps, healer, with at least a small group of followers including a few serious disciples and perhaps many interested listeners. It is conceivable that Jesus could have drawn crowds by his preaching and healing, though biblical accounts of thousands are likely exaggerated. But the fact that accounts of his life and teaching number in the hundreds is an indication that at the very least he was making a noticeable impact. What he taught was apparently revolutionary enough to both attract followers and incur resistance from the Jewish religious and political establishment. Some specifics of what he taught may reasonably be garnered from the various gospel accounts, both canonical and non-canonical, though each particular teaching quoted must be critically appraised and compared with the whole body of Jesus' teaching. Inconsistencies abound.

Jesus was a storyteller and used parables to both teach and challenge his listeners. Indeed, it may also be that in the latter sense, his whole life was a parable demonstrating life in the Kingdom of God and challenging the truthfulness and authority of the Jewish religious establishment. John Dominic Crossan argues that Jesus' parables are primarily challenge parables. They challenged biblical tradition, cultural norms, and call us to turn our world and assumptions upside down. He called this world God's divine kingdom and, for Crossan, Jesus was both the message and the medium. (Crossan, 2012, p. 29) This raises the question, what were Jesus' real purposes in his life and teaching? What are the bedrock objectives he was commissioned to fulfill? I believe there were two.

First, I believe he was sent by God to show us who God is. At this point in human history, the Jewish God, Yahweh, was generally conceived of by his Jewish followers as a jealous, vain and vengeful super-human with only occasional hints from a few of his more spiritually perceptive prophets that there was "something more" to God than fire and brimstone. At the turn of the millennium when Jesus appeared on the scene the human race was a toxic mixture of chaos and violence, and the gods modeled this highly dysfunctional human society. Even the followers of the Way, as the early Christians fancied themselves, were not able to fully escape the violence which was the societal norm. They gave Jesus many titles, one of them being "Prince of Peace," but the peace part of Jesus teaching was elusive. All they had ever known was violence. Violence was their way of life and though they acknowledged the ideal of peace, when there was controversy they resorted to the only "conflict resolution" methodology they knew—violent response. This is how they thought God acted and they acted accordingly. But Jesus spoke of a different kind of God—a God of peace and love, a Creator who loved her creation even with all its faults. "Father, forgive them, for they know not what they do." (Luke 23:34) Jesus didn't just say these words from the cross. He had lived them, demonstrating in his own life, the love of God for her creation. Jesus was doing what he came to do— to show us who God is.

For Jesus, God was love's fullest expression. He explicitly taught that we are to love God above all else, and to love others with the same kind of inclusive, indiscriminate, and unconditional love that God has for her creation—a creation in which even the fall of a sparrow does not go unnoticed—a creation which calls us to be *fully* human, fully the divine agents of God vested with the responsibility to love and care for each other and for all of God's creation—a creation which has no place for violence—a kingdom of peace.

The second of Jesus' objectives was to show us who we inherently are. Jesus understood that not only was he God's child but that we, too, are God's children in very much the same way. Jesus was different from the rest of us only in the sense that he was the Way-shower. Jesus was fully human; we, too, are called by God to be fully human. Jesus was fully divine; we, too, are called to be fully divine. Both Jesus and we are made of God stuff. To be *fully* human and *fully* divine is not a paradox. They are the same thing. Our failure to understand what Jesus in his "life as parable" was trying to demonstrate has meant that for virtually all of our human incarnation we have not known who we are. Have we been blinded by our own violence to who we really are? Jesus calls us to accept our identity in God and to live our lives out of that divine identity. As that happens—and it *is* happening increasingly on a world-wide scale—we will be the love we were made to be. The signs are all around us. It is to these signs we turn next.

The Journey Continues

There are signs on the horizon that a new dawn is upon us, that the dark ages of the past two thousand years are receding and that quickly. It would appear that we may be coming of age just in time to avert our immanent self-destruction. Some of these signs are:

1. A growing restlessness, particularly among Western Christians, Jews, and Muslims who are no longer willing to settle for faiths that have been tried and found wanting: The search for positive alternative religious understandings and

experience is becoming endemic to Western and Middle Eastern cultures. Secularism is on the rise as well, particularly as oncoming generations opt out of faith expressions that they believe are not only anachronistic but contribute to societal problems instead of solving them. Many of these seekers look for spiritual answers as they discover that materialism and secularism do not provide the answers they seek. All this is amply demonstrated by the burgeoning interest in spirituality even as there is diminishing interest in institutionalized religion.

2. A genuine and wide-spread alarm that the world is not the friendly environment we once thought it to be: Our failure to adequately care for our planet has brought us to the brink of annihilation. Domination as opposed to respectful caring and conservation is proving to be catastrophic. Our illusions of human superiority and dominance have now been shown to be just that—illusions. That awareness may lead to change.

3. The growing realization that if the planet does not kill us all first, then our technology may: Technology is neutral. In the hands of spiritually evolved peoples it may serve to bring us back from the brink. But it also can be used to push us over the brink by those who have no understanding or appreciation of what it means to be human. Unfortunately, even though a rising level of spiritual maturity may be in sight, we are not there yet. It may be a race to the finish line.

4. A refreshing and courageous honesty in the writings of many contemporary authors, including many Christian theologians, who have begun to have new insights on who we are and what we are about: Many of these are challenging our idols of the past two thousand years and are probing the possibilities of far-reaching religious, societal and cultural transformations. A number of these are cited in this book.

5. An abundance of age-old prophecies that appear to be converging on the present days—prophecies heralding great changes bringing either doom or a fresh start: It remains to

be seen whether any of these should be taken seriously or not, but if any of them are inspired by God, then I choose to believe that they herald a fresh start, a new hope, a new day, and a new humanity.

6. The increasing success that peace and justice activism has experienced in curbing the violence which has so characterized the last two thousand years: In the United States alone there are thousands of organizations addressing peace and justice issues in one way or another. Even though instances of human violence aimed at other humans is still unacceptably high—a fact accentuated by better and more wide-spread reporting—statistically the *per capita* incidents of violence are proportionally much fewer today than at any time in the past few centuries. Consequently average life spans are significantly increasing—at least in developed countries. In addition, the world is today awash in healing and beneficent organizations whose missions are the alleviation of human suffering. For all our missteps, some things we have done well. This is one of them. Now if we can just reign in our warring instincts....

7. People—particularly young people—are smarter today than were previous generations: IQs are rising, and educational programs are becoming more effective and available. Hopefully this will translate into better human decision-making as these young people enter the workforce and take up leadership roles in society.

8. A budding rapprochement between science and religion: On the table are a number of creative proposals by both scientists and theologians which have the potential for mutual recognition of our differing ways of knowing. Leading the way in the dialogue between science and spirituality is popular science/philosophy writer Ken Wilbur who, in Chapter 5 of his book, *The Marriage of Sense and Soul*, 1998, proposes a model that legitimizes *both* empirical and intuitive modes of knowing.

9. Evidence that we are in the midst of a global mind change: Willis Harman, in the second edition of his book, *Global Mind Change* (1998, p.viii), asserts that "People give legitimacy and they can take it away. A challenge to legitimacy is probably the most powerful force for change to be found in history.... To the empowering principle that people can withhold legitimacy, and thus change the world, we now add another: By deliberately changing the internal image of reality, people can change the world. Perhaps the only limits to the human mind are those we believe in." Pierre Teilhard de Chardin has written in the same vein that "The being who is the object of his own reflection, in consequence of that very doubling back upon himself, becomes in a flash able to raise himself to a new sphere." (Teilhard de Chardin 1959, p.165)

10. A growing recognition that we are not self-sufficient entities who have no responsibility for others: We are not a law unto ourselves. There are no "others". We are all members of the same race—the human race—and we were created for relationship. The existence of power—military, political, physical, judicial—does not legitimize its use for its own selfish purposes. If our lifestyles require that we deprive those less powerful or those unborn of a fair share of our world's wealth, then the belief that legitimizes those lifestyles must change. Belief in fairness as opposed to belief in the selfish right to unlimited acquisition is the order of the day if the human race is to survive. (See the appended World Citizenship Creed, Addendum IV.)

Our collective journey back to the heart of the Creator is well on its way. The more adventurous among us may lead the way, but do not linger along that way because you fear the unknown. Now is the time for courage, to acknowledge the darkness of our past and to strive for the dawning of a new day where peace, justice and God's Love replace the violence, inequality, and greed which have of late so characterized our world. There is, indeed a new day coming!

Chapter 2

THE MYSTICAL EXPERIENCE

Man is man because something divine is at stake in his existence. He is not an innocent bystander in the cosmic drama. There is in us more kinship with the divine than we are able to believe.
—Abraham Joshua Heschel

I know a man in Christ who fourteen years ago was caught up to the third heaven.
Whether it was in the body or out of the body I do not know.
God knows.
--Apostle Paul, II Corinthians 12:2 (NIV)

Mysticism is the name of that organic process which involves the perfect consummation of the love of God.
—Evelyn Underhill

How to Get on with the Journey—I

(1) RADICAL OPENNESS IN FAITH UNCONSTRAINED BY DOCTRINE;
(2) PERSONAL TRUST RELATIONSHIP WITH GOD; &
(3) PERSONAL SPIRITUAL INTENTION

In this chapter we will be looking at our spiritual journey from the point of view of some of the ancient Christian mystics as well as the models used by people of other faiths. Some things really do not change, and I think that in its basic premise and outline this is one of them. But I hasten to say up front, that applications of such premises do indeed change, depending on the time and culture in which they are being applied. The following application of Bonaventure's 13th century *Three Fold Path,* while preserving the basic outline, is, I think, true to the original vision, but its application is a thoroughly modern twenty-first century vision. It is a model of the spiritual journey which is just as applicable today as when it was first conceived. It is basically a model for individual spiritual journeys, but it definitely impacts institutional religious expressions.

The chart on the following pages is my systematic distillation of the Three-Fold Path followed by interpretive commentary on pages 35-51.

The Three-Fold Path, a Model of the Spiritual Journey
Attributed to Bonaventure (1221-1274), but may go back to Pseudo-Dionysius (late 5th to early 6th century)

34

Moving from left to right:

	first Stage–Purgation	second Stage–Illumination	third Stage–Union
(1)	Characterized by RATIONALITY–thus, doctrine is important.	Characterized by EXPERIENCES OF GOD–often gratuitous, unsought	Characterized by SILENCE–Acceptance
(2)	Dogma	Questioning Dogma	Enlightenment
(3)	God is a person	Evolving Understanding	God is All there is–Union
(4)	Relationship with Christ & self:		
	I (ego)–X (Christ) Ego centered	Ж (ego in Christ) Liberation from ego	X (ego death) & Ego transcendence, Divinity
(5)	Worship is Obligation	Worship is Desire	Worship is Reverence/Awe
(6)	Prayer is Verbal	Prayer is Communion	Prayer is Intuitive
(7)	Faith is propositional	Faith is demonstrative	Faith is inner certainty
(8)	Love is a duty–something you are supposed to do	Love is a desire to respond to & with God's Love	Love is Being–it is something you are
(9)	"Super spiritual"? Eschews passion; Kills compassion	Liberation from power of ego	Genuinely spiritual; Liberated emotion; Very Human; Very passionate; Very compassionate
(10)	Attitude > Fearful	Attitude > Hopeful	Attitude > Fearless

(11)	Attitude > Pride	Attitude > Ambiguous	Attitude > Deep humility
(12)	Attitude > Controlling/ Attachment	Attitude > Ambiguous	Attitude > Relinquishment/ Non-attachment
(13)	Rigid constraints/law	Personal freedom	Other centered freedom
(14)	Churches that are defined primarily by their doctrines	Churches that are defined primarily by their mission	No religious institutions are in this stage
(15)	Correlation of 3-Fold Path with the seven mansions of Teresa of Avila's Interior Castle: 1st mansion 2nd 3rd 4th, 5th, 6th, & 7th		

Interpretative Commentary on the Three-Fold Path

The 3-Fold Path is a map of the spiritual journey, conceived by Fathers of the early Christian Church as a progressive path through three Stages. In the above model the Christian pilgrims move from left to right, increasing in spiritual maturity as they move from stage to stage, but just because they begin the journey, there is no guarantee that, in this life, they will progress to the third Stage. Indeed, it is my observation that most never make it, in this life, to the second Stage. There are many reasons for this—bad or no teaching, ego, pride, and fear being the most common. Of those who make it to the second Stage, very few have the courage to progress to the third Stage which requires the death of one's ego. The few who make it into the third Stage have, as the Apostle Paul describes it, become a completely "new creation" (II Corinthians 5:17). My hunch is that if we do not in this life complete the journey, we may well have the opportunity somewhere in eternity to try again, but here I enter into the realm of speculation.

Please note that in the following descriptions, the experiences in each column are happening simultaneously. Each stage of the

36

journey is one whole and complex experience. It is here broken down into pieces to make it more comprehensible.

Line 1—Overall characterizations of the three parts of the path

<u>Line 1, Column 1</u>—This stage is characterized by *rationality* because this is the stage in which we are trying to make some kind of sense out of the religious teachings we have been given, whether by parents, culture, or institutional indoctrination. Religion fosters a "head trip" at this stage. We choose our dogma based on the best *information* we have at the time, information most often instilled in us by others who are still in the same stage themselves. "What am I supposed to believe?" That is the question foremost in our minds. It is my observation that most individuals never mature beyond this "religion of the mind" stage, at least in this life. Indeed, If Carl Jung is right that at mid-life we do or did not choose to individuate, thereby remaining open to the possibility of our own personal continuing evolution, we may tragically find ourselves unable to understand or accept the opportunities for change when they come to us later in life.

<u>Line 1, Column 2</u>—For the pilgrims who can receive them, *experiences of God* may be sought but are often given by God unexpectedly. They seem to "come out of the blue" as it were and are typically such as will challenge our religious assumptions. When this happens, it is usually our religious assumptions—our doctrines—that change. Many, perhaps most of us, *can* change our beliefs. We cannot change our experiences. Experience sits in judgment of our dogma.

There is no sharp line between Stage 1 and Stage 2. Pilgrims in Stage 2 still have doctrines, albeit some new ones, and they may vacillate between the two stages depending on how committed they were to their doctrines of the first Stage. But the change can be dramatic, as was the Apostle Paul's experience of the risen Christ on the road to Damascus. In this one experience, his religious (and political) dogma was virtually demolished (see his own account in the New Testament, Acts of the Apostles, chapter 22, verses 6-16).

His experience is by no means unique in the annals of religious history and is certainly not exclusive to Christianity.

<u>Line 1, Column 3</u>—This third fold of the path is characterized by *silence* because these pilgrims *know* that anything they believe or can say about God is neither adequate nor necessary. They know words cannot capture God, and that it is often better to say nothing than to say too little. Nor is it necessary to say anything. If these persons were to forget all of their doctrines it would not matter, because they are experiencing a depth of knowledge of God that does not depend on either rational thought or experiences. Theology, even mystical theology, is a diversion for which there is little time or interest for the pilgrim in the third Stage. Another way of looking at this stage is that it is a radical change in consciousness of a reality that cannot be fully expressed in words.

Line 2—The Place of dogma

<u>Line 2, Column 1</u>—For these pilgrims dogma is very important. It can be so important that they believe it is essential to survival and will defend it to the point that anyone who believes otherwise is considered a personal threat and is someone to be avoided and, if possible, silenced. There are entire religious associations—Christian denominations, Muslim sects, and divisions of the Jewish, Hindu, and other religions who assert that they, and only they, are the custodians of the truth and that all others are anathema. Some will even kill "in the name of God" or "Allah" or "Yahweh" those they believe to be religious apostates or heathens. Virtually all the committed members of such fundamentalist religions feel insecure in the presence of those who disagree with them. Fundamentalists require unanimity of belief and are unable to tolerate opposing views. Believing they have a corner on truth, they feel that if anyone should destroy their beliefs, they will lose everything. They will not lose everything, of course, but they do not know this. They are controlled by fear.

Admittedly, I have painted a pretty grim picture of, perhaps, a minority of participants in these religions. How true this characterization may be of any given individual may vary in degree if not in kind. Some participants in these groups may not share the deep commitment of others to particular beliefs, but if they do not, they likely know better than to express their "heretical" thoughts or questions openly. In any event, should they have an experience of God that calls their dogma into question, they will sometimes have to disassociate themselves from the religion because the religion is defined by its dogma.

Line 2, Column 2—Having made the transition from commitment to a particular dogma to questioning that dogma, a pilgrim may find that he or she has opened Pandora's box and consequently begins questioning all dogmas, eventually even those most pivotal to their former beliefs. Their bedrock has become the experience (or experiences) of God and they may find all their beliefs up for personal, critical review.

Line 2, Column 3—Both dogma and experience fade into irrelevance as enlightenment takes their place. In the mystical traditions of a number of religions, enlightenment is the goal of the journey. The pilgrims' goal is to experience the mind of God and to bask in the light of that knowing. These traditions include (but are certainly not limited to) Christian mysticism, the Jewish Kabbalah tradition, Hindu Yogic tradition, Muslim Sufism, and Buddhism. Virtually every religion, Western and Eastern, has a mystical component which often constitutes a separate branch of the religion.

Line 3—Perceptions of God

Line 3, Column 1—This pilgrim believes that "God is a person," but not just any person. God (male) is a person made in our image. Lacking the words to describe "him," these pilgrims use the only beings they think they know—themselves—and model their God on their own personal image. One difference, however, is that God is much bigger and much better than them in every way. "He" is also far away, answering prayers and pulling strings from a distance. God is, as it were, a super person. After all, Jesus spoke of God as Father, even *Abba*, daddy, and the only daddies we know are human. Literalism is the only way a first Stage pilgrim knows to think of God.

Line 3, Column 2—Depending on the spiritual experiences one has had at this stage of the journey, even though words are still inadequate for capturing God, the evolving understanding of God is expressed in phrases like "God is Love," "God is Light," and "God is Presence."

Line 3, Column 3—For the pilgrim in the third Stage, God simply Is. God is *all* there is. Gone are the illusions generated by our limited physical ability to perceive spiritual reality. Gone is the necessity for words. There is a knowing beyond words, and though this pilgrim relates to God out of this spiritual knowledge, he or she relates to others primarily through loving action, embodying the presence of God within.

Line 4—Relationship with Christ & self

Line 4, Column 1—Perhaps this pilgrim's relationship to Christ is best expressed in the popular poem, "Footprints in the Sand." The poem tells the story of a devotee of Jesus Christ walking alongside of Jesus on a beach, leaving behind a trail of two sets of footprints. Jesus is a friend with whom the devotee can carry on a conversation, asking for guidance for his or her journey. The clear but unspoken assumption of the poet is that the devotee and Jesus are two separate persons, walking together, but still two distinctly separated entities. Though separate from Jesus, the devotee in his or her ego centered identity has the implicit option of either following Jesus along the beach or going his or her own way. Jesus may continue to walk with devotee but perhaps only to a point. (This example is typical of new Christians. Pilgrims of other faiths will likely have similar experiences but within their own religious context.)

Line 4, Column 2—This Christian pilgrim's *experience* of Christ is much more the sense of Christ being within—with no separation between one's ego identity and the Christ within. In this scenario, it is impossible to go one's own way without Christ, because wherever the pilgrim goes, even if it is the wrong way, Christ goes with the pilgrim. For the pilgrim Christ's continuing presence within is experienced as liberation from the power of the ego. It is an experience of transformation, a transformation promised in the first Stage, but not fully experienced until evidenced by the indwelling of the pilgrim by Christ.

Line 4, Column 3—In this stage the Christian pilgrim experiences ego death in the sense that he or she has transcended ego identity and relinquished control of daily life. Transformation continues but at a greatly accelerated pace, as the person has lost the ability to return to the former stage, or to even think about returning. The moment of transition from Stage 2 to Stage 3 is somewhat like driving a car, letting go of the steering wheel while speeding down the road, and climbing out of the driver's seat before God climbs in. In less time than it takes to tell about it, the person ceases to be a follower of Christ and becomes an expression of Christ, fully integrated into the Christ persona, a mature divine being. In this respect, the ego transition is unlike the movement from Stage 1 to Stage 2, which may happen gradually, or a piece at a time.

Line 5, the experience of worship

Line 5, Column 1—*Worship* for the pilgrim in the first stage of the journey tends to be an obligation. We worship God, not because we really know who God is, but because others in our faith community worship and we are urged by both our religious leaders and our Scriptures to do so. But sometimes we get mixed signals as to how we should worship from both the Scriptures and from our religious leaders, so we worship whenever and however it suits us—or not at all. Who should I worship?—Jesus, God the Father, or the Holy Spirit? Will it make God angry if I choose the wrong one? Then there is the question of what kind of worship is acceptable to God? What if God doesn't like my worship? Should I continue to try?

Line 5, Column 2—Probably because we have at this stage had some kind of spiritual encounter(s) with God, we find ourselves *wanting* to worship. The "who" and "how" is no longer a concern. We worship from the heart rather than from the head. To worship has become a burning desire. Worship has become very personal and spontaneous. Participation in scripted worship services may continue but will be less than satisfying.

Line 5, Column 3—For these persons worship has become continual unadulterated reverence and awe—the only response possible to the *interiorized* presence of God. As a consequence the pilgrims have entered into that part of the journey where they have presented their "bodies as a living sacrifice, holy and acceptable to God, which is your spiritual worship" (Romans 12:1). These pilgrims have experienced ego death and have taken up their new divine identities. The Apostle Paul counsels us "not to be conformed [active tense], to this world but to be transformed [passive tense] by the renewing of your minds, so that you will discern what is the will of God—what is good and acceptable and perfect (Romans 12:2-3)."

Line 6, Prayer

Line 6, Column 1—Prayer is verbal. The important thing is what the pilgrim has to say to God.

Line 6, Column 2—Prayer is communion, listening. The important thing is what God has to say to the pilgrim.

Line 6, Column 3—Prayer is intuitive and never ceases. God within communicates silently, wordlessly. The pilgrim responds obediently and joyfully with full understanding and acceptance.

Line 7, Faith

Line 7, Column 1—For the novice pilgrim on the spiritual journey, faith is initially propositional, i.e. it consists primarily of a set of unexamined beliefs affirmed to be true. This is necessarily the case until one has spiritual experiences of God which either confirm or dispute these beliefs. Occasionally, one may adopt a set of beliefs as a consequence of spiritual experience, but more often than not, we come to a particular faith tradition already preconditioned by earlier indoctrination. For example, if one is born and raised in Israel, the high probability is that our first religious beliefs will be Jewish. Likewise, for North Americans, we will have been "born into" the beliefs of our family, usually one or another of the multitude of

Christian denominations. But *belief* is not the same thing as *faith*. The Greek origin of the word we translate as "faith"—*pistos*—actually means that for which we would be willing to give our lives.

I may believe that if I push a certain wall switch, a light will come on. But I probably would not want to stake my life on it. The light may have burned out, the switch may be defective, or it may be the wrong switch. But by the English definition of the word "belief," I still think the light will come on. Not so with *pistos,* the Greek word for faith. Our word "belief" is a poor translation of "pistos," but it is the best we have and it is a long way from expressing the depth of spiritual faith.

Line 7, column 2—With the growth of one's spiritual experience a pilgrim's faith takes on more of the meaning of its Greek predecessor. Faith becomes demonstrative; something we are willing to act on, perhaps even put our lives on the line for.

Line 7, Column 3—In this stage, faith has come to full fruition. There is an inner knowing, an inner certainty, that belies the common definition of faith. Can it be called a faith relationship when one knows God intimately? When one's identity is so entwined with God's that the two cannot be separated? The pilgrim, in the words of the Apostle Paul, will know God fully, even as he or she is fully known by God. (I Corinthians 13:13 paraphrased). Before, the pilgrim had to take God at God's word. Now the pilgrim speaks that word.

Line 8, *Agápe* Love

Line 8, Column 1—For the new spiritual pilgrim, love is something you are supposed to do. Jesus said it many times. So did The Apostle Paul. The problem is that the Love specified is *agápe*, the same inclusive, indiscriminate, unconditional, forgiving kind of Love with which we are loved by God. Furthermore, the ability to so love comes only as a gift of God. We can experience it, but we cannot muster it up on our own. Indeed, such love as we can muster is exclusive, discriminatory, loaded with conditions, and quite often unforgiving. Quite literally, we don't have it in us. If there is one supreme essential for progress on the spiritual journey, *agápe* is it. But we are frustratingly unable to make it happen on our own.

<u>Line 8, Column 2</u>—The pilgrim who has proceeded on the journey to the second stage has almost certainly experienced God's *Agápe* Love in continually transforming ways that are deeply personal. He or she is infected with a burning desire to be an instrument of that Love, feeling passionately for God and for the people God loves. We start with the people immediately around us, but the circle rapidly widens as we become more adequate vessels for the transmission of God's Love.

<u>Line 8, Column 3</u>—God is Love, and so is the pilgrim who has transitioned to the third stage of the journey. For the pilgrim who has progressed to this stage, loving is not so much something you *do*. It is something you *are*. Every thought is a thought of Love. Every one of our molecules, already initialed by God, is an instrument of *Agápe*. John, the author of the first New Testament epistle that carries his name, says that "...if we Love [*Agapáo*] one another, God lives in us, and his Love is perfected in us." (I John 3:12) When we Love with the Love of God, it is God doing the loving.

Line 9, Spirituality

<u>Line 9, Column 1</u>—How do you know if one person or another is "super spiritual"? You ask them. Anyone who thinks he or she is spiritually superior, as opposed to being simply a fellow pilgrim on the journey, is either deluded or a fraud. Do not follow in their path. It is particularly the case with anyone claiming to be in the third stage. To believe that you are in the third stage is one indication that you are not. Humility is at the heart of the pilgrim in the third stage. A lack of humility is an indication that the pilgrim is in the first stage.

Because of the temptation to take the journey into one's own hands the first stage pilgrim may try to deny his or her humanity, unaware that in so doing they also deny their divinity. To be *fully* human is to be fully divine. Our problem is that in denying our humanity we kill its essence, which is passion. We *fear* passion because we have difficulty controlling it. But we do not realize that if we kill passion, we also kill *com*passion. *If we cannot feel deeply, we cannot feel deeply for others.*

Line 9, Column 2—The pilgrims who have successfully moved into stage two have likely done so due to God-bestowed experiences that have liberated them from the tyranny of the ego. This, for the formerly self-absorbed egotists, is a sign of genuine spirituality and a major breakthrough on their journey to freedom. They are liberated to feel and consequently, to feel deeply for others.

Line 9, Column 3—The mature pilgrim in the third stage is fully human, and is therefore incredibly passionate, and is therefore incredibly *com*passionate. Articulated or not, he or she knows both an infectious joy in their humanity and a deep compassion for a world hung up on false pretensions and mistaken identity. The author of the biblical Letter to the Ephesians prays for his fellow pilgrims: "And I pray that you, being rooted and established in Love, may have power, together with all the Lord's people, to grasp how wide and long and high and deep is the Love of Christ, and to know this Love that surpasses knowledge—that *you may be filled to the measure of all the fullness of God."* (Ephesians 3:17-19, NRSV) The third stage pilgrim knows experientially what the biblical author is talking about.

Line 10, Innate Attitudes of Fear, Hope and Fearlessness

Line 10, Column 1—The pilgrim at this stage is often very fearful. Everything is new and confusing. What is my bedrock? Who do I believe? Do I take my Scriptures literally? What do I do with all the contradictions? There are answers aplenty, but which ones are right? Do I just go with my gut feeling? Or perhaps I should just follow someone else who seems to know the ropes. And what about sin? What is sin and what isn't? Will God still love me if I blow it? Does anybody know what is going on around here? These and countless other questions plague the novice pilgrim. It is hard not to be fearful.

45

Line 10, Column 2—Even a little progress on the journey instills hope. As long as the pilgrim remains open to the hidden machinations of the Spirit of God, there is hope that the questions will be resolved and that the confusion will be illuminated by the light of God's self-revelation. God's continuing manifestation through our experiences means that we are neither alone nor left to our own devices nor abandoned to our own hell. To have experienced God's *agápe* is to know that our Creator can no more reject her own creation than she can reject herself. Emanuel, God with us, is an eternal reality. This is the dawning truth that gives the pilgrim a profound hope.

Line 10, Column 3—The pilgrim in Stage 3 of the spiritual journey, as the consequence of his or her deep knowing, is completely fearless. It is a fearlessness born of the realization of one's divine identity. God has nothing to fear and God in us has nothing to fear. It is not courage. Courage is only needed when the outcome is in doubt. The pilgrim already knows the outcome of the journey so there is no need for courage.

Line 11, Innate Feelings of Pride and Humility

Line 11, Column 1—The Apostle Paul admonishes his Corinthian converts not to think more highly of themselves than they ought to think, but "to think with sober judgment, each according to the measure of faith that God has assigned." This raises the interesting premise that this is as much God's journey as it is ours, thus we have no occasion to take pride in it. It is a partnership in which we are the junior partners.

Line 11, Column 2—In this stage the pilgrim typically has ambiguous feelings. On the one hand, there may be the desire to take some of the credit for the newfound freedom and discernment. On the other hand, the pilgrim knows that whatever progress has happened, it is pure gift. The pilgrim's part is only to receive that which is given.

Line 11, Column 3—The pilgrim's only possible response to the initiatives of God is deep humility and gratitude, but it is not the false humility cowering before overwhelming power but rather the humility of an honest assessment of the goodness of God's work in one's life along with the humble acknowledgment that it is *God's* work.

Line 12, Control and Relinquishment

<u>Line 12, Column 1</u>—Initially the novice pilgrim looks upon this new idea of a spiritual journey as something he or she has to accomplish. It is conceived as a huge, possibly life-long, self-help project. There is attachment, not so much to the past, but to the journey itself. What has yet to be learned is that the only permissible attachment is to God; but this is difficult because the pilgrim's concept of God is so inadequate that it keeps getting in the way. There is the felt need to control the journey, lest God capriciously take the pilgrim in a direction he or she does not want to go. The truth that it is God's design to kill the pilgrim's ego is totally unacceptable.

<u>Line 12, Column 2</u>—The battle between the pilgrim's ego and God's will for the pilgrim, continues, sometimes leaning one direction, sometimes the other. This is a decisive battle, and neither side is assured of winning it. If the pilgrim successfully resists God, it is only because God chooses not to violate the liberty of the pilgrim to go his or her own way. There is no guarantee, therefore, that in this life the pilgrim will in fact reach the third stage.

<u>Line 12, Column 3</u>—Those pilgrims who relinquish their claims to be autonomous from God or to be independent agents of their own spiritual journey may eventually arrive at the point of accepting ego death. They make what can only be a scary decision to commit all they are and ever will be, like Christ on the cross, to the will of God. In ego death one gives up the right to self-determination and gives up all past attachments, spiritual and otherwise, in order to ascend in this life to the greatest treasure of all—the kingdom of God. Jesus speaks of this in a parable: "...the kingdom of heaven is like a merchant in search of fine pearls; on finding one pearl of great value, he went and sold all he had and bought it." (Gospel of Matthew, 13:45-46)

Line 13, Law and Freedom

Line 13, Column 1—The pilgrim in this stage is like a caged bird that has accepted its confinement, unaware that just beyond the bars of its cage is a whole world of glorious freedom. But the bird is well fed and its cage is kept clean, and it does not even know what it is like to soar. It does not know that it was created to soar. For the novice pilgrim, the law is like that cage. Religion abounds with laws which purportedly inform us as to what is safe and what is dangerous. It gives us well intentioned laws meant to guide us through a quiet and uneventful life, a life without ripples—at least that is the avowed purpose. But sometimes that is not the real purpose, which may be to protect the hegemony of the religious institution itself. Obeying the laws, the pilgrim may be safe, but he or she will never soar.

Line 13, Column 2—Initially the novice pilgrim looks upon this new idea of a spiritual journey as some-thing he or she has to accomplish. There is a higher law which is not nearly so confining—the law written on the heart by God herself. This is the law that the spiritual pilgrim is called to obey. It is not a law of rules, but it is a law which trusts the God-given instincts of every pilgrim on the journey. It is this law which allows the freedom to soar above the rooftops, above the trees, even above the mountains. It is not anarchy. It does recognize a higher, but benevolent, power that teaches that not everything that is labeled a sin is, in fact, sin. Indeed, many of the supposed moral lapses identified by religious "authorities"— homosexuality, for example—are not sins at all, but rather are God-created and blessed sexual orientations. Some of the spiritual illuminations of the pilgrim in this second stage will reveal the hypocrisy of such laws, based as they are on fear of the unknown, and the pilgrim will be released for untethered flight to soar where they have never soared before.

Line 13, Column 3—The pilgrim in this stage is subject only to the supreme law, repeated in one way or another in virtually every religion, "In everything, do to others as you would have them do to you, for this is the law and the prophets." (Gospel of Matthew 7:12) The author of the Gospel of John quotes Jesus as saying to his disciples, "I give you a new commandment, that you Love one another. Just as I have loved you, you also should Love one another." (Gospel of John 13:34) What kind of Love was Jesus talking about? It was *agápe*. (See commentary on Line 8, above.) These are the *only* laws for the pilgrim who has arrived at Stage 3. Anything else is just extra baggage to be abandoned.

Line 14, Religious Institutions

Line 14, Column 1—Among Christian denominations, virtually all churches are in Stage 1. This is because almost all churches are defined by their doctrines. Indeed, few churches even know there is a spiritual journey. It is more likely that most churches consider themselves to be the guardians of what they consider to be unchanging received truth. Anything or anybody who challenges this "truth" is thought to be hostile to the church. Individuals who progress to the second stage of the journey must either remain quiet or risk alienation, or even dismissal, from the church. In other religions the consequences of "heresy" can be much worse.

Line 14, Column 2—There are a few churches that are defined by their mission rather than by their doctrine. Depending on how tolerant they are of a variety of religious concepts, they may actually encourage spiritual journeys. Though it is unlikely that many or all of their members will consider themselves called to the journey, it is important to those who are thus called that they have the blessing of their church.

Line 14, Column 3—I have difficulty conceiving of any institutional religious group moving *en masse* into the third stage. I will not say that God *cannot* manage it, but I do think it is unlikely to happen. My reasoning is this: Inasmuch as each spiritual pilgrim is given the individual freedom to choose whether or not to go through the experience of ego death to enter into the third stage, it is inconceivable to me that a diverse group, (which likely includes children, older adults who long ago chose not to individuate, and spiritually immature adults still struggling with concerns of the first stage), I would be very surprised if all of these disparities could ever be brought together for such a voluntary and difficult joint experience. Nor am I sure that such a joint venture would even be desirable unless the group members were largely dispersed to be catalysts for other groups or individuals. I am willing to be proved wrong, but as of this writing, I do not know of any groups, large or small, that I would suspect of such an achievement.

Teresa of Avila's *Interior Castle* (see Line 15 above in the table, The Three-Fold Path)

Teresa of Avila (March 28, 1515–October 4, 1582) was a Spanish mystic, Roman Catholic saint, and Carmelite nun who conceived of the spiritual journey as a journey through an *Interior Castle* with seven mansions and many, many rooms. Though the content of the mansions is much more detailed, it very roughly correlates with the columns of Bonaventure's *Three-Fold Path,* with which Teresa would likely have been familiar. The seven mansions were labeled as follows in the commentary on the *Interior Castle* by Carolyn Myss, *Entering the Castle,* 2007 (see bibliography).

The First Mansion: The Power of Prayer, Humility, Chaos and Divine Seduction

The Second Mansion: God in the Details: Inner Vision and Soul Companions

The Third Mansion: Surrender: The Defeat of Reason, The Presence of God

The Fourth Mansion: The Mystical Heart

The Fifth Mansion: Dissolving into Holiness: From Silkworm to Butterfly

The Sixth Mansion: Essential Wisdoms and the Final Fire

The Seventh Mansion: Divine Marriage, Healing and Reentering the World

Teresa's descriptions of mystical experiences in the fourth, fifth and sixth mansions are particularly intriguing and informative as they concern the mystical realm of Bonaventure's *Three-Fold Path.*

I have been asked if I know of anyone who has entered into the third Stage of the *Three-Fold Path.* I am certain Jesus of Nazareth did, but I am not so certain about the Apostle Paul. Paul, at least during the time he was writing his letters to the gentile churches, still had unresolved issues with his concept of sin which I would have thought would be dealt with prior to the third Stage. Beyond that I speculate that there may be a handful of my contemporaries who have made that transition without ever having heard of the spiritual journey or the *Three-Fold Path.* I suspect that most would have been elderly because this is generally a life-long journey. I did, however, come to know one young woman, Victoria, who was in her mid-twenties and bed-ridden with serious illnesses for half her life. She died at age 29. She would not have known of the *Three-Fold Path* but her spiritual depth leads me to believe she not only was on it but had also completed it. Her life continues to illuminate my own journey to this day.

Matthew Fox, in a very free translation of part of St. Teresa's conclusion of her epic work on the soul, *Interior Castle,* quotes, "Now we've explored seven rooms in your soul, but in fact your soul has millions of rooms, most of which never have their doors opened. And in every one of them there are labyrinths and fountains and jewels and gems and gardens." (Fox & Sheldrake 1996, p. 87) Fox opines that we should open at least a million doors before we die.

Carolyn Myss, in her interpretive rendering of St. Teresa's *Interior Castle,* offers *"essential guidance for mystics outside the castle walls"* to those who have presumably completed the journey within the walls. Her counsel is here offered in summary fashion: (Myss 2007, pp. 342-346)

- *Maintain your work in the castle...* Revisit the rooms that need the most attention.
- *Practice illumination.* Do not treat your spiritual life as a hobby.

- *Develop and share the gifts of your soul...* Allow your inner guidance to alert you to act.
- *Keep alert.* Evil exists. Take refuge in your Castle.
- *Fly under the radar.* Never position yourself as an authority... Stay humble at all times.
- *Avoid power plays.* Your job is not to win arguments or prove anything to anyone.
- *Stop blaming others.* No human being is responsible for your choices.
- *Don't use the word "deserve."* To decide who deserves what in this world positions you as judge and jury over others.
- *Let your first response in any situation be, "What can I do?"*
- *Channel grace on a daily basis...* a channel for grace is a core part of your identity as a mystic.
- *Form a circle of grace with soul companions...* support one another's spiritual journeys.
- *Live congruently.* Make sure your mind and your heart are in agreement with your soul.
- *Be devoted to truth.* Mystics are Keepers of truth.
- *Stay active in the world.* Mystics are servants. Do not run and hide from this world.
- *You are a source for healing...* Visualize grace flowing through you and into the person who is speaking to you... Where there is tension, visualize grace flowing through you into the room.
- *Remain active in your castle...* Animate love in your life... See God in everything.

Carolyn Myss concludes her guidance through the *Interior Castle* with these final words: "Let your Castle become the sacred ground beneath your feet. Live the power of your soul. Listen to and follow the voice of your soul. You are not alone. No higher purpose in this life exists than to be called into mystical relationship with the divine." (op. cit., p. 346)

The Four Paths of Creation Spirituality

Matthew Fox, in his book *Original Blessing,* has outlined four paths to God based on the ancient tradition of creation spirituality, which "traces its roots to the ninth century B.C., with the very first author of the Bible (the Yahwist or J source), to the Psalms, to wisdom books of the Bible, to much of the prophets, to Jesus and much of the New Testament, and to the very first Christian theologian in the West, … St. Irenaeus (130-200 CE.)" The four paths are outlined as follows, but they are developed in detail comprising most of the book, *Original Blessing.* (Fox 1983, p. 11)

Path I, Befriending Creation, the Via Positiva

The ten themes or stopping places along the path of the Via Positiva:
1. *Dabhar*: The Creative Energy (Word) of God.
2. Creation as Blessing and the Recovery of the Art of Savoring Pleasure.
3. Humility as Earthiness: Our Earthiness as a Blessing along with Passion and Simplicity.
4. Cosmic, Universalist: Harmony, Beauty, and Justice as Cosmic Energies.
5. Trust: A Psychology of Trust and Expansion.
6. Panentheism: Experiencing the Diaphanous and Transparent God.
7. Our Royal Personhood: Our Dignity and Responsibility for Building the Kingdom/Queendom of God. Creation Theology as a Kingdom/Queendom Theology.
8. Realized Eschatology: A New Sense of Time.
9. Holiness as Cosmic Hospitality; Creation Ecstasies Shared Constitute the Holy Prayer of Thanksgiving and Praise.
10. Sin, Salvation, Christ from the Perspective of the Via Positiva: A Theology of Creation and Incarnation.

Path II, Befriending Darkness, Letting Go and Letting Be: The Via Negativa
1. Emptying: Letting Go of Images and Letting Silence Be Silence
2. Being Emptied: Letting Pain Be Pain; Kenosis.

3. Sinking into Nothingness and Letting Nothingness Be Nothingness.
4. Sin, Salvation, Christ in Perspective of the Via Negativa: A Theology of the Cross.

Path III, Befriending Creativity, Befriending Our Divinity: The Via Creativa

1. From Cosmos to Cosmogenesis: Our Divinization as Images of God Who Are Also Co-Creators.
2. Art as Meditation: Creation and Birthing as Meditation, Centering, a Return to the Source.
3. Faith as Trust of Images: Discipline—Yes! Asceticism—No!
4. Dialectical, Trinitarian: How Our Lives as Works of Art Spiral Beauty Back into the World.
5. God as Mother, God as Child: Ourselves as Mothers of God and Birthers of God's Son.
6. Sin, Salvation, Christ in the Perspective of the Via Creativa: A Theology of the Resurrection.

Path IV, Befriending New Creation: Compassion, Celebration, Erotic Justice, the Via Transformativa

1. The New Creation: Images of God in Motion Creating a Global Civilization.
2. Faith as Trusting the Prophetic Call of the Holy Spirit.
3. A Spirituality of the Anawim: Feminists, Third World, Lay, and Other Oppressed Peoples.
4. Compassion: Interdependence, Celebration, and Recovering Eros.
5. Compassion: Interdependence and Erotic Justice.
6. Sin, Salvation, Christ in the Perspective of the Via Transformativa: A Theology of the Holy Spirit.

One River, Many Wells

"One river, many wells," is Matthew Fox's apt phrase which he uses as the title for his book on the false distinctions we make between religions. In this book Fox "shows exactly how the different fingers of world faiths connect to a single hand" (Fox, 2000, back cover). He cites the observation of Burton Mack who says that "what was going on among the earliest communities after Jesus' death was an explosion of creative imagination that we would call myth-making." (cf. Mack, 1993, p. 207-ff.) Fox goes on to speculate: "One wonders if we do not need such an *explosion of imagination* today" and then proceeds to list *Eighteen Myths for Remythologizing Our Species;* though I tend to think that the following are myths only in the sense that their very literal truth can only be *spiritually* discerned (Fox, 2000, pp. 436-438). I share them here in somewhat abbreviated form:

1. All our spiritual traditions can learn from each other... the myth of Deep ecumenism.
2. All Creation is sacred and we humans are part of it.
3. All Creation is on fire with sacredness; the Buddha nature and the Cosmic Christ and the image of God reside in the very light (photons) present in every atom in the universe.
4. Community already is because all things are interdependent; nothing stands alone.
5. Whatever name we give the Source of sources, the Artist of artists, the Creator of creation, all are accurate and none is sufficient.
6. The Divine has a feminine as well as a masculine side. And so do we, made in her image.
7. Divine wisdom roams the world, "fills the whole earth," interacts with us and all Creation and calls us to supper.
8. The Divine, while present in all forms as emptiness, nothingness, and formlessness and... we experience... and can trust these.
9. The Divine "I Am" can be spoken by every one of us and by every creature and... this is our way of asserting our divine nobility.

10. We experience mindfulness, a state of being... fully present to the "I Am" and to our deepest self.

11. Our imaginations are holy...the Holy Spirit works through us when we create and participate in the ongoing Creation.

12. Joy is possible even daily; and... we have a right to it as well as a responsibility to search it out, prepare for it, and pass it on.

13. Suffering... comes as a teacher of wisdom and compassion.

14. Beauty is another name for the Divine, it is available everywhere.

15. Our sexuality is sacred; the body is no obstacle to Divine presence, and love-making is for the propagation of community and love as much as propagation of the species.

16. Our dying is as adventurous as our living, and what occurs at death and after death, whether we call it reincarnation or resurrection or regeneration, is mysterious but not final. No beauty dies; no grace is lost; no warmth is forgotten.

17. Compassion is the imitation of the Divine.

18. We are all spiritual warriors (or prophets) as well as lovers (or mystics). And this means that we struggle with self and... for social transformation. It also means that we work from the heart.

Dancing the Dream—A Native American Journey

It is in this spirit of deep ecumenism that I share the following insights of the Cherokee Indians on the "seven[7] sacred paths of human transformation". My primary source is my own several-year experience of Native American spirituality with my spiritual director, Sol Mockasin, a Cherokee elder. In Cherokee spiritual

---

7   Ancient religions have often made references to the number seven. In this review of the spiritual journey we have encountered St. Teresa's seven interior mansions and the seven Native American paths of initiation, and the seven *chakras* of Yoga. Beyond this, there were seven virtues in Catholic doctrine, seven sacraments, seven sins, and, biblically, the seven gifts of the spirit. In esoteric traditions seven is a magical number and persons or things to which it refers may be all-knowing, mystical or desire knowledge above all else. Seven signifies completeness gained through true insight. Seven is also the symbol of the philosopher or mystic and connotes an individual who is aloof, introspective and thoughtful, meditative, quiet and intuitive.

tradition this life is but the continuation of the life they experienced before their physical birth. It was a time of union with the Great Spirit. They are born into this life so that they may learn to dance the dream of union with the Creator. In so doing they accepted the limitations of embodiment. Thus to be human is to be on a sacred journey of discovery. To learn to dance and to feel, to experience reality in a human body is one of the purposes of this life. Another is to teach others how to celebrate their lives in anticipation of returning home to the Great Spirit.

The Medicine Wheel ceremony is one such celebration. The seven directions of the Medicine Wheel (East, South, West, and North plus Above, Below, and Within) correlate with the secrets of the seven paths. Ceremonially, the Medicine Wheel is performed by an individual moving around a 6-8-foot diameter circle of stones, stopping to face each of the seven directions to give thanks to the Great Spirit for the particular gifts that come from that direction. (For example, from the East: the gifts of awakening to a new day, the warmth of the rising sun, the banishment of darkness, the rising of the morning mists, the new energy from a night's rest, illumination, etc.)

Each direction in the life of the journeyer represents a new initiation leading ultimately to the inner depths of one's self. Thus the Medicine Wheel ceremony may be repeated to address the new challenges of each successive path of initiation. Another ceremony, called a vision quest, at least in Cherokee practice, is done alone with the involvement of one's spiritual mentor at the beginning and again at the end. The journeyer fasts during the experience and has only blankets to protect him or her from the cold and damp. No other creature comforts, such as flashlights or matches, tents or bedrolls, watches or cell phones are allowed. The duration of the initiation may be a period of one or two days and nights, though for some tribes it may be one or two weeks and becomes much more of a survival exercise. The goals of each vision quest will vary in content depending on the particular path of initiation one is on, but one hoped-for experience in each is the gift of a vision in response to the prayers to the Great Spirit.

The first path of initiation—East on the Medicine Wheel—is often a rite of passage from childhood to adulthood in Native American practice, and seeks readiness for change, illumination of spiritual synchronicity, the choice to be our personal best, and the choice to be of service. This is a path of openness, harmony, caring and innocence.

The second path of initiation—South on the Medicine Wheel—focuses on the healing of relationships and the return to trust. This is a path of compassion, loyalty, commitment and dedication.

The third path of initiation—West on the Medicine Wheel—is introspective, focusing on building self-esteem and personal balance. It is a path of commitment to learning, insight, meditation, and collaboration.

The fourth path of initiation—North on the Medicine Wheel—is concerned with the proper use of wisdom, unconditional Love, and compassion. This is a path of knowledge, curiosity, and intellect.

The fifth path of initiation—Above on the Medicine Wheel—is about moving in the spiritual realms and viewing infinity. This is the path of spirituality.

The sixth path of initiation—Below on the Medicine Wheel—focuses on reconnecting with the earth and the spirit in all things. Each person has a special song. Part of becoming a mature spiritual person is to discover your own song.

The seventh path of initiation—Within on the Medicine Wheel—seeks full awareness of the present moment.

These seven paths of human transformation practiced by Native Americans converge at a number of points with the seven mansions of St. Teresa's *Interior Castle,* though not always in the same order. The language differs, Teresa's being, I think, more overtly religious and the symbolism different from, but parallel to, the Medicine Wheel. The spiritualities have a lot of congruity with each other, even in the words used. In Matthew Fox's imagery, we draw water from the same river, but use different wells.

The ultimate goal of every journey, whatever its form or content, is union—whether it be with God or the Great Spirit or Allah or Yahweh makes no difference. It is in celebration of the union of our spirits with the Creator and with one another that we find our true selves.

Yoga, The Transcendence of Ego

Yoga is a Sanskrit word that can be translated "union". It originally comes from the root word *yuj*, which means 'to yoke,' to attach one's self "to a task at hand with ox-like discipline. And the task at hand in Yoga is to find union—between mind and body, between the individual and [his or] her God, between our thoughts and the source of our thoughts..." We sometimes confuse *Yoga* with *Hatha Yoga* which is an exercise system for the body and only one aspect of the *Yogic* philosophy. Elizabeth Gilbert points out that *Yoga* also means "trying to find God through meditation, through scholarly study, through the practice of silence, through devotional service or through mantra—the repetition of sacred words in Sanskrit." Though Yoga originated in Hinduism, "it is not synonymous with Hinduism, nor are all Hindus Yogis." The practice of Yoga "neither competes with nor precludes any religion. You may use your Yoga—your disciplined practices of sacred union—to get closer to Krishna, Jesus, Muhammad, Buddha or Yahweh." (Gilbert 2006, p.121-122)

Yoga teaches that human discontent is merely a case of mistaken identity that we wrongly think of ourselves as separated individuals, separated from each other and from God and that we are wholly our egos. Yoga teaches that we have a deeper, divine character, a supreme Self who is our true universal identity. Gilbert quotes the Greek stoic philosopher Epictetus: "You bear God within you, poor wretch, and know it not." (ibid, p. 122.) It is in Yoga that we encounter the concept of seven subtle, non-physical, energy centers called *chakras*. *Chakra* is Sanskrit for "wheel" or "disc." Each chakra correlates to a specific consciousness:

7. The Crown Chakra, the highest, represents our spiritual consciousness.
6. The Third Eye, or Brow, Chakra, located on the forehead between the eyes, represents our intuitive consciousness, imagination, and wisdom.
5. The Throat Chakra represents our creative consciousness, our ability to communicate and express our feelings.
4. The Heart Chakra, located in the center of the chest just above the heart, represents our ability to love and have compassion, joy and inner peace.
3. The Solar Plexus Chakra, located in the upper abdomen in the stomach area, represents our ego consciousness and issues of self-worth, self-confidence, and self-esteem.
2. The Sacral Chakra, located in the lower abdomen about two inches below the navel, represents our consciousness of desire, well-being, pleasure, and sexuality.
1. The Root Chakra, located at the base of the spine, represents our foundation, our sense of groundedness.

Yoga is all about being fully in the eternal present. Only from this vantage point can we leave the past behind and forgo our concerns about the future. Only then can we see the world as it really is—all of it a manifestation of God's creative energy. Human life is shown to be a very special manifestation because "only in human form and only with a human mind can God-realization ever occur. 'Our whole business in this life,' wrote St. Augustine, rather Yogically, 'is to restore to health the eye of the heart whereby God may be seen.'" (ibid. p.123)

From an Ashram in India to Augustine's Hippo Regius in North Africa to twenty-first century America; from before 3,000 BCE to 2013 CE, the "traditional purpose of Yoga... has always been to bring about a profound transformation in the person through the transcendence of the ego," (Feuerstein 2003, p.3) Yoga has had staying power. My inclination is to believe that it has had this power because there is within its basic teachings that which is truth, truth that has survived the passage of time; transcended national, cultural, and religious boundaries; and still, to this day, speaks to the yearnings for union of the human heart.

Traveling the Path of Love—The Islamic Sufi Mystical Tradition

The mystical path in the Sufi tradition is the soul's journey from separation back to union. On this homeward journey, the Sufi is seeking his or her own innermost essence, the pearl of great price that he/she has hidden within the heart. The Sufi travels three paths—the journey from God, the journey to God, and the journey in God; the Islamic equivalents of the Three-Fold Path in Christian mystical tradition. "The journey is towards your homeland... you are traveling from the world of appearances to the world of Reality." ('Abd'l-Khaliq Ghijduwani, quoted in Vaughan-Lee, 1995, p. 16)

The Sufi's journey, like that of the Christian mystics, is concerned with ego death. "Take one step away from yourself and—behold!—the Path." (Abǔ Sa'îd ibn Abî-L-Khayr, Vaughan-Lee, op. cit., p. 18) and "When you seek God, seek Him in your Heart—He is not in Jerusalem, nor in Mecca nor in the *hajj.*" (Yǔnus Emre, Vaughan-Lee, op. cit., p. 20) and "Lovers don't finally meet somewhere. They're in each other all along." (Rǔmi, Vaughan-Lee, ibid., p. 21) "Everything in the world of existence has an end and a goal. The end is maturity and the goal is freedom.... The final goal is returning to one's origin. Everything which reaches its origin has reached its goal. A farmer sows grain in the ground and tends it. It begins to grow, eventually seeds, and again becomes grain. It has returned to its original form. The circle is complete. Completing the circle of existence is freedom." (Nasafî, Vaughan-Lee, ibid., p. 30)

As far as I know the only route to maturity is through immaturity. No one is born mature. This applies as much or more to spiritual growth as it does to physical growth. Somewhere in eternity we were, each one, conceived in the mind of God and only then conceived *in utero.* It is from this common starting point that all people start this leg of their journeys. Whether one is born of Christian parents, Islamic parents, or atheist parents makes no difference. Furthermore the end goal is the same, which is to grow through immaturity to maturity, to eventually arrive back at our Source. *En route*, the details of our journeys will vary. The paths we take however, though uniquely our own, are similar. Some will complete their journey in this life; others may take a little longer. But we will all arrive at our Source.

What we will discover along the way to, or when we arrive at, our Source is that our common Source is *Agápe*, the unconditional, all inclusive, and eternal Love of God. It is only the spiritually immature who do not grasp this. In their immaturity, the goal is still too distant to apprehend. Theirs is the essence of fundamentalism which is, by definition, engagement with the fundamentals of life, faith, and myriads of relationships. It is a time of confusion exacerbated by false teaching and the innate *in*ability to conceive of so great a Love. The shorter this stage of development, the better, but few if any of us avoid it altogether. *We have to learn to Love, which is difficult when we are taught to hate.* Perhaps we all can learn from our Islamic brother, Rûmi, who, in his poem *"No Expectations,"* urges us to, "Be foolishly in love, Because love is all there is." (Rumi, Barks 2007, p.76)[8]

It matters not so much which path we take to return to our Source. It only matters how diligently we pursue it. We probably cannot avoid the path altogether but we can certainly prolong it by dallying along the way with detours that are dead ends and without merit. This is one reason why I think the concept of reincarnation may have some merit, because the pace of our journeys is such that it may require several lifetimes to finish the journey. (This, too, is a theme to which we will return later.)

How to Get on with the Journey—II

(1)-RADICAL **OPENNESS** IN FAITH UNCONSTRAINED BY DOCTRINE;
(2)- PERSONAL **TRUST** RELATIONSHIP WITH GOD; &
(3)-PERSONAL SPIRITUAL **INTENTION**

---

8 Biographical note: Rumi was a 13th-century Persian Muslim poet, jurist, theologian, and Sufi mystic. The testimony of the Apostle John in the Christian New Testament is that "God is Love..." (I John 4:8) It is not a huge leap of insight, combining Rumi's insight on love with John's insight on God, to come to the conclusion that *God is all there is*. (This is a theme which will be developed in chapter 8 of this book.)

For the sake of emphasis, I have repeated above the conditions for making progress in one's personal spiritual journey. The journey is not one that the pilgrim can control. He or she can only create favorable conditions for transformation to happen. I have called the first of these conditions *radical openness.* By definition, to be radical is to go to the root or foundation of something. In the theological context it means going to our root, which is God. This does not mean doctrines about God, but rather the God who Is; the primal Creator, the One who is ultimately indefinable and yet grants access to those pilgrims who approach with awe, trust, and desire.

The second condition, *trust,* is a huge stumbling block for those who have not learned to trust. If the pilgrim's approach to life is fraught with instances of betrayed trust, the journey will necessarily include healing of past injuries and learning to trust, first others, and then the One who is calling us on the journey.

The third condition, *spiritual intention,* is a requirement more of the heart than of the head. Heart intention is capable of humility, whereas spiritual intention ruled by the head is inevitably vulnerable to pride and consequent failure to progress on the journey.

Not only is it in the union of our spirits with the Creator and with one another that we find our true selves—it is also in that union that *we participate in God's dream.*

Chapter 3

GOD'S DREAM

"Where there is no vision a people perish."

—Ralph Waldo Emerson

I will pour out my Spirit on all flesh;
your sons and your daughters shall prophesy,
Your old men shall dream dreams,
and your young men shall see visions."

—Joel 2:28, NRSV

It is difficult to say what is impossible, for the dream of yesterday is
the hope of today and the reality of tomorrow.

Robert H. Goddard

You see things and say "Why?" but I dream things that never were
and I say "Why not?"

George Bernard Shaw

An Undigested Bit of Beef?

Charles Dickens had his miserly character, Scrooge, tell "the ghost of Christmas past," the first of the apparitions that came to him on Christmas Eve, "You may be an undigested bit of beef, a blot of mustard, a crumb of cheese, a fragment of underdone potato. There's more gravy than grave about you, whatever you are." Scrooge is not by himself. I cannot count the times that I have glibly asserted about one or another of my dreams, "It must have been something I ate." I am not serious when I say that, because I have done enough dream work to know better. As a general rule, however, our dreams *do appear* to be a bit of undecipherable mishmash not to be taken too seriously—and few people today do take them seriously.

This was not the case in the past. The biblical record is replete with accounts of dreams and visions which proved to be transformative, or even salvific, for those who took them seriously. Even when the dreams were a part of mythological stories, they reveal an openness to the likelihood that they communicate something of importance. Could it be that the pseudo-sophistication of modern thinking has blinded us to dreams as a source of guidance and truth, which we sorely need but ignore because we do not understand them?

Dreams have their own language, what I am inclined to call a language of the soul. They draw on the mundane experiences of our daily lives—the data stored in our memory—to speak symbolically of things present and future which need our attention. Our task is to decode the symbols in order to reveal the deep truths our soul wants to communicate to us. It is no wonder, then, that when we ignore our dreams, we are often left floundering, not knowing which way to turn.

Further, if my definition of soul as *that-which-is-of-God-in-us* is correct, then to ignore its attempts to communicate with us is tantamount to ignoring God. To recognize this can potentially be life-changing, opening us to the possibility of intelligent participation in the work of God in both our own lives and in the world. I believe that Carl Jung was in touch with a significant truth when he observed: *"the mystery of dreams [is] that one does not dream, one is dreamt."* (cited by Peter O'Connor, 1987, p. 87)

God has a dream, and we are both a part of the dream and implementers of the dream. In paying attention to our dreams we become co-creators with God of her dream. As such we can help make God's dream a reality. That is what we are here for, that is our calling. Because of our God-given identity—divine beings who demonstrate the presence of God in our lives and work—God's dreams are our dreams. They come to us unbidden and mysteriously, calling us to understand and incorporate them into our human/divine agendas.

It is not in the scope of this book to identify any given piece of God's dream with any particular person. This is something to be discerned by each individual, perhaps with the help of one's own spiritual mentor. But there are a lot of pointers to what God's big plan for the ages is. This information is, as it were, in the public domain.

What Is God's Dream?—A New Heaven and a New Earth

The Apostle John is credited by most biblical scholars with the most incredible vision found in all of Scripture (and perhaps in all of history). It is introduced by John as "the revelation of Jesus Christ which God gave him to show his servants what must soon take place; he [Jesus] made it known by sending his angel to his servant John, who testified to the word of God and to the testimony of Jesus Christ, even to all that he saw." (The Revelation to John, 1:1-2, NRSV) What follows in John's vision is an extraordinary visual and auditory production of twenty-two chapters, leading up to a climax in chapters 21 and 22, where John, continuing to report his vision, says:

> Then I saw a new heaven and a new earth; for the first heaven and the first earth had passed away, and the sea was no more. And I saw the holy city, the new Jerusalem, coming down out of heaven from God, prepared as a bride

adorned for her husband. And I heard a loud voice from the throne saying, "See, the home of God is among mortals. He will dwell with them as their God, they will be his peoples, and God himself will be with them; he will wipe away every tear from their eyes. Death will be no more, for the first things have passed away." (Revelation to John, 21:1-4, NRSV)

The end of suffering and death? God dwelling with her people? John apparently thought so. Taken literally, it has been a long time coming; countless billions of people have passed from the earthly scene without seeing any convincing evidence that it was coming, either soon or at all. But hope does not die easily, and it is upheld still by the tenacious belief that it *could* still happen just around the bend.

I would suggest that as long as there is hope for a new earth, the belief is justified and on some level is *realized*, at least by some. The alternative to hope is despair, which is unacceptable. The author of the New Testament Letter to the Hebrews writes, "Now faith is the assurance of things *hoped* for, the conviction of things not seen... By faith we understand that the worlds were prepared by the word of God, so that what is seen was made from things that are not visible." (Hebrews 11:1 & 3, NRSV) Hope is not "pie-in-the-sky" wishing. It is a psychological necessity and it is a requisite for its ultimate self-fulfillment. Whatever disparity there appears to be simply underscores the urgency that we human beings come to terms with our divine nature. Such visions as that reported by John must be owned, understood and, by the spiritual powers inherent in our God-given identity, implemented. The implementation of our/God's vision will come about not by some ethereal army, but by us. If it is a long time coming, then *we* have not been doing our part.

Our dreams and visions arise from within and may or may not be taken literally. They are given us by the God who is within. They are a spiritual gift and their meanings must be spiritually discerned. At the very least, they are expressions of the divine hopes of the divine beings we are. To repeat the inspired insight of psychologist Carl Jung cited above, *"The mystery of dreams [is] that one does not dream, one is dreamt.*" God does her dreaming through us and our dreams are, therefore, very significant.

What Is God's Dream?—Loving with the Love of God; Introduction to *Agápe*

Another one of God's dreams was reported in a piece of inspired writing by the mystic and apostle, Paul. Though he does not present this as a dream or vision, I believe it is, in fact, God's vision given through Paul. He speaks of Love (specifically of *agápe*), as a gift of God, recorded in his first letter to the Corinthian church as follows (edited by this author to indicate the use of *agápe* or *agápen* in original Greek): "If I speak in the tongues of men and of angels, but have not *agápen,* I am a noisy gong or a clanging cymbal. And if I have prophetic powers, and understand all mysteries and all knowledge, and if I have all faith, so as to remove mountains, but have not *agápen*, I am nothing. If I give away all I have, and if I deliver my body to be burned, but do not have *agápen* , I gain nothing...

"*Agápe* never ends. But where there are prophecies, they will pass away; as for tongues, they will cease; as for knowledge, it will pass away. For our knowledge is imperfect and our prophecy is imperfect, but when the perfect comes, the imperfect will pass away. When I was a child, I spoke like a child, I thought like a child, I reasoned like a child; when I became a man, I gave up childish ways. For now we see in a mirror dimly, but then face to face. Now I know in part; then I will understand fully, even as I have been fully understood. So faith, hope, *agápe* abide, these three; but the greatest of these is *agápe*." (I Corinthians 13:1-3, & 8-13 KJV, adapted)

To fulfill God's dream of *agápe* is the highest calling anyone can ever receive in either this world or in the life to come. As the divine children of God, we have the extraordinary privilege of being the purveyors of God's greatest gift, the gift of *agápe*. This is the goal of every spiritual journey and every spiritual discipline.

Agápe is the first gift listed by the Apostle Paul in his letter to the Galatians: "The fruit of the Spirit is *agápe*, joy, peace, patience, kindness, generosity, faithfulness, gentleness, and self-control." (Galatians 5:22, NRSV)

In English translation "love" is perhaps the most misunderstood term in the Christian vocabulary. Though rare, we do have a few exemplars of *agápe* in our world's history. The one that comes most readily to mind, especially for most Christians, is Jesus for whom *agápe* was both a taught and a lived reality. But he was not the first. About six centuries prior to Jesus, Siddhartha Gautama of Nepal, who was destined in time to become the Buddha, exhibited the same compassion and self-effacing attitude as did Jesus. In contemporary times, we have the example of Mother Teresa from Albania who responded to God's call to serve the dying in the slums of Calcutta, India. By the time of her death in 1997 her ministry of *agápe* had grown from her original 12 disciples in Calcutta to over 4,000 in 123 countries. All this was accomplished through the power of *agápe* love.

Closer home, we often see reported instances of *agápe* when one of our human family sacrifices his or her own life for another, at times even for a stranger. And we, ourselves, may have experienced moments when we have responded unselfishly to help meet another's need. In such experiences we may have tasted *agápe* and known the satisfaction that comes from acting selflessly. We may even find within ourselves a longing to be able to sustain such experiences, to make of them a kind of *persona*.

But even today, with these and countless other demonstrations of this same kind of selfless and unconditional love, there remains a lot of confusion about what it means to love. In addition to, or instead of its biblical usages, *love* has acquired in our secular societies other baggage which confuses, and usually contradicts, the biblical meanings and standards. The following comparisons of the secular and biblical usages will illustrate the differences[9].

---

9 From an unpublished manuscript currently being rewritten by the author.

	Love in Secular Usage, usually *eros*	*Love* in Biblical Usage, almost always *agápe*
1	Love is something we generate	Love is a gift of God
2	Love is sweetness, moonlight and roses	Love is always vulnerable, risking great pain
3	Love is carnal	Love is Spirit and enables our spirits to grow
4	Love is something you fall into	Love is a decision to express the grace of God and to allow our barriers to fall
5	Love is exclusive, selective, conditional, and unforgiving	Love is inclusive, indiscriminate, unconditional, and always forgiving
6	Love is an unattainable ideal	Love is a commission
7	Love is something we do	Love is something we are
8	Love is cheap, requiring little or no commitment	Love is costly, requiring deep commitment
9	Love is possessing	Love is giving and receiving
10	Love is weakness	Love is strength
11	Love is binding, entrapping	Love is freeing, freedom giving
12	Love is fearful for itself	Love is hopeful for others
13	Love's objects are divisible, selective	Love is for the whole person—body, mind and soul
14	Love is sex	Love is expressed in many ways, including *eros,* sex
15	Love is only human	All love is of God

16	Love's expression is limited	Love's expression is limited only by the other's ability to receive it and the other's good
17	Love is blind	Love knows its way is hard and loves anyway
18	Love is transitory, open to re-negotiation	Love is permanent and non-negotiable
19	Love is just a feeling	Love is a way of life, encompassing the whole
20	Love is only a relationship	Love, in its essence, is shared identity
21	Love is a fantasy world	Love is reality in its most exquisite expression

A Brief Word Study on *agápe, eros,* and *phileo*

The English word "love" has its root in the Indo-European *leubh* and its archaic English progeny, *lief.* Its root meaning is "to find pleasing" plus the Old English derivative meanings, "affectionate" and "lovable". Thus, the English word "love" does convey some of its root meanings in secular usage. A problem arises when it is used to translate not one, but all three Greek terms for love. The only one of the three Greek words, translated in English as "love" for which it is an adequate translation, is the Greek term *eros* (erotic or sexual love). The other two Greek terms which we translate "love" are *agápe* (Godly love) and *phileo* (brotherly love). *Agápe* is the predominant word for "love" in the New Testament (used 221 times), and it specifically refers to that self-sacrificing, unconditional love characteristic of God's way of relating to us.

Phileo (used thirty-one times) is found particularly in the Gospel of John, as in God's love for his son (John 5:20), and of Jesus' love for Lazarus as in "Behold how he loved him!" (John 11:36). *Eros,* sexual love is not found in the New Testament at all, but *agapáo* the verb form of *agápe,* is used in place of *eros* which has no verb form. In Ephesians 5:25 and 28, *agapáo* is used specifically of the physical union of husband and wife and, analogously of the union of Christ and the Church. The image of the bride and the bridegroom in Revelation 19:7-9 likewise speaks of the sexual dimension of Divine Love.

Thus, it is my conclusion that "*agápe*" in the New Testament speaks not so much of form as it does quality. *Agápe* predominates precisely because God's Love for us and through us is of a deeper, more intense quality than that found in other human relationships. *Agápe* has no form of its own but is dependent on the forms of *phileo* and *eros* for its expression. But the intensity of that expression, when it is *agápe* being expressed, is as different from the forms it uses as is light from darkness.

How tragic our loss, and how impoverishing, when we settle for the secular definition of love; on the other hand, how immeasurable is the gift of *agápe* when we allow God to love others through us! How rich are our lives and how enriched are the lives of those we love!

What Is God's Dream?—The Dream of Jesus

"...You shall love the Lord your God with all your heart,
and with all your soul, and with all your mind,
and with all your strength."
"...You shall love your neighbor as yourself."
— (Gospel of Mark, 12:30 & 31, NRSV)

Jesus was a visionary. He had a vision of the Kingdom of God. It was actually more than a dream. It was a vision based on his own experience of the kingdom. He wanted it to be our vision as well. Even though he never had more than a handful of committed followers, his teaching drew crowds large enough to incite the envy and hostility of the religious leadership of his day. He also concerned the Roman occupiers who were alarmed by his teaching of a kingdom other than the Holy Roman Empire. *This Kingdom of God was another of Jesus' visions, another one of God's dreams.* Jesus' teaching concerning the Kingdom of God permeates all his teaching. The Kingdom is already present, and is yet to come. It is nearby, even within. It is good news, but also contains secrets. It is entered easily by children, and it is a kingdom for the hungry and thirsty, the stranger and the naked. It is the inheritance of those who mourn, the meek, those who hunger for righteousness, the merciful, and the pure in heart, the peacemakers and the persecuted. It is a kingdom of compassion and *agápe.* It is a kingdom both on earth and in heaven.

Contrary to popular characterizations of the Kingdom of God, it does not refer to a place so much as it does a spiritual consciousness or awareness. It is specifically the continual awareness of the presence of God within oneself. It is a kingdom wherein there is no separation from God and no separation from God's creation, including other human beings. Jesus not only taught about the Kingdom, he lived it out in practice. For him a king was no more important than a pauper, nor an intellectual giant more important than a child. For him this equality of people was more than just a moral proposition. It was a keen awareness of what *is*. He saw all people quite literally through the eyes of God.

When challenged by the Jews, "If you are the Messiah, tell us plainly." Jesus answered, "...the Father and I are one." (John 10:24 & 30)   Jesus, then, in defense of his claim, quoted the Hebrew scripture, "Is it not written in your law, 'I said, you are gods?'" (John 10:34) Jesus was quoting Psalm 82:6, the full text of which says, "I say, 'You are gods, children of the Most High, all of you.'" (Psalm 82:6, NRSV) The message of the Kingdom is, according to Jesus and the Psalmist, "We are gods, all of us." That we don't know this is simply an indication that we have been blinded by our sin, which is the illusion of separation. To be sure, we came by this sin honestly. Our culture does not support such an idea, just as the Jews were not supportive of the idea in Jesus' time. But it is something that we were probably aware of at the time of our birth. Very small children often do not lose their God-consciousness for sometimes three or four years after their birth. If they knew the words to tell us of their awareness of God during their first year of earthly life, they could undoubtedly teach us much of what we have forgotten. As it is, we have to find our own way back to our own Godly origins in a climate that is most often hostile to such recollections. But the message of Jesus is that the Kingdom of God is here, right *now*, awaiting our entry, and we do not have to enter physical death to re-enter. All that is required is the recognition that God is in no way separate from us. Once we accept that reality—that the almighty Creator is quite literally inside of us—that changes everything. God's dream in Jesus is of our literal return home to the Kingdom within.

What Is God's Dream?—The Vision of Archbishop Desmond Tutu

Archbishop Tutu also has a vision of God's dream, which he shares with the youngest of readers by way of a colorful picture book. Its story involves people who reach out and hold each other's hands, but sometimes get angry and hurt each other—and say they're sorry and please forgive me. It's a vision where everyone will see that they are brothers and sisters, no matter their way of speaking to God, no matter the size of their nose or the shade of their skin. (Tutu, Desmond, and Douglas Carlton Abrams; LeUyen Pham, Ill. *God's Dream.* Cambridge, MA: Candlewick Press, 2008.)

The magazine, *What Is Enlightenment?,* asked seven Nobel Peace Prize laureates to "speak about their hopes for humanity's next step." Archbishop Tutu was among them. His response: "I hope that we can begin to realize that all of us are created in the image of God, *that all of us are God-carriers.* The evolution that people are speaking about is the recognition of our essential goodness. And that we are made, surprisingly, for transcendence, for beauty, for joy, for caring. So many of us are unaware of our heritage. Some of the bewildering things that happen drive us back to our source, to our roots. When we realize that we are vulnerable, that we are not omnipotent, then maybe we will see where our true security lies." (Emphasis mine. From "For the Sake of the Future: 7 Nobel Peace

Prize Laureates Speak about their Hopes for Humanity's Next Step,"
What Is Enlightenment?, Spring/Summer (2002): 130.)

What Is God's Dream?—The Dream of Martin Luther King

The lyrics of a song titled *Martin's Dream* by Jean and Drew Adams
(published by the General Board of Discipleship of the United
Methodist Church, 1989) accurately reflects the vision that gripped
Martin Luther King, Jr. right up to the time of his assassination in
Memphis on April 4, 1968. It uses many of his own words.

Martin's Dream

My name is Brother Martin, I have a dream today;
a dream that someday, somewhere all races shall be free.
We look ahead for healing to put behind the past.
We'll walk as sister, brother, and we'll be free at last.

I dreamed my little children will live within a world,
where they will not be judged by the color of their skin.
I dreamed we'd work together, I dreamed, "Let freedom
   ring."
We'll learn to trust each other and then let peace begin.

We're marching on for freedom and peace throughout the
   land,
where ever there's injustice, that's where we'll make our
   stand!
From Colorado's mountains to every lake and sea,
one dream, one hope, one vision: oh, won't you walk with
   me?

I may not get there with you, we've many miles to go.
I will not fear the future, my Lord's with me, I know!
The road will lead to heaven where all the saints have trod,
where black, white, brown, and yellow walk hand in hand
   with God.

Others dream of a day when religious people will learn to appreciate and learn from each other. Martin's death did not kill the dream. It still flourishes, I believe, because it was not just Martin's dream. It was God's dream.

What Is God's Dream?—Dreams Abound

The Old Testament prophet, Joel, is quoted by the Apostle Peter in a sermon shared in *Acts of the Apostles*: In the last days it will be, God declares that "I will pour out my Spirit upon all flesh, and your sons and your daughters shall prophesy, and your young men will see visions and your old men shall dream dreams." (Joel 2:28-32; Acts, 2:17) Are these those last days promised by God through Peter? We can hope and dream, and we can work to bring our dreams to fruition.

Some people today are having visions of a new day when peace will reign on earth, and wars will cease.

Some envision a day when politicians will cease their bickering and get back to the work of governing justly and wisely.

Some dream and work for a day when poverty will be forever abolished and no one will be without shelter and plenty to eat.

Some have visions of a time when the human race will no longer be divided by economic, cultural, racial, sexual or national differences, and when all people will be a global community, interdependent and mutually responsible for our physical and social environments.

Still others dream of the time when the supreme worth of each person will be affirmed and the dignity of all humanity celebrated.

Dreams Pull us from the Future

For the Creator to dream is to create. This is likewise true of the human conveyors of the dream. *If we can dream it, we can create it.*

The dreams pull us towards the envisioned reality. This is just the opposite of the case with Darwinian evolution. There it is past experiences which drive the changes in the life of a species. If something works, the individual creature keeps doing it over and over, forcing an adaptation in future generations. Whatever past need and experience dictates drives the needed changes to the fore. With *Homo sapiens*, however, both the ability to dream and to see a different future pull us towards that future. We have a unique ability to see future possibilities and the capability to bring them to pass. (This is yet another argument to support the thesis in the Introduction to this book, that human beings are a special case in evolutionary theory; that we have evolved parallel to other humanoid species rather than having descended from them.)

The Importance of Our Dreams of the Future

I am convinced that the really significant dreams for our spiritual journeys, the ones that pull us from and to the future, come from the divine presence in us for whom there is no past, present or future. Time is a concept of our own making, as a way of marking our progress from now to then. For God the future and the past are all *now*. Indeed, all possible futures are now. We are the ones who are nearsighted, not God. So when our souls communicate dreams of the future, we had best remember them and act on them. Our failure to do so will not change the future, which is already here in any event, but it may deprive us of the hope, or even the joyful anticipation, of its fulfillment. Diarmuid O'Murchu notes that "Just as the past provides the basic patterns upon which nature builds, it is the lure of the future that gives direction and purpose to every development. The future, not the dead past, is the foundation on which the world leans." (O'Murchu, 2008, p.221) O'Murchu quotes the American theologian John F. Haught, "God forever promises, and God never fails to fulfill what has been promised.... Theologically speaking, a promising God who opens up the world to the future, is the *ultimate* explanation of evolution" (Haught, 2003, pp.164, 128).

This may well have been one of the more critically important gleanings of Henry David Thoreau's reminiscences during his twenty-six month sojourn at Walden Pond: "I learned this, at least, by my experiment: that if one advances confidently in the direction of his dreams, and endeavors to live the life which he has imagined, he will meet with a success unexpected in common hours. He will put some things behind, he will pass an invisible boundary; new, universal and more liberal laws will begin to establish themselves around and within him; or the old laws be expanded, and interpreted in his favour in a more liberal sense, and he will live with the license of a higher order of beings. In proportion as he simplifies his life, the laws of the universe will appear less complex, and solitude will not be solitude, nor poverty poverty, nor weakness weakness. If you have built castles in the air, your work need not be lost; that is where they should be. Now put the foundations under them." (Thoreau 1854, p. 285) In his conclusion, Thoreau echoes the evolutionary theology of Teilhard de Chardin.

Pierre Teilhard de Chardin, the dean of theologically astute evolutionists, thinks of the future "as that dimension which provides direction and goal for cosmic, planetary, and human evolution" (Teilhard de Chardin, 1969). And O'Murchu affirms that "The Spirit that allures us from the perspective of the ever new future also awakens our hearts' dreams for a future that will often look threatening to the guardians of conventional reality" (O'Murchu, 2008, p. 222). Threatening or not, the future is upon us and it is what it *will be*. The Spirit leads where it will. It is our responsibility, as the divine humans we are, to seek and implement the future we are given.

Precognitive Dreams

Precognitive dreams are a fairly rare phenomenon which cross the boundary of temporal experience into what is called the "eternal now." In the eternal now past, present, and future are all *present.* The only example of a precognitive dream that I have personally encountered was related to me by a person well known to me. I was her spiritual counselor when she shared with me this incredible dream the week following her experience of it. I share it here in abbreviated form:

In her dream she saw a young professional woman give the teenage babysitter last minute instructions as she was leaving her suburban home for work. She explained that her toddler had not yet awakened and was still in her crib. The mother left and the babysitter settled down in the front room. In the meantime the child awakened, climbed out of her crib and slipped out of the house through the back door, which had been left ajar. She crossed the back yard, wandered into an adjoining park and fell into a deep drainage ditch. It began to rain hard and the ditch began to fill with water. End of dream.

My friend awoke from her disturbing dream to find it raining. Two hours later she left to do some early morning shopping at a home decorating store in a nearby mall. It was raining harder. When she entered the store she was greeted by one of the sales staff—the same lady she had seen in her dream just before she awakened a couple of hours earlier. Astonished, she immediately asked the sales lady if she had a toddler daughter. Yes. Then she asked if her home adjoined a park. Again the answer was yes. In a state of panic, she told the incredulous sales person that her daughter was in peril and that she did not have a moment to lose. The two of them rushed to the woman's home and found the child, just as my friend had dreamed, in the drainage ditch filling with water. The child was cold and wet and crying, but otherwise unhurt.

Precognitive dreams are deliberately given, I suspect, for just such occasions as this. They are probably also given to such persons as my friend because she was known to take her dreams seriously. Of course this raises all kinds of questions, such as what is the source of our dreams? What are their purposes? How do we know which ones to take seriously? Though the purpose of most dreams is clearly not as blatantly obvious as in the above example, we may never know what the Spirit of our Original Source may be trying to communicate with us through our dreams, if we pay no attention to them. I do not believe all our dreams have life-transforming significance. I do believe that some of them, however, may well have that potential.

There was a time that I paid close attention to all my dreams and learned techniques for remembering and analyzing them, sometimes as many as five or six in a single night. I found such extensive dream work exhausting and time consuming. I have found since a workable compromise where I pay attention to (1) dreams that are particularly clear when I awake, (2) lucid dreams (i.e. dreams where I am aware I am dreaming while I am still asleep, and (3) dreams that are repeated. Some of these dreams, though not all, have indeed been helpful in working through or supplying answers to problems which were bugging me. I do not know their source—the Mind Field, Universal Consciousness, Holy Spirit, God, Original Source, the Mind of Christ—all of these are candidates. But whatever the Source, it has proved to be a trustworthy one and something quite a bit more than "an undigested bit of beef."

What about Nightmares and Bad Dreams?

Apparently our ability to dream has a dual function. Not all our dreams are visions of the future. Some of them function as correctives of self-destructive thoughts and emotions. Unpleasant dreams can serve as a sort of release valve for stress and depression. It is not even necessary that we remember such dreams. They accomplish their purpose whether or not we are aware of them. Years ago I came across research conclusions that were summed up thus: If our dream patterns are disrupted by some outside circumstance for one twenty-four hour period, we will be mildly mentally disturbed; if the disruption continues for another twenty-four hours, we will become neurotic; but if the condition persists for yet another twenty-four hours, we will become psychotic. To whatever extent this is true, it underscores both our psychological need for "bad" dreams but also illuminates the dual function of dreams, which is to address both the present and the future.

As a preadolescent child, I learned two curious things about bad dreams, particularly recurring nightmares. First, I learned that the dream itself was essentially harmless—even if it is unpleasant, no physical harm would come to me from the dream. I learned, secondly, that if I want to stop the recurrence of the nightmares, I need only confront the beast or whatever it is attacking me. If a tiger was about to leap on me (a dream that terrified me for months) I needed only to stand pat and not run or try to defend myself. Once I summoned the courage to try this approach, I never had this nightmare again. Not only did the tiger disappear forever, my nightmares generally became exceedingly rare. I have had few, if any, such dreams in the past seventy years.

The Dream of *Pleroma* (Greek, πλήρώμά)—the Ultimate Dream

Pleroma refers to the totality of divine powers. The word is translated "fullness" in English and is used seventeen times in the New Testament. One use is in the Letter to the Colossians, where Paul, writing of Christ Jesus, says: "For in him all the fullness of God was pleased to dwell..." (Colossians 1:19, NRSV). It could also be translated: "For in him the totality of divine powers was pleased to dwell." This is fairly widely accepted Christian theology. Such is not the case, however, in Ephesians, in a letter attributed to the Apostle Paul (but debatably not from his hand), where the author, praying for the Ephesian saints, says: "I pray that you may have the power to comprehend, with all the saints, what is the breadth and length and height and depth, and to know the Love of Christ that surpasses knowledge, so that you may be filled with all the fullness [*pleroma*] of God." [or with the totality of the divine powers of God] (Ephesians 3: 18-19). On this score, Christian theology tends to be silent! This is strange, especially given the fact that we are the ones who have had the audacity to create God in *our* image. Since we cannot conceive of the biblical application of *pleroma* to human beings, have we chosen to lower God to our level of incompetence rather than simply accepting God's gift? But I believe that *this gift of the totality of divine powers, too, is a part of God's dream for his human/divine progeny.*

I recently had a dream, (the dream located at the retreat center I founded with my wife many years ago) in which I saw the center developed far beyond the stage at which we left it. In my dream we had built a new mountain-top lodge from which we had views that seemed to go on forever. In point of fact such a facility was, indeed, once envisioned, but I thought it was so far beyond our capabilities that it was never attempted. Would we have attempted it if I had known then what I know now? If I had known that God's gift of *pleroma* would have enabled us to bring the dream to fruition, would that mountain-top lodge now be a reality? I believe now that it would have been possible, but for my lack of faith. It is not so much that we do not have the totality of divine power at our disposal, but that we do not *believe* we have that power. I am not yet sure what, specifically, my recent dream is trying to tell me, or what the symbolism of the dream is preparing me for, but I have been put on notice that something is afoot that I should be prepared to take seriously whatever it is when it becomes apparent. I also hope that my faith is now equal to the task!

So, what dreams have you either dismissed or put on hold? What is God's Spirit trying to tell you to do? Whatever it is, *never let the dream die for lack of faith.* Instead ask God to increase your faith sufficiently for you to fulfill the dream—God's dream.

God Is Still Speaking

Because it is God's dream, you can know certain identifying aspects of the dream up front:

1. Its fulfillment will likely require skills that you have already acquired. Unbeknownst to you, God may have been preparing you for this call for some time. When the moment comes it will be necessary for you to grasp it in trust that God knows what she is doing.
2. God's dream will be as much or more for the benefit of others, than for you. You are typically called for service, not self-indulgence.
3. For you, the dream's implementation will likely be a transforming "mountain-top" experience, exceeding your wildest expectations.
4. The dream's implementation will be its own confirmation, as you repeatedly see firsthand the Spirit of God at work, going

before you, clearing the way and opening doors of opportunity.

5. The dream's implementation will likely require all the energy and Love you can pour into it. You cannot expect God to do *all* the work.

6. The dream's beneficiaries will likely draw on all the *agápe* you can bring to them. Since God's dreams are for others, you will be God's loving presence to those you serve.

7. Depending on the specifics of the dream, others of God's children may be drawn to join you in the dream's implementation, in both active and supportive roles. You probably will not even have to look for them. They will simply appear on your doorstep, already having heard God's summons.

Dreams are one of God's ways of communicating to her children. This has been true through the ages and is no less the case today. Sometimes our pseudo-sophistication or our false humility or pride may interfere with our ability to receive God's communications, but *God is still speaking.* And when she does, we need to be listening.

Chapter 4

ON BEING A CO-CREATOR WITH GOD

"It is wise to learn; it is God-like to create."

—John Saxe

*"Had I been present at the creation of the world
I would have proposed some improvements."*

—Alfonso X of Castile

*"To see a world in a grain of sand
And heaven in a wild flower,
Hold infinity in the palm of your hand
And eternity in an hour."*

—William Blake

Unlimited Creativity

The creative genius of human beings apparently has no limits, except such as may be God/self-imposed. In this sense, we mirror the work of our Creator God, for whom we ourselves are her creation. We are God's progeny, made in her image; thus, we are the creative result of God's imagination and heirs of that same power to visualize that which we cannot physically see or which may not even exist. The ability to convert our mental images into apparently concrete reality is one of the hallmarks of our divine/human identity.

Creativity is so much a part of our identity that we often do not think of it so much as a process as it is just something that happens. It comes as a flash of insight or sometimes as a vision in the night. It may come as a song or a symphony, as it were, out of thin air. In our minds we hear it, visualize it, or have a new understanding which, seemingly, rises out of the depths of our being. We may know not from whence it came, but we know enough to receive it with gratitude and then, using such skills and tools as we have at our disposal, to commit it to paper or clay or canvas, or life or conversation or community building.

The portrayal of the composer, Wolfgang Amadeus Mozart, in the movie *Amadeus* resonated deeply within me. I was awed by the spontaneity and magnitude of his creative process. In one of the final scenes where Mozart, on his death bed, is committing to musical notation his own *Requiem,* he was feverishly dictating what he was obviously hearing in his own head. This combination of compositional competence and inspired listening has ever since prompted me to be more intentional in my own listening for the promptings of that Spirit within, whatever or whoever it may be.

Though we may not know for certain the source of *our* creative inspiration, it is not a bad bet that the divine Spirit within us, believed in or not, had something to do with it. Whether the impulse to create originates with us or with *that-which-is-of-God-in-us* is a case of splitting ontological hairs. If our soul is, as I believe, *that-which-is-of-God-in-us*, then it is useless to try to separate us from God, and it becomes clear that the impetus to create anything specific lies with God. As God's children, we are simply carrying on the family tradition.

Co-Evolution

Co-evolution, in the context of co-*creation,* is concerned with the partnership between God and the co-creator for his or her own continuing creation. Much of this creation occurred *in utero* or before, when our DNA was first determined. It is a partnership that was forged before we were born. The place and circumstances of our birth were either determined for us or *with* our consensual participation. The partnership continues throughout life as we are increasingly formed in the image of God, who created us in the first place.

It is in the empowerment to create *ex nihilo* [out of nothing] that we most readily glimpse our divine/human partnership. We are co-creators with the prime Creator. This is evidenced in our own evolutionary development, but also in the arts, technology, the sciences, language, our literature, our relationships, our innate religiosity, our visionary capabilities, our apprehension of beauty, and in our powers of procreation. There is little or nothing about us that does not, in one way or another, reveal the Creator.

Based in part on the understanding of our identity as divine/humans, who are in continual relationship with the Creator God, I am prompted to reflect about what this alliance of the human and the divine means for the big picture. I have been ably assisted in this endeavor by the works of Diarmuid O'Murchu, who writes, "...our story is not about evolution, but co-evolution. It is a story with several actors and many intriguing plots.... The hardest lesson to learn for the human participants is to realize that without the big and inclusive picture of this complex and intriguing landscape, we are in danger of misunderstanding our fundamental role within it. Consequently, we are in danger of misconstruing our engagement with it, with possibly deadly consequences both for ourselves and for the natural world we inhabit. The story of co-evolution is indisputably a story of cooperation and collaboration." (O'Murchu,

2002, p. 17) Evolution accepted, mistakes are forgiven and are understood as simply a part of the process of learning. As we are open to the Spirit's teaching, whether directly or mediated through community with others, our "sin" is precisely what the word means—missing the mark—and we continue growing into our future as led by the Spirit of God.

Moving "...across the entire spectrum of evolutionary unfolding we need to keep in mind the scientific principle that 'the whole is greater than the sum of the parts,' while also keeping in the forefront of our consciousness that the whole is contained in each part." Furthermore, "...evolution is about the awakening of consciousness. It is the inner intelligence of co-evolution that pushes toward greater complexity and creativity." And finally, "Evolution is biased toward the future. It is the future rather than the past that gives evolution its foundational meaning." (ibid. p.19 & 22) The goal of the evolutionary process itself unfolds amidst the horizons of promise that know no limits. As co-creative creatures engaging with our co-creative God, we are forever stretching the horizons of possibility.

Humanity's evolutionary success is obvious when we stop to consider how modern humans have evolved into the social organization and technological savvy we now demonstrate. We have not become the top predators of the amazingly diverse planetary biota entirely by accident. Ever since the hunter-gatherer milieu of evolutionary history, creativity has been the engine that has driven us to the top of the food chain. This is a process that is still unfolding, most evidenced perhaps in first century tribal societies, but in developed nations as well. No matter where we are developmentally, the inner drive to create is still the primary force which moves us forward in a never-ending spiral of human achievement. We are still tool-makers, but the tools we make have become increasingly complex. We are still survivors, but now instead of fighting to survive wild beasts, we fight to survive each other.

Our instinct for art, once demonstrated in story-telling drawings on the walls of caves, has become a domain for creative genius unrivaled by any other species. It is perhaps in our art that our creativity in all its depth of understanding and complexity reaches its zenith. It still is a tool of communication, but what it communicates so far exceeds the former stories of the hunt that it leaves us in awe of its profundity and beauty.

On virtually every frontier of our history creativity has been the engine of our evolution. Whether the frontier be in our technology and art, or in our politics and religions, or in our language and scientific endeavors, or in our life-skills and global relationships, we have evolved, and are still evolving, into who we will be. The only limit to our evolving creativity is our imagination—and even that is expanding exponentially. The not-so-simple truth is that if we can imagine it, we will eventually evolve enough to create it.

In this respect, we are like our Creator, who imagined us before there was a "before." This is the image in which we were created. We, like our Creator, are also creators, and, like our creator, if we can imagine something, we can create it. Or is it the Creator *in us* doing the imagining and creating? If so, this would tend to substantiate God's message to the Hebrew prophet, Isaiah: "I form the light and create darkness: I make peace, and create evil: I the Lord do all these things." (Isaiah 45:7, KJV)

In as much as the various translations of the Hebrew terms differ in the above quote, there are apparently no adequate terms in English with which to convey the exact meaning of the original Hebrew text. The Revised Standard Version, for example, has God saying "I make weal and create woe" while in the New International Version, God is quoted as saying "I bring prosperity and create disaster." However, the gist of the message is the same--that God is the Creator of all that is: good and evil, peace and war, sunny days and stormy weather.

Co-Evolution and Culture

We tend to buy into reality as generally perceived by the culture into which we are born and develop. It is in our culture that we see the *communal* aspect of co-evolution most clearly. Every human being is in the process of creating herself or himself and our *cultural heritage* plays a huge role in our process of becoming. Culture impacts our worldview and our beliefs, and consequently influences how we perceive the world around us. We make our own reality consistent with our inherited cognitive map and consensual reality. This is often seen in our choice of religious beliefs. Thus, if our culture believes in the miraculous, we will likely not only share that belief but our senses will perceive the miraculous, blocking any perceptions to the contrary.

Rarely, if ever do our senses perceive reality as it in fact is. *Our sensory perceptions skew the reality and thus skew our worldview.* In other words, we live in our own world of illusions, and the illusions become our reality even to the point that our brains create the reality we are preconditioned to perceive. The brain has no way of separating vision from visions. To our brains, both physical sight and inner visions are equally real, and we choose that which best supports our already ingrained existing communal worldview, thereby creating our own reality.

Our consensual realities are not necessarily wrong. There is much that is real that our physical senses cannot perceive. An adequate worldview needs to make room for two kinds of reality, the concrete and the imaginal. Concrete reality is such as can be scientifically verified as true. Imaginal reality is such as can be intuitionally verified. The latter way of perceiving is preeminently in the realms of co-creation and co-evolution. God works with us and in us to determine the kind of reality we may best exemplify.

The Joy and Responsibility of Co-Creators

If we are created in God's image and are, therefore, co-creators participating in the creative activities of our Creator, then the Isaiah text cited above, "I form the light and create darkness: I make peace, and create evil: I the Lord do all these things." (Isaiah 45:7, KJV) explains our capability to imagine and create both good and evil. It also means that the act of creation is apparently morally and ethically neutral. The choice of what specifically to create may be more a matter of creative freedom, also given us by God, in order that we may choose responsibly that which we create. This freedom to create may give birth to either joy or woe. In a positive take on our creative activity, Matthew Fox calls attention to the declaration of the Upanishads of ancient India concerning the joy of creativity: "Know the joy of creating. Where there is joy, there is creating. Know the nature of joy. Where there is the Infinite, there is joy." He continues, "Thus the joy of creating comes from the *Godself*." (Fox, 2002, p.69) Or, in the terminology favored by this writer, the joy of creating comes from our soul—*that-which-is-of-God-in-us*.

To choose responsibly may be the greatest challenge of our day—and also the greatest need. Our poor choices of the past have put the whole evolutionary endeavor at risk. God's message to the people of Israel, cited by the writer of Deuteronomy, of ancient Hebrew history, is still applicable to humanity today: "See, I have set before you this day life and prosperity, death and adversity... Choose life so that you and your descendants may live..." (Deuteronomy 30:15 & 19, NRSV) Never before has the choice been so stark; never before have we created the possibility of our own mass annihilation. At this moment in our long evolutionary journey, just as we are able to glimpse the goal on the horizon, we still have the opportunity to choose life over death, good over evil, and the continuation of our journey over its premature end. Therefore, choose life!

Such is the enormous challenge of our day: to accept the role of co-creators with God, to imagine and create responsibly, and to exercise our prerogative to choose Life. God is our Creator, the very Source of our being. As the progeny of God it is our privilege to follow in the footsteps of our Divine Father/Mother, to become co-creators in the work of God's kingdom, and not in name only, but in practice. This is manifested in many ways, not the least of which is our sexuality.

Human Sexuality and Procreativity

It is in the area of procreation that we find the greatest expression of our role as co-creators with God, because in this area we find the totality of our being-ness—mind, heart, body, and soul—employed as the vehicle for the pinnacle of creative endeavor. But in many religious associations, sexuality has been denigrated as something at best bordering on the immoral, and certainly something not talked about in civil discourse. Certainly it has been our modern human experience that sex has become scorned and perverted on the one hand and brazenly exploited on the other. Our social mores leave us in the impossible position of condemning the very thing that gives us life and enables our creative endeavors. We have come to regard sex as immoral.

How Did Sex Become Sin?

At least some of the responsibility for the sorry state of affairs in Christian societies falls on the church fathers who, in defense of their patriarchal hegemony, defamed sexuality in general and women in particular. They did this with the help of the Apostle Paul, who was, I believe, so fearful of his own sexuality, that he thought any expression of it outside of very narrowly defined marital limits was tantamount to flagrant sin. Even in the context of marriage, he found sexual expression for any purpose beyond procreation so tainted with sin (*porneia*), that he recommended celibacy over marriage for those unable to control their sexual appetite. Of course, in his vilification of sex as sin, Paul also effectively redefined sin (Greek, *hamartano*) from "missing the mark" to "immorality" (Greek, *porneia,* one of the root forms for the English word "pornography") which is typically used for sexual practices which debase sexuality, thus cheapening and distorting it. Thus to treat *persons*, made in God's image as sacred divine beings, as *objects* to satisfy one's own sexual needs is immoral. To use sex to assert power over another is immoral. To force sex upon another is immoral. Anything that cheapens or devalues our sexuality is immoral. But it is no less immoral to treat sex and sexuality as something inherently debased, to deny its goodness, and to limit its expression by societal norms based on fear or prudishness.

Eros, An Expression of God's Love

To limit the term *eros* to exclusively sexual expression is to largely misconstrue the breadth and power of the term. I find expressed in it a compelling drive toward intimacy, and, thus, toward community. As such *eros* is infinitely more than sex. It is that which enables human beings to know and be known by one another, to plumb the depths of each other's thoughts and aspirations. It opens to us new vistas of possibility and understanding, connection and fruitful cooperation. It is a force within for creative endeavor, compelling us to push back the night and enter a new day of appreciation and discovery. But in our fear of its power and our twisted human application of *eros*, we have limited its meaning to sex alone. We have thereby turned a priceless gift of God into something demeaning and missed the limitless horizons it offers.

In this latter regard, Diarmuid O'Murchu has observed that "Throughout the 1980's, we experienced another quantum leap which has not yet been acknowledged publicly: intimate relationships, whether between male and female, male and male, or female and female tend to become quite erotic and veer toward genital expression. Genitality is no longer reserved for heterosexual monogamous relationships, never mind for marital union. It has become a dimension of human intimacy in many different situations in which people seek to express tenderness, affection, and mutuality." O'Murchu goes on to suggest that the "real havoc... is not in the behavior itself (whether in its range of delightful or deleterious consequences) but in the massive denial whereby these new developments are perceived and treated [by churches and governments] as adversarial forces to be opposed, subdued, and conquered." (O'Murchu 1997, pp. 190-191)

Citing the writings of Carter Heyward, Episcopal priest, teacher, and theologian, Alexander Irwin lists five characteristics of eros (Irwin 1991, pp, 126-133), summarized as follows:

> 1. "*Eros is joy.* In contrast to many representatives of the masculine intellectual tradition, pleasure is neither a dirty nor an insignificant word. Carter Heyward writes of the imperative to transform the 'body-despising, woman-

fearing, sexually repressive religious tradition' that Christians have inherited.

2. *"Eros is a source of knowledge.* A mode of cognition, a way of gaining deep and intimate knowledge of persons, things and ideas.... Erotic knowledge... is a form of wisdom that puts us in touch with the deepest levels of life itself.... Erotic 'knowing by heart' establishes a relationship between knower and known that transcends the simplistic subject-object duality and opens the way for transforming action rooted in 'relational power.' Such knowledge is not detached and dispassionate but passionately involved.

3. *"Eros is relational.* Although it touches and transforms the individual in her deepest and most intimate dimensions, *eros* is not a private experience.... *Eros* can be characterized as 'the power of our primal interrelatedness, which 'creates and connects hearts,' involving 'the whole person in relationships of self-awareness, vulnerability, openness, and caring.'

4. *"Eros is a cosmic force.* As a cosmic force of creativity and love, *eros* can be imaged in non-theistic ways. In the work of secular poets and theorists, *eros* is often described as 'life-force,' a suprapersonal, empowering energy on which individuals can draw, in pleasure and struggle.... 'God is erotic power,' a truly Christic—liberating, healing, transformative—energy.

5. *"Eros is political.* Eros connects deep feeling, wisdom, and responsible action. It shapes the tone and quality of moral behavior..."

Jungian analyst June Singer has written, "If a new worldview is in the making, as I believe it is, sexuality has not yet been incorporated into that vision. Current sexual practice can no longer be explained by the old theories and we do not yet understand it in the light of the new ones.... We may as well begin drawing new maps. This is the first step in the process of re-visioning sexuality, a step which I believe is necessary to our personal growth and collective evolution." (Singer 1990, p. 10)

We should have learned by now that arbitrary suppression and condemnation of those caught up in the sexual revolution of the 1960s and 70s has not worked, and to continue in our denial, rather than engage in rational dialogue, is more a symptom of our own fear and sexual repression than it is of the morality of those we condemn. Tragically, when we repress *eros* because of its sexual dimension, we also repress our capability for intimacy and community generally, along with all its inherent promise of human/divine accomplishment.

One place we see the suppression of sexuality is in the Christian Gospels, the New Testament writings purportedly about the life and teachings of Jesus. From these accounts one can discern little of the humanity of Jesus. A casual reading of these texts leaves the intended impression that Jesus was unmarried and celibate, and that his relationships with women were strictly platonic, devoid of any sexual activity or interest. We are left to surmise that Jesus was either not really human or that he was in gross denial of his sexuality—and this in spite of his being in the presence of women at every turn. However, a closer reading of the text reveals instead a fully virile young man, who was married, probably, to Mary Magdalene, at Cana. (John 2:1-12) Two biblical texts in particular, Luke 7:38-50 and John 11:2 reveal an episode in Jesus' life in which he received, quite willingly, the sexual overtures of Mary from Magdala. Two other gospels, which did not make it into the biblical canon, the *Gospel of Mary* (Robinson 1988, p.525) and the *Gospel of Philip* (ibid., p. 148) both speak of the sexual love Jesus and Mary Magdalene had for each other.

Biblical scholar and theologian, Barbara Thiering, makes a strong argument that Jesus and his parents belonged to the Essenes, a radical sect of Judaism. In that context, she has observed that "When the Essene marriage rules are brought together with the passage on the woman with the ointment, [Mary Magdalene] the actual history becomes clear. This was not a purely spiritual relationship, but a real marriage, following the rules of the dynastic order. Jesus had to marry in order to continue his family line, and in his case it was all the more necessary in order to affirm his legitimacy..." (Thiering 1992, p. 88)

The failure of the early Church Fathers and/or the Gospel writers to acknowledge the marriage of Jesus and his sexuality reveals more about their sexual mores than it does about Jesus. They were part of a patriarchal hierarchy more concerned to keep a lid on women and sexuality and to maintain their positions of power in the budding church. Not much has changed in the ensuing two thousand years of church and cultural history, though there are signs on the horizon that patriarchy is not as good as it has been cracked up to be. Perhaps women can do better; but better yet, women and men working together in committed relationships, loving and being loved, promises an even more fruitful evolvement into the persons we are called to be.

Joan Timmerman, professor of theology at the College of St. Catherine in St. Paul, Minnesota, has observed that the "...incarnation, in a real sense, is not complete until the community of people discovers God disclosed in their own humanity; just so, an element of Christology is lacking until we can allow ourselves to formulate images of Jesus entering as deeply into the passion of his sexuality as we have done regarding the passion of his suffering." (Nelson/Longfellow 1993, p.92)

Some Western and Eastern societies alike are abysmally hypocritical in our and their efforts to deny and control the expression of sexuality. Far from celebrating it as a wonderful gift from God, we try to suppress it, contain it, and pretend it doesn't exist. Nonetheless, it is forever breaking out of our imposed limits, a force for good or evil, which scares us because it will *not* be repressed or denied. We have sown the wind, and reaped the whirlwind.

To celebrate sexually with another person the life and pleasure of our God-given sexuality is not only moral, it is essential to our psychological well-being, our creative instincts, and our eventual evolution as a species into the fullness of our divine identities. Sex is not only good, it is good for us. It is holy, precisely because it is of God. The crying need of our time, and in most cultures, is to lay aside the fear-based prejudices of our forebears, to own our personal sexuality as the gift of God that it is, and to enter into committed sexual relationships with unabashed joy and ecstasy.

Openness to God requires openness to all that God has created, to love her creation, and to find in it the explosion of creativity that is our legitimate role as co-creators with God. Inasmuch as we are sexual beings, all our creativity is sexual in nature and, in this sense sexuality is at the very heart of spirituality. The bringing to birth of other children of God is the embodiment of spirituality as we relate to one another as spiritual beings. God is born anew every time a baby is born. This is the preeminent creative act, the culmination of lives devoted to being co-creators with God. The creativity continues as together with God and each other we nurture our infant son or daughter to mature adulthood. The wheel of evolution is unending as we live on in our progeny and they live on in theirs, *ad infinitum*.

It is, perhaps, because of this power of *eros* (sexual love), that the New Testament writers never use the term, even when the context clearly indicates that sexual love is the intended subject. Instead, they use the terms *agápe* (noun) or *ágapáo* (verb), indicating that *eros*, too, is Godly love. God gives him/herself to us fully through *eros*. As divine co-creators, we, too, are called to love unconditionally through whatever expressions of love are appropriate and can be received. The power of *eros,* especially in conjunction with *agápe,* is such that its expression can be overwhelming and, therefore, its expression by the divine lover may need to be moderated to a level that can be received. This sensitivity, too, is an expression of *agápe*.

A further consideration is, unfortunately, the cultural milieu in which the divine lover is loving. Though you may know that cultural limitations on the expressions of love are inconsistent with your freedom to express the legitimate love you feel, it may be a constraint you need to respect, lest the culture crucify both you and the one loved. You may have to be content to observe the societal norms while loving as fully and as best you can within the cultural limits. But never try to deny or suppress the feeling you have for the one loved, for by so doing you will abdicate the primary role for which you were born. You were born to be a co-creator with God.

"Instead of eroticism being an obstacle (temptation) to spiritual growth, it may be the creative wellspring of spiritual unfolding... The repressed psychic and sexual energies of centuries, especially the last few hundred years, explodes upon our world, releasing instinctual forces of unrestrained intimacy, passionate justice, unstinting compassion, but also fiery eroticism, phallic projection, consuming passion, and self-destructive narcissism." (O'Murchu 1997, pp. 191-192)

Beyond the procreative aspect of sexuality is the experience of ecstasy. As Joan Timmerman notes, "As important as intimacy to test the rightness of a lifestyle, so is the availability of moments of ecstasy. Excitement, adventure, being beside oneself with feeling are not luxuries but are the essential integrators of human life. Ecstasy is the experience of the temporary dissolution of boundaries. The moment... is one in which some otherwise distant reality is glimpsed as here and now, one with oneself."... This "'unitive glimpse' is capable of completely reorganizing a life..." (Nelson/Longfellow 1993, p. 102) Such is the power of sexuality to recreate our own lives into the image of God. We are ourselves both the creators and the created as we pursue the spiritual journey. Recreate and cultivate your own life, as Jesus did, as an act of *agápe*. Study Love. Think long and hard about how best to express it. Give yourself to it. Examine your motives, and then trust the Spirit's leading. Experience the ecstasy!

The expression of *agápe* is your highest calling. Whether it takes the form of *eros* or *phileo* makes little difference. Whatever its form, it is essential to our lives as fully embodied divine beings.

Art as an Act of Co-Creation

There is no art without imagination, and imagination is the essential foundation of our creativity. To be an artist is to employ learned techniques, the inspiration of others, and our inherent ability to envision that which does not now exist. Indeed, imagination is that which makes creation possible. To create without imagination is simply to repeat that which has been done before.

There is nothing wrong with repeating what has been done before, as long as the objects being copied are worthy of repetition. This was the route great artists have followed. Pablo Picasso once observed that "[I]t took me four years to paint like Raphael, but a lifetime to paint like a child." Repetition may be necessary in the learning of artistic techniques, but techniques alone do not constitute art. It is only when the techniques are wedded to the creative imagination that true art is born. It is in this wedding that the artist realizes the glory of artistic endeavor. It is also in this uniting of imagination and technique that an integral part of human/divine evolution is realized, for unless there is first an articulated vision of what can be, there can be nothing for which to strive. Without the imaginative vision of the artist as a first step in the creative process, the rest of us are left bereft of a clear evolutionary goal. Art, and therefore, the artist, are absolutely essential to the unfolding of new life in any society.

Change is the essence of growth. Without change we cannot grow. As *Homo sapiens* continue to evolve into our God-given human/divine identity, we must embrace positive change as the price of becoming formed more fully into the image of our original Artist and Creator. The status quo is not only unacceptable; it is the way of death and the abdication of our calling.

When we reject change or denigrate the artistic imagination, whether actively or passively, we choose the way of death and stagnation. When we eliminate art in the education of our young, we choose the way of death. When we stymie the artistic inclinations of our children, we choose the way of death. When we replace the artistic imagination with total immersion in technology, we choose the way of death. When we ignore the prophetic imaginations of our artists, we choose the way of death. Western and Eastern societies continue to choose the way of death and stagnation, even in the 21st century.

Is it too late for rebirth? No, it is not, but for new life to come into being, we must once again honor the creative imaginations of our artists. We must also encourage the imaginative capabilities of our children, capabilities which may bring about the salvation of their parents. We must free our young to follow their own paths to the future, some to be the purveyors of creative imagination, others to be the fulfillers of those prophetic dreams. Painters, dancers, sculptors, writers, poets, musicians—whatever their God-given talents may be—must be honored, and the fruit of their creative imaginations taken seriously. Then, and only then, will that essential next step in our evolutionary development as divine/human beings be possible.

Music Is the Language of God

"How wonderful is the human voice! It is indeed the organ of the soul! The *intellect* of [human beings] sits enthroned upon the forehead and in [the] eye; and the *heart* of [humankind] is written upon [the] countenance. But the *soul* reveals itself in the voice only, as God revealed himself to the prophet of old, in 'the still, small voice,' and in a voice from the burning bush. The soul of [humankind] is audible, not visible. A sound alone betrays the flowing of the eternal fountain, invisible to [humans]!"   (Henry David Longfellow, cited in *Elbert Hubbard's Scrapbook*, p.228, emphasis added)

Music is the language of God. This was my intuitive conclusion many years ago. But now it has been confirmed from an unexpected source—string theory. Michio Kaku, one of the founders of string theory, explains: "Traditionally, physicists viewed electrons as being point particles, which were infinitesimally small. This meant physicists had to introduce a different point particle for each of the hundreds of sub-atomic particles they found, which was very confusing. But according to string theory, if... we could peer into the heart of an electron, we would see that it was not a point particle at all but a tiny vibrating string.... This tiny string, in turn, vibrates at different frequencies and resonances. If we were to pluck this vibrating string, it would change mode and become another subatomic particle, such as a quark. Pluck it again and it turns into a neutrino. In this way we can explain the blizzard of subatomic particles as nothing but different musical notes of the string. We can now replace the hundreds of subatomic particles seen in the laboratory with a single object, the string." (Kaku 2004, p. 18)

Kaku continues the analogy: the laws of physics come down to the "laws of harmony written for strings and membranes." The laws of chemistry equate to the melodies one plays on the strings, and "the universe is a symphony of strings." And the *Mind of God*, "which Einstein wrote eloquently about, is cosmic music resonating throughout hyperspace." (ibid., p. 18) Who would have ever thought that music, an art form, might also have had a scientific role in God's original act of our creation!

Al Young, an African American music critic, was reflecting on the music of saxophonist Coleman Hawkins. "Thirty-nine, forty, fifty, a hundred, thousands—who's to say how many rosy-chilled Octobers have befallen us, each one engraved in micro-moments of this innocent utterance, electrically notated, but like light in a photograph, never quite captured in detail, only in essence. Essence in this instance is private song, is you hearing your secret sorrow and joy blown back through Coleman Hawkins, invisibly connected to you and played back through countless bodies, each one an embodiment of the same soul force.... All poetry is about silent music, invisible art, and the clothing of time for the ages." (Young, *Bodies & Soul*, p. 4)

I have often wondered why I have found great music to be so emotionally moving and even the creation and participation in not-so-great music to be so satisfying. Is it because it brings one so close to the very heart of creation and, thus, to God? It is the music itself that moves me and not the just the words that may accompany it. Few things have moved me so emotionally as a live performance of Gustav Mahler's *Ninth Symphony* performed by Knoxville Symphony Orchestra some months ago. Why did it affect me so, unless it somehow put me in touch with my rootedness in Creation itself? Looking back on the experience, I think I knew myself to be in the presence of such raw power and enormous beauty, a beauty that so transcended whatever human scale I could apply to it, that I surely must have been in the presence of the Creator herself.

If music is, indeed, the language of God, then to create music is to use God's language—a divine language—to communicate with God and with each other about divine things. This is surely why music has played so large a role in our religious practice through the history of Christianity, Islam, and Judaism. It is one of our primary ways of communicating with God, and to create music is to co-create with her in God's own language.

The Creation of Beauty / The Beauty of Creation

He looked at his own Soul with a telescope. What seemed all irregular, he saw and shewed to be beautiful Constellations; And he added to the Consciousness hidden worlds within worlds.

—Samuel Coleridge

Beauty is the measure of creative genius. Artists envision it, musicians communicate it, scientists and crafts persons bring it into being. All of these comprise the teams which create and preserve beauty. God, however we define God, has gone before us to give us myriad examples of incredible beauty. What we call the "natural" world is exemplary of such extravagant beauty as to leave those who are not yet among the living dead, virtually speechless with awe and wonder. We are constantly enveloped by beauty, surrounded by it and filled with it. *To be human is to be beautiful.* We do not have to look far to find it. We need only to have eyes to see it, ears to hear it and hearts to respond to it. It is our response that reveals whether we are alive or dead. *Webster's New World Dictionary* defines beauty as "the quality attributed to whatever pleases or satisfies the senses or mind, as by line, color, form, texture, proportion, rhythmic motion, tone, etc. or by behavior, attitude, etc." I find this definition to be completely lacking of any satisfying explanation of just exactly *what* beauty is. Better, I think, are the much longer attempts of John O'Donohue, recent Irish poet, philosopher, and Roman Catholic priest, to define beauty:

> Nature is full of hidden geometry and harmony, as is the human mind; and the creations of the mind that awaken or recreate this sense of pattern and order tend to awaken or unveil beauty. Symmetry satisfies us and coheres with our need for meaning and shelter in the world. Indeed the notion

of symmetry is central to the beauty of mathematics and science.

More often than not it is the inner beauty of heart and mind that illuminates the face. A smile can completely transform a face. Ultimately it is the *soul* that makes the face beautiful. [Emphasis mine.]

There is something in the nature of beauty that goes beyond personality, good looks, image and fashion.

There is profound nobility in beauty that can elevate life, bring it into harmony with the artistry of its eternal source and destination.

...if our style of looking becomes beautiful, then beauty will become visible and shine forth for us. We will be surprised to discover beauty in unexpected places where the ungraceful eye would never linger, for beauty does not reserve itself for special elite moments or instances; it does not wait for perfection but is present already secretly in everything. (O'Donohue, 2004, pp.14-19)

It is my theory, given my conviction that we are divine, and thus eternal beings made in God's image, that our perception of beauty is simply the hazy reflection of bygone, timeless days when once we participated with God in whatever was the spiritual realm in which we existed, or, to quote Hermann Broch (cited by O'Donohue), "Beauty was a reversion to the pre-divine lingering in man as a presence of something that existed before his presence... prior to the gods." In this sense, beauty becomes a longing for home—but a home we cannot remember with any clarity. We only know that it reminds us of something wonderful, and we yearn for whatever it is. This is also the message of neurosurgeon Eben Alexander in his book *Proof of Heaven* about his near death experience (NDE).

For those sufficiently in touch with the yearning, to first become aware of beauty here and now in this earthly milieu, and then go on to be co-creators with God of like beauty in these earthly circumstances, is to assuage the pain of our separation from our former life in God. It is interesting that one of the experiences common to those who have an NDE (near death experience) is exposure to a time and place of such peace and beauty that they do not want to return to the chaos and violence of this life. Further, upon their return to this life, they no longer fear death, but look forward to its promise of release to that paradise they once briefly tasted. (see Moody, 1976; also see Ring, 1980)

Another way of looking at our yearning for beauty is the often unacknowledged presence of God within us—namely our soul. Our soul is *that-which-is-of-God-within-us*, and it may be that continuing presence working in our subconscious that continually tempts us with vague remembrances of the awesome beauty we once knew. However it happens, apprehension of the beautiful gives this life meaning and direction and, as such, is on a par with our experience of *agápe* and God's grace as an indication of who we are and that which is our destiny as *Homo sapiens.*

The Creation of Relationships

It is demonstrable that *to be human is to create.* There is a sense that much of what we do is an exercise in creation. Preeminent in our creative activity is the practice of forming relationships, some casual, some deep. Virtually every human being has relationships that we have created and nurtured for years. Even for the very old among us, the creation of yet more relationships is not an unusual occurrence. I would submit that the creation of formal and informal networks of people is one of humanity's most beautiful and productive creative activities. To thus create the opportunities for the practice of Love and compassion between persons has to be very close to the heart of the primary Creator, who also creates loving and compassionate relationships with her Creation, probably through us. Since we are all created by God, thus filling the earth with co-creators, it is inconceivable to me that God could be anything but a universalist, loving and compassionate toward all humanity and, beyond that, loving the whole of creation. Matthew Fox states unequivocally that "All creativity is meant to serve compassion, not projections. The result of Christ's compassion is a 'New Creation' and a new relation to creation wherein we are reunited with the whole, and our powers, including our creativity, serve the loving purpose of the whole." (Fox 2002, p. 95)

All of these demonstrate our primary relationship—a relationship we did not initially choose. We were instead chosen by the One who, by whatever name we use, created us as God's children. My religious tradition uses the names God and Creator and Holy Spirit. The name does not matter as much as the fact of our relationship. What does matter is that, because every person in all places at all times is also God's child, each one is my brother and sister—as are you. We are one family no matter your religion or race or nationality or culture. We are all one human family, the sons and daughters of one common progenitor. It will be a glorious day when each of us can sit at the same table with any of the rest of us, in genuine love and appreciation for each other. This is our Creator's goal as well.

In the meantime, while we are still here in this earthly tabernacle, if we would be co-creators of beauty with God and with others, we need to be alive and responsive to the beauty that already exists around us and within us. Having become aware of whose and who we are and our reason for being, the next step is to take seriously our God-inspired role as co-creators of beauty with God. The opportunities for each of us to do this are virtually endless. I have spoken here of only six such opportunities: the creation of self, procreation, the creation of art, the creation of music, the creation of beauty, and the creation of relationships.

When Creators Go Bad

Just because we have the power to create does not mean that we will always use that power to good effect. For starters, we have the freedom and the capacity to create hurt as well as healing, injustice as well as peace, ugliness as well as beauty, greed as well as compassion, and fear as well as hope. *If we do not know who and whose we are, we are as likely to create bad as we are good.* The power of our imagination is neutral. We can imagine terrible deeds and their consequences, just as easily as we can imagine the good. We also have the power to choose to act on that which we imagine, whether good or bad. This is the necessary consequence of our freedom. To recognize our errors and to make the necessary adjustments may also be an essential aspect of our learning process.

To make mistakes is an aspect of growing. I have yet to meet a mature person who did not first go through *im*maturity. To grow from irresponsibility to responsibility is part of what it means to be human. Forgiveness by those hurt by our mistakes is both warranted and healing—for *both* parties. To fail to forgive another, even repeatedly, is to block whatever healing needs to take place. This is a testament to the nature of our relationships as human beings. We are *not* independent beings answerable only to ourselves. Our maturing into who we are called to be is a community project with the participation of three parties—the self, other people, and God. The bond that holds us together is inclusive, indiscriminate, unconditional and forgiving love—*agápe*.

What is *not* necessary is that we always choose the bad over the good. The power to create evil is a two-edged sword in that it hurts indiscriminately and hurts most the one wielding it. Whether we choose to hurt others as an act of ignorance of who we and they are, or as an act of grievance or revenge for some imagined wrong, or as a display of self-pride and rebellion, the result is always the same. We destroy the very things that make us human, blemishing the image of our Creator in us and in others. Thankfully, our Creator does not respond with this same kind of destructive vengeance. The *agápe* Love of the One who first imagined us demonstrates a maturity we have not yet attained. Consequently, Her reaction is one of reasoned and hopeful confidence that Her investment in us will, in time or eternity, bear good fruit.

It may be that patience with both ourselves and with others is one of our critical needs as co-creators, as we choose from among the imaginations of our hearts that which we will create. It is essential that we recognize that we are capable of choosing both good and evil. To accomplish this requires first an honest assessment of the choices, then a determination to choose the good. The biblical term for this is *repentance*. Often, following repentance, an acceptance of our need for help in making necessary changes in basic attitudes is required. In many ways, at this stage of our spiritual development, we are like little children. We need mature, loving guidance from others who have traveled this way before us. We also need the healing and empowering of our Creator, whose very essence is to choose good over evil. The more we strengthen this spiritual connection to our Source, the more consistently will we be able to choose to create good. The biblical term for this is *regeneration*.

Our Source of Creativity

"Source" is another way to think of the prime Creator. I very often feel that I am drawing on knowledge that I never knew I had. This is certainly true of the little bit of song writing I have done. But the same feeling has persisted through the writing of this book and other writing I have undertaken. It is a sense of being supplied the thoughts I have as they are needed for the work at hand. I do not want to make too much of this, but to the extent that it may be true, it could mean that the term "co-creator" is really analogous to "scribe" for who- or whatever is on the other side dictating to me. Since I am not always sure how to identify the Source, it may or may not be synonymous with Co-Creator or God or some source in a parallel universe using me to say what it may otherwise be unable to speak. At least the existence of parallel universes is now a viable conversation taking place in some quarters of scientific cosmological exploration (See Greene, 2011). I may not be losing my mind, after all!

Citing the Roman philosopher, Plotinus (C.E. 205-270), James Hillman writes, "That all happenings form a unity and are spun together is signified by the Fates.... It is the task the gods allot us, and the share of glory they allow; the limits we must not pass; and our appointed end." (Hillman 1996, p. ix) Creativity is not only the task which God allots us; it is through our creativity that we become one with the basic foundation of the universe.

If Plotinus is right, there may be both solace and consternation in his assessment of our source. On the one hand, I would like to believe that we are free agents who have the final say about our destiny as co-creators with God. But on the other hand I confess to some ambivalence because I am quite sure that I am also prone to entertain illusions about how much freedom I actually have *in this life*. Such evidence as I can point to (as I did in the preface to this book) sometimes makes me wonder if we are not all subject to delusions of either grandeur or inadequacy, or both, plagued by both unwarranted pride and fear. I have exercised, on occasion, spiritual power. But was I its source? Not likely. I have also designed and added a beautiful sun room to my house. I confess to being pleased with it, but am I really the source of the beauty? I do not think so. It is much more likely the case that, at best, I am but the conduit of whatever I create and as such I simply carry out the design of my life accepted by me before my birth. This makes me truly a *co*-creator. I am satisfied that, *by myself*, I create nothing good. I am beholden to God *and* those whose DNA I share for both that which I am and, I suspect, for whatever good I accomplish.

Carolyn Myss speaks of "each person's spiritual chronology, a personal mythology that had begun *even before they entered their physical lives.* These images were archetypes, energy guides that could direct people toward their spiritual purpose, their Contracts." (Myss 2001, p. 14, emphasis added) Given the eternal aspect of our divine nature, the idea that we may have, indeed, made a contract with our Creator prior to our birth does not seem to me an unreasonable proposition. Since I have no other explanation for the existence of the archetypes which support our personal development *and* are demonstrated within each of us in ways which define our individual identities, I find it a conceptually more reasonable premise that I accepted the arrangement beforehand than that it just happened by chance. The larger question may be how detailed and specific are these archetypes when it comes to the choices we make on a day to day basis.

Shakti Gawain, the New Age author and promoter of the "creative visualization movement" writes that, "One of the most important steps in making your creative visualization work effectively and successfully is to have the experience of coming from 'source'. Source means the supply of infinite Love, wisdom, and energy in the universe. For you, source may mean God, or the universal mind, or the oneness of all, or your true essence. However we conceptualize it, it can be found here and now within each of us, in our inner being." (Gawain 1978, p. 39) I would add to her list "soul" or "that-which–is-of-God-in-us." As soul God is both within and beyond us. Soul is our connection to each other and to every other who has ever lived. Soul may also be our connection to all we need to know at any given time.

However it happens, to listen and to respond to our creative intuitions is a calling we dare not ignore. Whether your talent is writing, composing music, inventing new technology, solving problems, creating and nurturing relationships, preparing nourishing food, painting or sculpting beauty, or any one of a myriad of other creative endeavors—if we are to have a beautiful world and fulfilling lives, we must respond to those creative urges we receive and claim our identities as Co-Creators with "that-which-is-of-God-in-us," our Holy Souls.

Chapter 5

THE HUMAN DIMENSION OF DIVINITY

We are mirrors of God, created to reflect him.
Even when the water is not calm, it reflects the sky.
—Ernesto Cardenal, (born 1925)

Our Lord says to every living soul, "I became man for you.
If you do not become God for me, you do me wrong."
—Meister Eckhart (1260-1329)

Man still stands in the image of God—twisted, broken, abnormal,
but still the image-bearer of God.
—Francis Schaffer (1912-1984)

Learn to hold loosely all that is not eternal.—Agnes Maud Royden

"And I will do whatever you ask in my name, so that the Father may
be glorified in the Son.
You may ask me for anything in my name, and I will do it."
—John 14:13-14 (Today's New International Version)

"...the Kingdom of God is within you."
—Luke 17:21 (New International Version)

"The [Father's] imperial rule is within you and it is outside of you."
—Gospel of Thomas 3:3

"...the seed of true humanity exists within you."—Gospel of Mary 4:5

Just Who Are We, Anyway?

There is a curious anomaly in the writings of the Apostle Paul. In his letters to the Romans and to the Corinthians he spends a significant amount of ink on their sinfulness. On the one hand, much of his concern with sin is in the first seven chapters of his letter to the Roman Christians, and his first letter to the Corinthian church was so filled with warnings and dire predictions of God's judgments on their sinful ways that he had to write a second letter to apologize for the first (see II Corinthians 2:1-4). On the other hand, his first two letters, Romans and I Corinthians, were addressed to those "called to be *saints*" (*hágioi* in the original Greek text, meaning "holy ones"). Paul's second letter to the Corinthians is addressed simply to "the church of God that is in Corinth, including all the saints (*hágioi*) throughout Achaia."

So how can the Christians in Rome and in Corinth be both sinners and saints? The two terms are not mutually exclusive. In the first instance, Paul is addressing their misbehaviors. But in his salutations he was addressing their *basic identity* as holy ones. They were saints who sinned, to be sure, but their basic identity was saints. They were saints who sin, *not* sinners who "saint." This is a crucial distinction because it is out of our sense of identity that we act. If we identify ourselves as sinners, we will act out of that identity by sinning. But if we think of ourselves as holy ones, then our actions will more likely reflect that belief by saintly behavior.

I repeat here an analogy I used in the Introduction: if a bird thinks it is a fish, it is likely to neither swim very well nor fly very well. It may even fear flying. But if a bird *knows* it is a bird then it may fly very well indeed and may even soar to great heights. One of the reasons we are so often plagued by our sin is that we believe that is our real nature. But that is a serious error. We were created in God's image, and that image is one of holiness and separation *to* (not from) God. We were born to soar!

The Greek term *hámartia*, usually translated "sin," literally means "missing the mark," not immorality. There is another Greek term available to translate "immorality," *porneia,* a term also used by the

Apostle when the circumstances dictate its use. A problem arises when we use the term "sin" to translate both these Greek terms. We do, indeed, *miss the mark*, when we think of ourselves as separate from God. The truth is that we can no more separate ourselves from our Creator than a clay pot can separate itself from the potter who is forming it. Wherever we are, God is. Whatever we do, right or wrong, God is still with us, in us, and molding us. We do not have the option of separating ourselves from God, even at our worst. Separation is an illusion fostered by our mistaken sense of identity as sinners.

This, of course, calls into question the entire Christian doctrine of sin and redemption. If sin is missing the mark, then the needed corrective is not redemption, but reorientation. This means, too, that Jesus did not come to redeem us but rather to show us who we already are and who, in the caressing hands of our loving Potter, we are becoming. Jesus, a divine child of God, is showing us that we, too, are divine children. We are immature, perhaps, and often rebellious and unruly, surely, but for all that we are no less God's children in the same sense in which Jesus is. We, too, are heirs of our heavenly Father, as is Jesus. We, too, are potentially capable of selfless, holy living, as is Jesus. Jesus was our teacher and model and is still our cheerleader on a journey that will last at least one lifetime and perhaps more (if the Hindus are right). In any event, like Jesus we are eternal spiritual beings who have always been and who will always be. Our given task in this life is to learn who we are as children of God made in God's image.

Original Blessing, Not Fall and Redemption

Most of us who grew up in the Evangelical Christian tradition learned well the theology of sin, fall, and redemption. We may not have known all of these theological terms but we clearly got the gist of it—salvation from Hell. How well I remember reading the sermonic imagery of Jonathan Edwards, an 18th century theologian and preacher, who portrayed an angry God gleefully dangling sinners over the fiery pits of Hell. His was not a loving God or a God to be loved in return, no matter what Jesus may have said to the contrary. But Edwards' fire and brimstone messages did not fall on deaf ears. Hundreds, if not thousands, of the people of his day were scared into the Kingdom by his preaching. And his influence is still to be seen in some evangelical circles to this day.

Edwards had apparently not read the writings of Meister Eckhart, who preceded him by about five centuries. Eckhart was tried as a heretic by Pope John XXII's inquisition, around 1327 C.E., for teachings that would have roundly contradicted the venom spouted by Edwards. He taught that we must let go of many religious traditions of his day. "Only those who dare to let go can dare to reenter," he wrote.

Matthew Fox, picking up on Eckhart's theme, notes that "what religion must let go of in the West is an exclusively fall/redemption model of spirituality [which goes back not to Jesus, but to St. Augustine, four centuries later]—a model that has dominated theology, Bible studies, seminary and novitiate training, hagiography, [and] psychology for centuries. It is a dualistic model and a patriarchal one; it begins its theology with original sin, and it generally ends with redemption [or hell]. Fall/redemption spirituality does not teach believers about the New Creation or creativity, about justice-making and social transformation, or about Eros, play, pleasure and the God of delight. It fails to teach love of the earth or care for the cosmos, and it is so frightened of passion that it fails to listen to the impassioned pleas of the *anawim* [a Hebrew word that refers to *the poor who depend on the Lord for deliverance*], the little ones, of human history. This same fear of passion prevents it [fall/redemption spirituality] from helping lovers to celebrate their experiences as spiritual and mystical. This tradition has not proven friendly to artists or prophets or Native American peoples or women." (Fox, 1983, p. 11)

The doctrine of sin, fall and redemption has been the cornerstone of evangelical teaching. As such it has skewed our understanding of the Church as a community of unconditional Love and acceptance, our understanding of the person, mission, and teaching of Jesus, and our understanding and acceptance of ourselves as the Beloved of God. It has substituted fear for Love, terror for joy, and despair for hope. It has made of God's creation something ugly to be trashed and despised. In our day, it has become a stumbling block for those who would otherwise be devoted to the God revealed in Jesus.

It is past time for a major theological reassessment of what God is about in the world and in our lives, individually and collectively. Some theologians and an assortment of other spiritual writers have begun to beat the drums of theological reform. Note that I do not say "renewal." Renewal of the tried and untrue theologies of the past is decidedly *not* what we need. What we need is to go back to square one, to the first century Jesus, peel away the layers of legends which have made him anything but what he is, and, beginning with the Apostle Paul's writings and the Gospels, separate the mythical Christ from the real man Jesus. These efforts are well under way, but need to be continued, not by those already beholden to sin, fall, and redemption fictions, but by those who see the need to start afresh from the very beginning of the Christian era—and who have the courage to do so.

There have already been a number of prophetic voices along the way. Meister Eckhart is one, his disciple, Matthew Fox (21st century) is another. Irenaeus, Bishop of Lyons (2nd century) was one, John Woolman (18th century Quaker) another. Hildegarde of Bingen (12th century mystic) was one, Thomas Aquinas (13th century theologian) another. Dietrich Bonhoeffer (20th century prophet) was one, Martin Luther King (20th century prophet) another. The list goes on and on. We have not been lacking for prophetic voices anytime along the way.

If God Is Life, *per se* Life (Aquinas); *and* Spirit (Apostle John)

Thomas Aquinas, 13th century philosopher and theologian, wrote that "God is life, *per se* Life." Life is, by definition, intrinsically God. God = Life = God. Jesus said *"God is spirit*, and those who worship him must worship in spirit and truth." (Gospel of John

$4:24)^{10}$ The same has been said of other dimensions of being. The Apostle John wrote that "God is Light" (I John 1:5) and that "God is Love" (I John 4:8). Perhaps John and Aquinas are speaking metaphorically in each instance, but in as much as the only body that God is reported to have has been his embodiment in his creation, Life and Spirit and Light and Love may not be metaphors at all, but accurate perceptions of God's imbodied identity. Could it be that God's embodiment is to be found only in his creation and perhaps primarily in human beings in the form of Soul and Spirit and Life and Light and Love? If so, we may be closer to God than we realized.

Webster defines life as "1) that property of plants and animals that distinguishes them from inorganic matter or dead organisms... specifically the cellular biochemical activity or processes, the storage and use of energy, the excretion of wastes, growth, reproduction, etc." There follow sixteen more derivative definitions, none of which address anything remotely spiritual. Roman Catholic theologians Karl Rahner and Herbert Vorgrimler, on the other hand, note that "...in a theological context life is defined as (1) a "gift of God" and (2) is manifested in 'personal spirit.' Spirit they define as, "That entity which is characterized by an openness towards being and at the same time by an awareness of what itself is and is not. These two fundamental aspects of spirit correspond to these two opennesses, to universal being and to itself: transcendence and reflexivity." (Rahner and Vorgrimler, 1981, p. 485)

Between the two definitions, one of life, the other of spirit, presented by Rahner and Vorgrimler, we can begin to discern what Aquinas and the Apostle John are getting at. If God is the possessor of that life we experience as a divine gift which manifests itself as personal spirit, then what we receive in our spirit is the gift of God of her own self. This then is what the New Testament writers mean when they speak of being "filled with the Spirit" (see Acts 2:4 and Ephesians 5:18) and "baptized with the Holy Spirit." (Acts 1:5)

---

10 In the spirit of full disclosure, it must be noted that many biblical scholars do not believe that Jesus actually said this, but that these words represent the perspective of a later or different tradition, added perhaps by the author of the gospel.

They are speaking of being filled with God and being immersed in God. And life becomes not that cold, mechanistic collection of physical processes described by Webster, but rather the inheritance of God herself—or, in a word, *soul, that-which-is-of-God-in-us*, filling us and immersing us.

Our representations of God as a larger-than-life human being are anthropomorphic projections resulting from our inability to visualize God in any other acceptable form. It has been said that "In the beginning God created us in his image, and then we returned the favor." The ancient Jewish religious authorities, aware of the inadequacy of such a representation, prohibited the making of images presumed to be of God. We, too, have known that our human images of God were inadequate, but we use them anyway. The primary Hebrew term for God, Yahweh, was written without vowel points as YHWH, thereby making it unpronounceable. Presumably, even vocal representations of the divine One were also deemed to be so inadequate as to be sacrilegious. (I cannot imagine the communication problems this posed for Jewish theological scholars, whose primary responsibility it was to think and teach about YHVH.) Yahweh can be translated in English "I am who I will be." Perhaps the best we can do is to think of God as "She who is" though I suspect that even the implication of gender also leads us astray. For us "God" presents both a conceptual and a linguistic dilemma. We conceptualized Her, and now we don't know what to do with Him.

But perhaps our anthropomorphic images are not so unreasonable, after all. If "God-in-us" is the only fully embodied form of God we have come to know, then our anthropomorphic representations of God in our form are not entirely inappropriate. It may not be hyperbole to assert that God has no hands but our hands and no feet but our feet, that God has no physical manifestation but our bodies, male and female. In this light, the Apostle Paul's startling assertion in his second letter to the Corinthian takes on a new depth of meaning:

"...all of us, with unveiled faces, seeing the glory of the Lord as though reflected in a mirror, *are being transformed [metamorphosed] into the same image from one degree of glory [manifest presence] to another*, even as by the Spirit of the Lord." (II Corinthians 3:17-18, NRSV; annotation and emphasis added)

If God is Life then we are virtually and tangibly surrounded by God. To see God we have only to open our eyes to behold God's handiwork in every bird that flies and every blade of grass. Our ears behold God's creativity in the songs of the birds and in the rustling of the grass. We can feel God's loving care in the warm, feathery down of a young bird's plumage and in the cool grass nurtured by morning dew. If God is Life then all creatures, including our own species reveal God's creative genius. But if God is *intrinsically* Life, then we need look no further than ourselves to discern the actual *presence* of The Divine. If God is Life then we must rejoice in it, plunge into it, and partake of God's goodness. If God is Life, then to live fully is to live fully in God and the glory of God will be humanity fully alive.

If God is the essence of *Spirit* then as spiritual beings we are expressions of the Divine. We partake of God when we pursue the spiritual journey. To be baptized in the Spirit, is to be baptized into God. I have noticed an interesting confluence in the work of the Spirit and the work of Jesus as they are described in the gospels. Virtually everything that Jesus is reported to have done, is likewise said to have been done by the Spirit. Jesus heals, the Spirit heals; Jesus speaks, the Spirit speaks; Jesus drives out demons, the Spirit drives out demons. Jesus and the Spirit are one; we, likewise are one with the Spirit. That we can squash the work of the Spirit in our lives is amply demonstrated, and when we do we render ourselves weak and ineffective by denying our true identity. But when we free the Spirit of God in us, we are empowered to do the miraculous, bringing challenge, change and hope to all around us.

If God Is Light, *per se* Light

The Apostle John exclaimed, "God is light and in him is no darkness at all." Is John speaking metaphorically or intrinsically here? If the former, then he is saying that God has the characteristics of light. If he is speaking intrinsically, he is saying that light is of the essence of God's nature. I propose that John is here speaking intrinsically.

In the past few decades modern physics has come to some provocative conclusions about the elemental nature of matter. Brian Greene writes that "Quantum mechanics establishes that, somewhat as water is composed of H_2O molecules, a field is composed of infinitesimally small particles known as the field's *quanta*. For the electromagnetic field, the quanta are photons, and so a quantum theorist would modify the classical description of your light bulb by saying that the bulb emits a steady stream comprising 100 billion billion photons each second... the mathematics of quantum field theory describes these particles as *dots or points that have no spatial extent and no internal structure.*" (Greene 2011, p.76, emphasis added)

Heinz R. Pagels[11] has described fields, particles, and reality as "a coherent, unified, and experimentally correct picture of material reality.... To understand atomic particles one has to go beyond the old idea of matter as a 'material stuff' that can be known through our senses to descriptions of particles in terms of how they transform when subject to various interactions. *It is how material objects respond when acted upon that tells us what they are...*" Likewise, "as we describe the field concept it should become clear that particle and field are complementary manifestations of the same thing... That light is a form of energy is clear to us simply by standing in the sun. The heat that we feel was once energy in the form of light— electromagnetic fields—transmitted across interplanetary space from the sun. But light also carries momentum—a small but observable push" [a possible kind of propulsion for future space travel]. (H. Pagels 1983, pp. 236-237)

Pagels continues, "...there were two dualisms that had to be overcome before the modern concept of matter could develop. First was the dualism of mass and energy, which were seen as distinct.

---

11 Heinz R. Pagels was formerly Director of the New York Academy of Sciences and adjunct Professor of Physics at Rockefeller University.

This dualism was overcome by Einstein's relativity theory, which showed that mass and energy were convertible; mass was simply a form of bound energy. The second dualism was that of field and particle, often referred to as the wave-particle duality. This dualism was overcome by the new quantum theory, in which fields and particles were no longer seen as distinct but as complementary." When the "dualisms of energy and matter, particle and field" were understood, it became clear that material reality was only "the transformation and organization of field quanta—*that is all there is.*" (ibid., pp. 238-239, emphasis added)

And, apart from the soul, that is all there is to *us* as well—the transformation and organization of photons. We are bundles of energy—light energy. We are beings of light, whirling masses of organized photons, trillions of photons. Add soul (*that-which-is-of-God-in-us*) and we take on creative capabilities we have not yet even dared to dream. Though the first and second century Apostle John surely did not know the details that the 20th century physicists have figured out, he certainly nailed their conclusion that we are light. We are light just as God is light, which is yet another way of saying that we were created in God's image. He makes the same point in his Gospel about Jesus whom he quoted as saying, "As long as I am in the world, I am the light of the world"—just like God. (John 9:5, NRSV) This, then, raises the question, what happens when Jesus is no longer in the world? We get our answer, from another gospel writer, Matthew, who quotes Jesus as saying, "You are the light of the world..." (Matthew 5:14, NRSV) Jesus was reportedly speaking to his disciples. He was teaching us that we are as he is—*light*.

If God is Love, *per se* Love

Once again it is the astute disciple of Jesus, the Apostle John who, writing before his time, said "...everyone who loves is born of God and knows God. Whoever does not love does not know God, for God is Love." (I John 4:7-8, NRSV) Here he is using the Greek term *agápe* (Godly Love). In both Chapters 2 and 3, I wrote at some length of the human manifestation of *agápe* and will not repeat what I said there. At this point, however, I wish to emphasize that Love is not so much something we do as it is something we intrinsically *are*.

We were born to love; to love deeply, universally, and unconditionally; to be the embodiment of Love, just like God. Everyone is born of God, but we have forgotten who we are, and therefore whose presence we should be manifesting. Love is a soul matter; the lack of love is soul sickness. This is not a new problem, but it is a problem that in our day has reached critical proportions. If we will but own our true identity as Divine Lovers, wars will cease, poverty will be eradicated, joy will replace fear, governments will serve the common good, the earth itself will join in the chorus of ecstasy, and we all will join in the heartfelt praises of the One who calls us to unity *as* the Holy Lovers of people and God.

The musical adaptation of Victor Hugo's *Les Misérables* is a modern parable of agápe. The leading character, Jean Valjean, at his death, cites his guiding truth, *"To love another person is to see the face of God."* In as much as all of us bear the imprint of God upon our *"beingness,"* then the statement is literally true. To love other persons is, indeed, to see them for who they are—children of God, with a soul which is *that-of-God-within-us*, made in God's image.

God
Creator of worlds, Designer of universes,
Artist of nature, and cosmic Potter!
Great Spirit of evolution, Nurturer of the seeds of Life
Sharer of visions and sacred Inspirer!

Humankind
Eternal, transcendent, luminous and living!
Purveyors of truth and Bringers of hope!
Benefactors of earth and willing partners
In union with God and with one another.

God's Spirit
Beyond us, within us and as us,
Filling us with Life and Love and Light!
Embodied Presence, divine Lovers
Making lives sacred, souls full and infinite!

Are we not called to honor and praise God as the Holy One *embodied* in her creation? Is this asking for too much? Not if we are willing to forgo our delusional thinking that we are somehow separate from God. Change our thinking and we will change those around us. Love with the love of God and we can change the world. Love our enemies and we will have no enemies. Love passionately and we will be passionately loved. *Agápe* begets *agápe*. If we are love, we can start an epidemic of love. This is my dream!

The Mind of Christ

The Apostle Paul, in his first letter to the young Corinthian church, makes the case for spiritual maturity: "My speech and my proclamation were not with plausible words of wisdom, but with a demonstration of the Spirit and of power, so that your faith might not rest on human wisdom but on the power of God. Yet among the mature we do speak wisdom... we speak God's wisdom, secret and hidden... 'For who has known the mind of the Lord so as to instruct him?' *But we have the mind of Christ."* (I Corinthians 2:4-7 & 16, NRSV) To be spiritually mature is to recognize and accept that we have the mind of Christ.

Just as there are several words in New Testament Greek which are all translated "love," there are several words in Greek—three primary ones being *nous, phroneo,* and *dianoia*—which we typically translate with the English word "mind." It does not help matters that the English term "mind" has multiple definitions such as memory, thought, will, brain, consciousness, the unconscious, care, intention, obey, opinion, understanding, intellect, etc. So when the Apostle Paul writes to the Philippian church "Let the same mind be in you that was in Christ Jesus..." (Philippians 2:5, NRSV), was he talking about Jesus' brain or will or intention or memory? Our English translators here settled on the generic word "mind" to translate *phroneo*, which is generally used in Greek in the sense of "intention" or "mindedness." Thus, Paul was exhorting us to have the same "intention" or "like-mindedness" as Jesus, this same Jesus who "being in the form of God, thought it not robbery to be equal with God." (Philippians 2:6, KJV), this same Jesus who came to show us who *we* are!

Earlier, in Paul's first letter to his brothers and sisters in the Corinthian church, he tells them "But we have the mind [*nous*, meaning 'understanding'] of Christ (a translation which agrees with Jesus' purpose in his teachings about the Kingdom of God). Jesus was trying to help us *understand* that God's Kingdom was not a particular place but an *awareness* of this world in which there is no separation between God and humans. Jesus "...'saw' with his everyday mind (consciousness) that he was completely united with the God others in his audience merely thought they should worship. Indeed, in his refutation of dualism, Jesus was reflecting the ancient teachings of the Hindu Yogis, who believed the whole of Creation was one with Brahma, the eternal essence of the universe.

Another Greek term which warrants our attention is the word *syneidesis* which is translated variously into English as "consciousness," "mindful," or "awareness." Its only use in the New Testament is by the Apostle Peter: "One is approved, if mindful [conscious] of God..." (I Peter 2:19). "Consciousness" was not a well developed concept in the first century. Even today, it is not well understood. Timothy Ferris[12] has posited that consciousness is, "...the totality of thoughts, feelings and sensations presented by the brain to that segment of it that is conscious. But... consciousness forms a much smaller part of the operations of the brain than we once supposed. Mind is not the all-knowing monarch of the brain, but a little circle of firelight in a dark, Australia-sized continent where the unconscious brain processes carry on." (Ferris, 1992, p. 74). It is this vast and mysterious region of the *un*conscious, which has proved virtually impregnable to the probing of science, to which Jesus calls us. He seeks to enlarge significantly "the circle of firelight" by bringing to our consciousness the ever present and enfolding Love and *union* we have with God. This is not a mystery science will ever solve, yet it is readily apparent to the eyes of faith as we follow the Spirit's leading deeper and deeper into our own unconscious.

---

12 Timothy Ferris is a prolific science writer, a Fellow of the American Association for the Advancement of Science, and Emeritus Professor of Astronomy at University of California.

"The Kingdom of Heaven[13] that Jesus saw so well is a vision of this world that sees no separation (duality) between God and Humans." And, secondly, *"The Kingdom of Heaven that Jesus saw so well is a vision of this world that sees no separation (duality) between human beings."* (Marion 2000, p. 8) Jesus wants us to live in the constant consciousness of God's sovereign presence... where?—within us! The first and second century Christians inherited the scourge of Greek dualistic philosophy, a philosophy which has been passed down through the centuries to us. In fact, God is neither here nor there; she is both. Like God, we are *intrinsically* not here *or* there, not good *or* evil, not mind *or* body, and not Spirit *or* matter, not me *or* you, not male *or* female—and we are not God *or* human—we are all of these all of the time. The Kingdom of God is not a Kingdom of opposites, but a Kingdom of total unity which includes all of us and all we all bring to it.

To the Galatians Paul wrote. "There is no longer Jew or Greek, there is no longer slave or free, there is no longer male or female; for all of you are one in Christ Jesus." (Galatians 3:28, NRSV) *There is no duality in the Kingdom of God—only unity.*

God is within all of us and all of us are within God. This is the consciousness, the mind, the *syneidesis* that Jesus was trying to awaken within all of us. When we realize that we are and always have been the totally loved and accepted divine children of the divine Creator, *this* is the Kingdom of God.

It is our calling, even our evolutionary destiny, to accept the mantle of divinity, to accept the mantle of Godhood, because that is who we intrinsically are. That is the teaching of Jesus, the teaching of Paul and the teaching of Christian mystics through the ages. It is also the teaching of Hindu Yogis, American Indian medicine men, and spiritually astute quantum physicists. And it is the teaching of Yoga, Hinduism and Buddhism. To arrive at this understanding of oneself is *satori* in Zen Buddhism, *bodhi* in Hinduism and *metamorphosis* in

---

13 The phrase "Kingdom of Heaven" is generally thought by biblical scholars to be a euphemism for Kingdom of God, used by the Jewish author of the Gospel of Matthew so as to avoid offending Jews, for whom the gospel was written and for whom the name of God was too sacred to be uttered or written.

Paul's Christian teaching. In the words of Christian mystic Meister Eckhart, "In this breaking through I find that God and I are both the same."

Freedom to Be, Freedom to Do

A further expression of our divinity is our freedom to choose whatever or whoever we want to be. Freedom has not always, or even usually, been the watchword of either religious or political authorities. Depending on the power of such authorities and how much they have vested in maintaining that power, real liberation is eyed negatively on a scale ranging from beneficent toleration to disdain to anathema. Virtually no one who is infected with this kind of power over others is immune to its abuse. In the oft quoted words of John Acton, "Power tends to corrupt, and absolute power corrupts absolutely." Rare is the politician who does not yield to the temptations of political power. The same is true of other forms of power as in the military power of empires and the economic power of corporations. Abigail Adams, writing to her husband, President John Adams, cautioned, "I am more and more convinced that man is a dangerous creature; and that power, whether vested in many or a few, is ever grasping, and, like the grave cries, 'Give, give!'" She further cautioned, "All men would be tyrants, if they could..." (Abigail & John Adams 2002, *The Book of Abigail and John: Selected Letters of the Adams Family, 1762-1784)*. For these kinds of power, freedom is anathema.

There is however, another kind of power that protects both those who use it and the powerless—the power of Spirit. Spiritual power reveals wealth, privilege and greed to be weak and futile and corrupt. This spiritual power is the power of the liberated spirit of the children of God. Not even death can defeat it. Spiritual power eviscerates and renders helpless the exercise of malicious power. It is the power of liberation from ego and illusion.

Peace activist Daniel Berrigan has said that "the [malicious] spirit of *control* [is] ego run amok." The freedom of the mature child of God, of whatever religious persuasion, is the freedom of un-entangled ego. The pilgrim on the spiritual journey experiences increasing liberty the further he or she travels the Way of the Spirit. The extent of our freedom is the measure of our surrender to the liberating power of God's Spirit. When we surrender our minds and hearts and wills to God, we discover the strength we need to do whatever needs to be done.

The author of the Letter to the Ephesians exclaimed, "How very great is his power at work in us who believe. This power working in us is the same as the mighty strength which he used when he raised Christ from death and seated him at his right side in the heavenly world." (Ephesians 1:19-20, NRSV). I have long favored a transliterated version of the 19th verse which says "How very great is his *dynamite* in us..." (The Greek term *dunameos* is the root from which we get our English word, "dynamite.")

The freedom of the child of God is grounded in power, but only the power to do good to others and to resist evil. It is the freedom of the knowledge of who we are and whose we are; and it is also the freedom of the sure knowledge that our greatest nemesis, death, has already been defeated. The Apostle Paul exclaims that "neither death, nor life, nor angels, nor rulers, nor things present, nor things to come, nor powers, nor height, nor depth, nor anything else in all creation, will be able to separate us from the Love of God in Christ Jesus our Lord." (Romans 8:38-39, NRSV) I would add to his list that neither we ourselves, our mistakes, our lack of faith, our fears, nor anything else can separate us from the Love of God. Even when we fail to appropriate the freedom given us, we are still the liberated children of God.

Those in the third stage of the *Threefold Path* are subject only to the supreme law, repeated in one way or another in virtually every religion—"In everything do to others as you would have them do to you, for this is the law and the prophets" (Matthew 7:12). The author of the Gospel of John quotes Jesus as saying to his disciples, "I give you a new commandment, that you love one another. Just as I have loved you, you also should love one another" (John 13:34). What kind of love was Jesus talking about? It was *agápe*. These are the *only* laws for the pilgrim who has arrived at Stage 3. Anything else is just extra baggage to be abandoned.

The only persons who need to fear the freedom of God's children are those who try to control or oppress us. We are an irrepressible, rebellious bunch who, having tasted true liberty, are not about to let it be taken away. We know where our freedom lies. *God is our Liberator*. God has set us free to pursue and fulfill our calling to be divine lovers in a world desperately in need of all the *agápe* we can bring to it. This means loving our foes and making them our friends. It means forgiving and praying for those who try to make our lives difficult. It means, quite literally, being the presence of God in a world of greed and injustice. It means letting our hearts be broken by the things that break the heart of God.

Finally, our freedom is the freedom of resurrection. We are already living the resurrected life. In the resurrected life death has already been vanquished and our growth continues forever. There is no power on earth that can take it away. When we leave this earthly life we return home to the rest and company of those who have preceded us. We will be loved and we will be Love. That is the destiny of divine beings.

Ordinary Mystics

To be a mystic is to live intentionally into the mystery. (And we are not lacking for mystery to live into.) Contemporary scientists, particularly in the fields of physics and cosmology, are making great strides in *understanding* how the world and the universe really work on both the micro and macro levels. Their problem is that the more mysteries they solve, the greater unsolved mysteries they find. Both world and cosmos are so incredibly complex that their mysteries apparently stretch on forever. And *that* is one of the mysteries. So far science has no clues as to what "forever" is. It is seemingly bigger than time (another mystery) but it cannot be quantified. To say that the cosmos either has boundaries beyond which nothingness goes on forever *or* that the cosmos itself goes on forever are both unfathomable and unquantifiable and, therefore unacceptable options. This is truly a dilemma for those committed exclusively to scientific methodology.

However, for the mystic, "forever" is not a problem—at least no more than God is a problem. It is not a problem because the mystic's way of knowing is through *intuition* rather than scientific verification. Concepts like eternity and forever are known in a different way from that of the scientist. But because science cannot account for intuition either, it has to relegate it to yet another unsolved mystery.

Still another concept, "infinity," is one in which mystics and scientists can agree, at least in definition. It can, for example, be demonstrated that two straight parallel lines, extended forever in either one or both directions, will never meet. This is true by definition and can be verified, to an extent, by observation. But the scientific jinx to this conclusion is that there is no way yet discovered to follow the lines to their end because there is no end. Thus it must presumably "forever" remain a theorem, not a verifiable fact, in spite of mystic and scientific agreement.

Divinity is yet another scientifically unverifiable reality. Though generally acknowledged by most people as a reality referring to an ill-defined entity we call God or Allah, divinity is not generally applied to individual people. By definition it may be used not only of God, but of anything thought to be holy or sacred. But the existence of God or divinity is not something that can be scientifically verified. It does not help matters that even the religious community cannot agree on who or what God or Allah is. Even the New Testament Scriptures and the Hebrew Bible are not in complete agreement about God, differing primarily on whether God is a benevolent or a judgmental being. Differing opinions between religions tend to be even more stark. But most of us who take our cue from Jesus of Nazareth understand God to be the ultimate expression of *agápe*, the Creator and Sustainer of all that is, and the source of Life here and hereafter. None of this can be proved, but it all can be known intuitively and experientially by ordinary mystics.

The above examples are but the tip of the iceberg of the different ways of perceiving by the scientist and the mystic. But as ever deeper and deeper mysteries continue to unfold and proliferate in the scientific search for reality, it is becoming apparent, even to some scientists, that scientific method has its limits and will not by itself be able to answer all their questions. Mystics, on the other hand, may not know all the answers, but they do know much of reality otherwise inaccessible to those who would equate mysticism with fantasy.

Mysticism is concerned with both spiritual and physical realities inasmuch as the physical is seen to be a manifestation of the spiritual. Spirituality is all-encompassing. All creation is spiritual and, for the mystic, this is self-evident. The only reality is, therefore, mystical reality, some of it understood, most of it not. To see reality as anything other than spiritual is to accept an *illusion of reality* rather than reality itself. Non-mystics can usually get along quite well living with the illusion. On the surface illusions usually work pretty well, but when one is drawn more deeply into spiritual realities, and the illusionary quality of our perceptions become apparent, one is faced with the necessity of either becoming a mystic or learning to live with the contradictions that our new mystical consciousness dictates.

The world is becoming less religious and more spiritual. This is indicated by the waning interest in institutionalized religions which fail to meet deeply felt spiritual needs. At the same time, interest in spirituality is growing, presumably because spiritual perceptions are proving capable of addressing otherwise unanswerable spiritual and moral questions. In such a spiritual revolution, only those religious institutions which take seriously the challenge to address the mystical dimensions of reality are likely to survive. Change is the order of the day.

As ordinary mystics, we are the harbingers of the change that is already underway. We are the way-showers. Our own personal spiritual journeys have equipped us to meet the challenges of the ever unfolding mystical reality. Our work is to demonstrate by concept and action the way forward for those just joining the journey. Ordinary mystics are the expressions of *divinity*.

Saints, The Holy Ones of God

The Apostle Paul consistently refers to the followers of the Way as *hágiois* (άγίοι, "holy ones" or "saints" in Greek). Its meaning is simply "those separated or consecrated to God." This has little to do with morality which, at most, is a derivative sense based on the lives of some particularly righteous saints. In fact, Paul does not spare the saints in Corinth severe criticism of their apparently immoral behavior. Paul apparently understood that to be a saint has everything to do with God's designation, not ours. We do not create saints, God does. Thus, to be a saint also has *nothing* to do with being officially appointed saints of the Roman Catholic Church. We are all saints. God's criteria for sainthood are, quite simply, her designation of her created human beings to be the agents of reconciliation for the whole of creation to herself. As thinking, spiritually receptive human beings, our work as saints in the Kingdom of God is to combat the illusion of separation from God, thereby reconciling the whole of creation to God.

To be a saint is to live in union with God. Sainthood is not something that we humans confer on just the exceptionally good and loving members of our species. It was conferred on all of us when God created us in God's own image. Both God's Love for the creation and the conferral of sainthood are unconditional. It is not God, but we, God's creation, who in error seek to put conditions on what God may or may not do. We do not have veto power over God's decisions. Nor do we have the whole picture. There may come a day when, in the Apostle Paul's words, "we shall know even as we are known," but probably not in this life. At this point in our respective journeys most of us are still seeing "in a glass darkly" and are consequently blind to how utterly radical the *agápe* Love of God really is. We are also blind to the reality of the whole creation's total unity with God. Oneness with God is not just the reality for a privileged few.

One of our favorite scapegoats for our own inadequacies, the person we would most like to drive out into the desert carrying our own misadventures with him, is Adolf Hitler. We have identified him as the very epitome of evil, ignoring all the while the thousands of supposedly God-fearing people who were complicit in his attempted genocide of the Jews. Granted, Adolf Hitler was a psychopath, was mentally deranged, and was a threat to the lives of millions. But the difference between any one of us and Hitler is one of degree, not of kind. Did Hitler need to be stopped? Yes! Did his war machine need to be stopped? Yes! But so do the people of our own nation who we euphemistically refer to as "hawks" need to be stopped! We who are complicit in the violence surrounding us daily, we who are complacent and silent—we need to be stopped! Violence against each other is never acceptable and to resort to it, either actively or complicitly, simply points to our colossal failure to bring to bear the incredible power of *agápe* on the needs of a hurting and dangerously disoriented world. We collectively bear no less responsibility for the misdeeds of Hitler than does he. We all need a course correction. As long as we persist in believing that we are separated *from* God instead of one *with* God, the atrocities will continue. There have been and will continue to be other "Hitlers" and we will have no one to blame but ourselves. This is *our* sin, *our hamartia*—that we continue to reject our essential oneness with God, thereby denying that we are created to be instruments of sustaining, inclusive, non-judgmental *agápe* Love.

Jesus saw a vision of this world where there is no separation (duality) between God and humans." And, *Jesus also saw so well a vision of this world in which there is no separation (duality) between human beings."* The Kingdom of God is within us. This is what makes us saints!

It is fortunate that we have eternity on our side, for it may take an eternity for all of us to comprehend the reality of our union with God and to consequently live the *agápe* Love of our Creator. But it is happening. Every time a hungry person is fed and a naked person clothed, every time a prisoner is pardoned, every time a sick person, or tree, or animal is healed, God's reign is evidenced. Every time we reach out in *agápe* to another, God is present. Every time we choose life over death, we affirm our union with God. And for those of us who have open eyes to see this reality, which has always been, there is hope for a new dawn.

Eternal Life

One further human dimension of divinity is *eternal life*. We are not just an experiment of God. We are not just an hypothesis of what reality is. *God is not limited by a need for scientific verification of the viability of humankind as an enduring expression of divinity.* God and God's creation are more than just co-existent. They are the same thing. As human beings we participate with the rest of creation in God and therefore share in that most defining aspect of God—life, and that eternal. Those who question human eternal life, confuse humanity as persons somehow separate from God, existing in a separate reality from God. This kind of separatist thinking is at the root of our difficulty in accepting eternal life as the reality of our existence. We might as well doubt our existence at all as to doubt the eternal dimension of our God-ness.

All of the debate about what happens after death is a *red herring* inasmuch as it treats human reality as somehow different from God's reality. The question is not whether there is life after death, or whether or not heaven is just a projection of our imagination or wishful thinking. Unless the entirety of the theological enterprise is to be discarded and the reality of God herself denied, there is life eternally for the whole of the creation. We cannot participate in something which does not exist. If God does not exist, we do not exist and there is no life of any kind, eternal or otherwise. But I opt to believe, with René Descartes, that because I am a rational thinking entity, I exist. And because I exist (and that along with all other human beings), God exists.

In addition, there is a serious case to be made that time itself is a creative human fiction. Its existence as anything more than a convenient metaphor for our limited perception of reality is in the process of being debunked by the quantum physicists of our day. But it is not just the physicists, but the theologians who are questioning whether "time" and eternity can co-exist. For God time certainly does not exist, nor does it exist for the creation that is in God. A reality that is eternal, cannot co-exist with a temporal "reality." Either all of reality is eternal or none of it is. But as so-called "temporal reality" is proven to be an illusion, then the only reality left is eternal—and so are we, our limited perceptions not withstanding.

As eternal, God has an infinite amount of opportunity to accomplish her intention. There are no grounds for assuming that God will not finish what she has started. Humankind, as an apparently significant part of God's intended creation, will continue maturing until we all realize that we are each a part of the whole, which we call God. And as all of us are a part of the whole, we are also one with each other. Our attainment of unity will eliminate all sense of otherness of both God and people. Our transformation will be complete.

131

Chapter 6

RECONCILING EARTH AND HEAVEN

To reconcile man with man but not with God
is to reconcile no one at all.

—Thomas Merton

A love of reconciliation is not weakness or cowardice.
It demands courage, nobility, generosity, sometimes heroism,
and overcoming oneself rather than one's adversary.

—Pope Paul VI

The Created world is but a small parenthesis in eternity.

—Sir Thomas Browne

After all, it is no more surprising to me to be born twice
than it is to be born once.

—Voltaire

The soul is partly in time and partly in eternity. We might remember
the part that resides in eternity when we feel despair over the part
that is in life.

--Thomas Moore

The Ministry of Reconciliation

If the Apostle Paul is right, human beings have an incredibly larger role in God's plan for the universe than we may have realized—perhaps even a key role. He writes, "The creation waits with eager longing for the revealing of the children of God; for the creation was subjected to futility, not of its own will but by the will of the one who subjected it, [so] *that the creation itself will be set free from its bondage to decay and will obtain the freedom of the glory of the children of God.* We know that the whole creation has been groaning in labor pains until now..." (Romans 8:19-22, NRSV)

Paul continues, to the Corinthians: "So if anyone is in Christ, there is a new creation: everything old has passed away; see, everything has become new! All this is from God, who reconciled us to himself through Christ and *has given us the ministry of reconciliation; that is, in Christ God was reconciling the world [cosmos,* Greek, κόσμον] "to *himself"* (II Corinthians 5:17-19, NRSV).

Some four hundred years earlier, the Greek philosopher, Plato, had applied the term "cosmos" to the whole of the observable universe. Paul, as a well-educated first-century Roman citizen, would have undoubtedly shared the Platonic understanding of "cosmos" as the whole ordered system of the universe, both earth and the firmament of the heavens. God was not just reconciling the earth unto himself, but the whole universe. This passage is *not* a teaching about the work of converting "the heathen" to Christ. If anything, it is about God using humanity (all of us) to bring about the *unity* of the whole of creation. God in Christ got the unification process going, and human beings of all faiths and no faiths, working both locally and universally, including men and women, theologians and scientists, cosmetologists and cosmologists, have been working on it ever since.

Only in recent decades have we seen dramatic outreach to the stars and planets. Let us hope that our message to them is, "we come in peace," as emissaries appointed by God to bring unity through reconciliation. Even at this point in our extraterrestrial exploration, it is difficult to see where we are headed and how we will finally get there. Perhaps the answer will finally be more in the realm of spirituality than in science, though in the last few centuries science has certainly been leading the way. It is likely, however, that spirituality and science *together* will show the way to universal reconciliation and unification.

Reconciling Science and Religion

Ken Wilber has been one of the authors leading the way towards reconciliation of science and spirituality. He speaks of the "marriage" of science and religion as a "difficult marriage," citing the following reasons: (Wilber, 1999, pp. 15-17; quotes from Wilber in italics)

1. *Science denies any validity to religion.* This is a prescription for no marriage at all.

2. *Religion denies any validity to science.* This, likewise, is a conversation stopper. Both these views reflect close-minded fundamentalist thinking which is so threatened by differing views that neither can tolerate the possibility of truth on the other side. On the part of science, skepticism is warranted by past history, when religion made claims for scientific truth which have subsequently been proved by science to be utterly false (flat earth for one example; the earth as the center of the universe for another). On the part of religion, it has been demonstrably correct in claims initially ridiculed by science (the efficacy of prayer and meditation, the power of faith to transform and overcome, for example.) It is also true that, in spite of its devotion to scientific method, science has often been blind to its own errors. However...

3. *Science is but one of several valid modes of knowing, and thus can peacefully coexist with spiritual modes.* This was the generally accepted worldview until modern times, when science, but not the general population, concluded that it was *passé.*

4. *Science can offer "plausibility arguments" for the existence of Spirit.* It has become increasingly evident to science, especially with the advent of quantum physics, that there are some phenomena that are not amenable to analysis by

"scientific method." For these phenomena intuition is often the only way of knowing applicable.

5. *Science itself is not knowledge of the world but merely an interpretation of the world and therefore it has the same validity—no more, no less—as poetry and the arts.* Poets and artists have, I think, always known this, but for scientists it can be a bitter pill to swallow.

Wilbur goes on to demonstrate through explication of "The Four Quadrants" of the universe how there are differing ways of knowing that are mutually exclusive, but which together account for the whole range of human knowledge. He identifies these ways as 1) Interior-Individual (Intentional), 2) Exterior-Individual (Behavioral), 3) Interior-Collective (Cultural), and 4) Exterior-Collective (Social). The Interior quadrants are in the domain of religion or spirituality, facilitated by intuition. The exterior quadrants are in the domain of science facilitated by observation and measurement. All are valid ways of knowing and all are necessary for a potentially complete apprehension of reality. In practice, all of us use all four ways whether or not we acknowledge them, or employ all four intentionally. (Wilber 1999, pp. 63-66)

Jungian analysts David Keirsey and Marilyn Bates, in their use of Jungian typology, demonstrate not only the *different* ways of knowing but also that we each employ *all* the ways, differing in our preference for some ways over others. For example, a person designated as INFP (introverted, intuitive, feeling, judging) favors intuition (N) over sensing (S), while one designated ESTJ (extroverted, sensing, thinking, perceiving) uses sensing as the way of appropriating knowledge. This INFP person prefers to make decisions on the basis of feeling (F) rather than thinking (T). Likewise, a person who favors perceiving (P) over judging (J) is more tentative in arriving at conclusions than his or her decisive opposite. The point is that all these ways are valid ways of knowing. Ideally, the person who falls close to the middle of the intuitive-sensing and feeling-thinking and perceiving-judging scales has more strengths to draw on than one who is heavily biased one way or the other. Balance is the key to understanding and explaining the whole. (Keirsey/Bates 1978)

Ken Wilber posits that there are, *"at least* the three basic eyes of knowing: the eye of flesh (empiricism), the eye of mind (rationalism), and the eye of contemplation (mysticism), each of which is important and quite valid when dealing with its own level, but gravely confused if it attempts to see into other domains" (Wilber, 1998, p. 18). These ways of knowing are comparable to the Jungian personality types discussed above, which have been shown to have similar success rates in ascertaining the accuracy and plausibility of various conclusions whether arrived at empirically, rationally, or intuitively.

The only thing blocking the acceptance of the above rationale for the reconciliation of science and religion, is a lack of openness on the part of scientific empiricism to modes of knowledge other than the empirical, particularly the *mystical* mode which addresses areas of experience and knowledge inaccessible to scientific methods of validation. Scientists, in particular, are prone to dismiss spirituality and mysticism because they, themselves, are blinded by their own devotion to scientific method. I hasten to acknowledge that scientific method has served humankind very well and continues to do so *in the realm of the empirical.* But as experiential evidence, appropriated by an increasingly large portion of the population, continues to mount, the scientific enterprise will lose its credibility as the exclusive harbinger of truth.

It is inevitable that the age-old phenomenon of holonic[14] development, seen in virtually every aspect of scientific and human development, will catch up with us and be manifested in an evolving population, breaching the divide between empiricism and mysticism. Mystical knowing will become a valued way of knowing, not replacing but incorporating scientific truth in the same manner of all other holons. I can see no reason why this aspect of human development should be an exception to the general rule. It is at the point of the incorporation of empirical science into the mystical

---

14 A holon is something that is simultaneously a whole and a part. It is derived from the Greek term *holon,* meaning "whole" and was first used in Arthur Koestler's 1967 book, *The Ghost in the Machine.* As used above, "holon" refers to the process of human development in which we are the culmination of all that we have ever been. Nothing is ever lost.

dimension of reality that the centuries-old standoff between science and mysticism will be reconciled.

Reconciling Jesus and the Christ

In 451 C.E., the Roman Catholic Church held what has come to be known as the Council of Chalcedon. It was in this council of the church's bishops that the doctrine of the two natures of Jesus Christ was addressed, supposedly for the last time. The conclusion of the council was that Jesus was totally human and totally divine:

> Therefore, following the holy Fathers, we all with one accord teach men to acknowledge one and the same Son, our Lord Jesus Christ, at once complete in Godhead and complete in manhood, truly God and truly man, consisting also of a reasonable soul and body; of one substance [ὁμοούσιος] with the Father as regards his Godhead, and at the same time of one substance with us as regards his manhood; like us in all respects, apart from sin; as regards his Godhead, begotten of the Father before the ages, but yet as regards his manhood begotten for us men and for our salvation, of Mary the Virgin, the God-bearer [θεοτόκος]; One and the same Christ, Son, Lord, Only-begotten, recognized *in two natures, without confusion, without change, without division, without separation;* the distinction of natures being in no way annulled by the union, but rather the characteristics of each nature being preserved and coming together to form one person and subsistence, [ὑπόστασις] not as parted or separated into two persons, but one and the same Son and Only-begotten God the Word, Lord Jesus Christ; even as the prophets from earliest times spoke of him, and our Lord Jesus Christ himself taught us, and the creed of the Fathers has handed down to us." (Bettenson, 1963, p. 73, emphasis, Bettenson's)

This is not the time or place to thoroughly critique this relatively ancient creed, except to note that some of its claims are less than factual. On the whole it is a fair representation of the theology of most of the bishops in attendance at the Council of Chalcedon. Though they did not speak of paradox in the creed, their prior 70 plus years belaboring the issue clearly indicate that they were thinking of Christ's identity as a paradox that needed to be defended.

Did the Chalcedonian Creed finally end the debate? Not really. It only settled it in the sense of making it the official doctrine of the Roman Catholic Church. Since that time it has apparently been accepted widely and uncritically by Protestant denominations. Eastern Orthodox churches (including their autocephalous Orthodox brethren, the Russian Orthodox Church, et al.) split from the Roman Catholic Church at the Council of Chalcedon, having been the dissenters on the question of the dual nature of Jesus Christ. The division was formalized in 1054 C.E., when the Roman and the Eastern churches excommunicated each other, never having reconciled their theological differences.

I will presume to offer a slightly different *slant* on the identity of Christ that agrees with the basic conclusions of the Creed, but questions the insinuation that it was a paradox. I believe that the *"two natures, without confusion, without change, without division, without separation"* is not a paradox at all, but that they are *synonymous—that to be fully God and fully human are the same thing!* Thus, rather than resorting to an assumed paradox to reconcile the human Jesus with the Divine God, the reconciliation happens by virtue of its actualization of the essence of what it means to be fully human—its entelechy. This is what Jesus demonstrated both in his life on earth and in his teaching. Thus, in the true sense of the Greek term *hamartia*, usually mistranslated "sin," but meaning "separation," Jesus was indeed without sin. He was without separation from God.

This has enormous implications for the rest of us humans, whose major problem is that we have not yet discovered what it means to be *fully* human. Jesus knew what it meant, and tried to show and teach us, but we have been blinded by eons of falling so far short of the ideal of fully human adulthood that we have substituted a lie for the truth about our own relationship to our Creator. The lie has been passed on from generation to generation to generation. Jesus came to teach us the truth—about us!

Reconciling Evolution and Creationism

The Psalmist, purportedly David, reflecting on mysteries far beyond his ken, wrote, "When I look at your heavens, the work of your fingers, the moon and the stars that you have established, what are human beings that you are mindful of them, mortals that you care for them?" (Psalm 8:3-4, NRSV)

What, indeed! In the roughly three thousand years since David penned these words, the mystery has only deepened. The work of creation is even more astounding than David could have imagined. For starters the establishment of the universe was not an event in either time or space. Time and space did not exist. Something or someone who existed outside of time and space created existence out of whatever was before existence. It was effectively creation out of nothing (Latin, *ex nihilo*). In one quintillionth (that is, $1/1,000,000,000,000,000,000^{th}$) of a second, all the matter of the universe and all the organizational principles which were to govern the evolving, not only of David's moon and stars, but of ourselves as well, were brought into existence. Before that *nothing* existed. Existence itself was created. What was not created then, does not exist now. The "originating power," as Brian Swimme and Thomas Berry prefer to call the Creator (Swimme & Berry 1992, p. 17), was doing a new and awesome and spectacular thing fifteen billion years ago. In that infinitesimally short moment between nothing and everything, the photons which were to become the foundation of all that is were hurled into an abyss of nothingness. They were hurled with such power that the universe is still expanding exponentially, constrained only by the gravitational and mysterious attraction of each particle for every other particle. This same force of attraction, laid down at the very beginning of time, is what keeps planets and stars in their orbits, and draws human beings to one another. Thus the universe is both "out there" in the far horizons of outer space and "in here" within the minds and souls of living beings.

Is it any more of a wonder, then, that at the appointed time, in the complex coming-together of the original design of the Creator, that we are identified in every cell of our bodies with the initials of our primordial Source? Having thus created us out of the energy of that original fireball of creation, the Creator has given us the critical role of maintaining the whole of the created universe. I believe we are just now beginning to glimpse our reason for being. Our evolution, though in many ways similar to that of other living beings, has a providential dimension which translates into a divine responsibility for the care and nurturing of the whole created order. We are agents, not by dint of our own choice or ability, but agents nonetheless, of the Originating Power, the Creator, the Prime Mover, the Uncreated One, the Word, God. We are God's presence in time and space, doing the work of God within the framework established at the beginning of time. We are the connecting link between time and eternity, and between space and whatever other non-dimensional arrangements may or may not exist.

We know of no other intelligence within time and space sufficient for the role for which we have been formed. The Old Testament prophet Isaiah was prescient in his reporting of the Creator's intent: "Thus says the Lord who made you, who *formed you in the womb* and will help you"; "I made the earth and created humankind upon it, it was my hand that stretched out the heavens, and I commanded all their host." (Isaiah 44:2 & 45:12, NRSV) It is the work of paleontologists and anthropologists to discern *how* we have evolved as *Homo sapiens.* Their work is not yet finished. It is the work of prophets and seers, sages and mystics to discern *why* we have evolved as we have, into the only known creatures in the panoply of creation who know or care enough to ask the questions of role and purpose. Ours is a holy calling because we have been endowed with the gifts we need to be able to accomplish the task of reconciling the creation to its Source.

One of these endowments is the gift of prescience demonstrated by Isaiah and other prophets, who foresaw a day when all of creation would come to a unity in understanding and purpose—a day when the principles of attraction put in force at the very beginning of time would draw the whole of creation back to its Source. What these forerunners saw afar off, we can begin to see more clearly. We are also seeing more clearly what our failures of the past are putting at risk. The quest for unity in freedom has too often devolved into the freedom of license and individualism, and personal and corporate greed. As a species, we have not yet acquired the sense of responsibility foreordained by our Creator to forgo separatism and egocentrism in order to be wholly one with the Creator and the creation.

Another, very much related endowment, is the gift of *agápe,* God's inclusive, indiscriminate, unconditional and forgiving Love. This has been demonstrated a number of times in our *Homo sapiens* sojourn on earth, so we know what it is. It is not for lack of knowledge that we have failed to broadly employ the gift of *agápe.* But when we do, the transformation of the whole of creation will continue with the unabated pace that we now observe in the expansion of the universe.

Evolution is God Pulling Us from the Future

When we learn to Love, we will discover that far from creating us and leaving us to shift for ourselves, the Creator has been both with us and ahead of us, pulling us from a future that was created in that first astronomical blast. Herein is our hope. Despite all our missteps, we cannot derail the future first decreed by the Creator. To even entertain that presumption is audacious beyond comprehension. It is not in our power to destroy the dream of God, whatever we do.

That God keeps her promises is implicit in the covenants God makes with humanity. The Greek term which we translate "covenant"— *diatheke (διαθήκη)*—is a one-way contract; a legal term used in wills, and as such is thus incontestable. It is a covenant in which God says, "This is what I am going to do. Period." The person on the receiving end is given no choice. God will do what God will do, whether we agree with it or not. The covenant is binding, but God is the only active participant bound by it. In Hebrew Scriptures, God is said to have made such a covenant with Abraham, to make of his lineage a great nation, but Abraham was asleep when God informed him of the covenant. He had no say in the matter at all. (Genesis 15:1-5) In the words of theologian John F. Haught, "God forever promises, and God never fails to fulfill what has been promised. (O'Murchu 2008, p. 221) God draws us from up ahead, attracting us forward into the future. A promising God who calls us to be open to the future is the ultimate cause of evolutionary change. (cf. Haught 2003, p. 128) We are part of a universe, the end of which has forever been in its beginning. We have the ironclad promise of God that all that she has promised will come to pass. The outcome was determined from the beginning of time. We may complain and drag our feet, but we cannot change one *iota* of the promise of God. We cannot contest it. It makes life easier to cooperate with the program. God will finish what she started.

This is the message of Genesis—both the genesis of the universe and the first book of the Bible. "God saw everything that he had made, and, indeed, it was very good." (Genesis 1:31, NRSV) Our ending is in our beginning. As we began in eternity, so shall we end in eternity. God, herself, is drawing us thither. And it will be very good.

Reconciling Time and Eternity—The Eternal Now

In eternity there is no time, at least not as we conceive it to be. Time is a creature of our own imagining, a construction of our minds meant to bring order to an otherwise apparently chaotic universe. *There is no past and no future but only the present infinitesimal moment.* The past has no *present* reality. The future is just as unreal and is at most an illusory construct based on imagination and guesswork. But the present is eternally real, even when our perceptions of it may not be. We live in the eternal *now*.

The eternal now, because it encompasses all time, gives us access at *any* time to whatever is happening *any* time. Past, present and future are all *now*. When you look at the night sky, you are seeing it as it was in the past, not as it is now. In the movements of the stars the past is to our eyes the present and, could we physically see far enough, we could actually see our origin as if it were happening in the present. Astronomers have, indeed, through new and incredibly powerful space-based microwave instrumentation[15], been able to create a detailed picture of the early universe "when it was a mere 380,000 years old." (Kaku 2004, p. 6)

Similarly, seers, who live in the eternal now, can "prophesy" concerning happenings in the future which are in reality happening now. English biologist Rupert Sheldrake conceives of the eternal now as a morphogenetic field (somewhat like a gravitational field or an electromagnetic field, or even the eleven dimensional hyperspace, in the sense that they are invisible to any of our human sense perceptions), but like these other fields, the morphogenetic field has a huge impact on the lives of us earthbound humans, impacts of which we are generally totally unaware. Perhaps Sheldrake's morphogenetic field is but one of many unknown-to-us parallel universes, all simultaneous creations of "the originating power" some of us call God. Or, alternatively, these other universes may be manifestations of the eternal now impinging on time and space and redirecting our understandings of reality.

We know, for example, that gravitational fields not only exist but that they constrain the outward thrust of the universe, thereby making it a viable host for life forms such as ourselves. What we do *not* know is just exactly what gravity *is*. We can identify it only by its action, the force of attraction of celestial bodies for all other celestial bodies. We also know that it is what keeps us from falling off the earth. But we still do not know *what* it is.

Nor can science define a morphogenetic field. We only know of it through its actions, and thereby postulate its existence. "The term [morphic fields] is more general in its meaning than morphogenetic field, and includes other kinds of organizing fields in addition to those of morphogenesis... The organizing fields of animal and

---

15 The Wilkinson Microwave Anisotropy Probe (WMAP) is a satellite launched in 2001 that has created precise and detailed pictures of the very early universe when there was still microwave radiation left over from the original "big bang" of creation, what has been called the echo of creation. According to Michio Kaku, the findings of the WMAP satellite represent "a rite of passage for cosmology from speculation to precision science."

human behavior, of social and cultural systems, and of mental activity can all be regarded as morphic fields which contain an inherent memory." (Sheldrake 1989, p. 113) In the case of a morphic field of mental activity, a mind field, as it were, it could account for much of what we usually call intuition, knowledge that comes from we-know-not-where. This could also give new meaning to the quip, "the ancients have stolen my best ideas." Carl Jung's postulation of archetypes may be yet another example of parallel, invisible worlds. (See Anthony Storr's *The Essential Jung*, Parts 3 and 4; also see C. G. Jung: *Four Archetypes: Mother/Rebirth/Spirit/Trickster*).

Not only can we live in both dimensions—the illusion of time and the quantum reality of eternity—simultaneously, but we, in fact, already *do* live in both. Our awareness of this fact can only increase our utilization of both realms, bringing us one huge leap forward in our own evolutionary development from *karma* to transcendence.

Reconciling *Karma* and Transcendence

In Hinduism and Buddhism, *karma* is the universal law of cause and effect. It is an action seen as bringing upon oneself inevitable results, good or bad. We can see it in both physical and social phenomena, either in this life or in a reincarnation. According to its law we do not transcend *karma*. We reap what we sow. If we do good, then good comes back to us. If we do evil, we pay for it. That's the law. And it is supported both observationally and by social policy. The penal codes in most, if not all countries, try to insure that we pay for our misdeeds, in this life if possible. If we fail to exact retribution in this life and we do not believe in reincarnation, then the law of *karma* may not be carried out. In such an instance, we may feel that it needs the assistance of our law enforcement and criminal courts. But what happens when "justice" does not prevail? Can we beat *karma*? Can we legitimately conclude that it will catch up with us in the next life if not in this one?

Beginning with a quote attributed to Voltaire, "To understand all is to forgive all," Elizabeth Lesser observes that "The more we understand how our karma intersects with the karma of others, and how all karma exists in a web of meaningfulness, the easier it becomes to forgive ourselves and others. But forgiveness is an action, not an idea. We *understand* karma, we *practice* forgiveness." (Lesser 1999, p. 362) To forgive, both ourselves and others, is to break the chains of *karma*. It requires a choice to forgive, not just once but time and again, wherever and whenever it is needed. Such forgiveness is characteristic of *agápe* Love which is itself a gift of God. The secret then to cultivating a predisposition to forgive, is to first understand and accept God's unconditional *agápe* Love for one's self thus rendering ineffectual the prior claims of *karma,* thus freeing yourself to forgive others.

The New Testament concept of justice is to make right that which is wrong. If one person kills another, and we apply the Old Testament concept of judgment, we must kill the killer. But to kill the killer does not bring the person he killed back to life. So what is made right? Nothing! Two wrongs do not equal one right. Instead, Jesus taught the law of Love, including Love for enemies. Love does not murder another, *ever*, even with state approval. The *agápe* Love of God for her creation transcends *karma*. We are not to be the instruments of judgment here, and God is not its instrument hereafter. In short, in God's kingdom, *karma* doesn't happen. In God's kingdom, our errors are forgiven, corrected, and transcended—not revenged.

Our intentionality is the key to this transcendence. We only see what we expect to see. Rather than "seeing is believing," believing is seeing. In a quantum world, all possible worlds exist all the time. The material world around us has been created by thought. God spoke the universe into existence. If we do not like what we have created thus far, we can *re*create it by thought. The same is true of human relationships. Vision and intention are the keys. As a person "thinketh," so is he or she. If violence is our intent, we create it. If peace is our intent, we create it. Energy (thought) creates both good and evil, both community and separation, both love and hate. We change our reality by changing our thoughts. By energizing a vision of a new reality of beauty and spirit, we can thereby change both ourselves and our enemies.

We create our own future through our vision of it. Future, too, is a mental construct, as is time. It is fluid, elastic, capable of constriction and expansion depending on our thoughts—our vision. Time is simply a mechanism for accounting for sequence, hence *con*-sequence. The future will thus be the consequence of whatever we envision it to be. The crucial thing is to recognize that our inner reality determines our outer and quantum reality. The new creation happens first internally, enabling the movement from *material* illusion to spiritual reality. The *process* of enabling the new perception of reality is entirely internal.

In quantum reality, matter is not a substance. It is rather a whirling mass of electrons—energy. Thought, likewise, is a form of energy—the electrical firing of synapses in the human brain. Matter can thus be construed as a form of thought. Thought creates matter. What we intend creates what is. Bring our intentions under control and we can transcend anything. In point of fact, we are always transcending. For example, we are not the same person we were seven years ago. Every cell in our body will have been replaced by another many times over in an average life span. Even our personalities have changed. Transcendence has been our way of physical and mental life ever since our conception. It is only credible that, lacking evidence to the contrary, our transcendence continues after our death.

None of the above is magical thinking. It is simply the acknowledgment of who we are as divine beings and the reality of the *quantum* creation of which we are a part. The only *karma* to which we are subject is that in which we believe. If we change our beliefs, we *transcend* the illusion of *karma*.

Reconciling Reincarnation and Salvation

Reincarnation: "Rebirth of the soul in another body, as in Hindu religious belief..." (Webster). However, it is not just Hindus who believe in reincarnation. It is a belief common in New Age circles as well as in early Jewish and Christian writings. Though it may be too much to claim that the Bible contains "proof" of reincarnation, it is clearly not too much to say that the *belief* in reincarnation was shared widely in first century Judaism, and in the early Christian church. Such a belief was evident repeatedly in the teachings of both Jesus and the apostle Paul, not so much as a specific doctrinal teaching as it was an assumed underlying reality. Following are a sampling of a few of the New Testament passages suggesting a belief in reincarnation:

Matthew 11:13-14 (NRSV): In this passage, Jesus identifies John the Baptist as Elijah: "For all the prophets and the law prophesied until John [the Baptist] came; and if you are willing to accept it, *he is Elijah* who is to come." (Critical biblical scholars are in broad agreement that Jesus did not actually say this, but that it reflects a later theological tradition. Whether it was inserted by the author of the Gospel or yet another "editor," it remains indicative of a prevailing first century Jewish and Christian belief in reincarnation.) Following Jesus' visionary mountain-top conference with Moses and Elijah, Jesus' disciples, Peter and James, seek clarification: "And the disciples asked him, 'Why then do the scribes say that Elijah must come first?' But he answered them and said, 'Elijah indeed is coming and will restore all things. But I say to you that Elijah has already come, and they did not recognize him, but they did to him whatever they pleased. So also the Son of Man is about to suffer at their hands.' Then the disciples understood that he was speaking to them about John the Baptist." (Matthew 17:10-13, NRSV) (The origin of this text, too, is questioned by critical scholarship, but even if Jesus was not its origin, Christian storytellers were, indicating that the early Church fathers were conversant with, and accepted, reincarnation as a valid phenomenon.)

Indeed the scribes had spoken, purportedly quoting Yahweh: "Lo, I will send you the prophet Elijah, before the great and terrible day of the Lord comes." (Malachi 4:5, NRSV)

Jesus, stating clearly, (purportedly) declared that John the Baptist (forerunner of the long-awaited Messiah) was Elijah who had returned. Whoever the source of the text may be, the statement is an unequivocal assertion of a belief in reincarnation, a belief later *rejected* by the Roman church, which amounts to their rejection of either Jesus' teaching or of their own redaction of the Gospel of Matthew. This, in turn, calls into question the church's acceptance of the Malachi passage as a Messianic prophecy applied to Jesus, meaning that the prophecy is either wrong or that Jesus is not the prophesied Messiah.

In the Gospel of John there is the following account: "And as he walked along, he saw a man blind from birth. His disciples asked him, 'Rabbi, who sinned, this man or his parents, that he was born blind?' Jesus answered, 'Neither this man nor his parents sinned; he was born blind so that God's works might be revealed in him.'" (John 9:1-3, NRSV) Jesus went on to make this the occasion for teaching his disciples about the necessity of getting on with the works "of him who sent me..." But aside from this, their question reveals an assumption that the blind man might have sinned before his birth, thus causing his blindness. The question assumes a prenatal existence, suggesting either that he sinned 1) in the womb, or 2) in some kind of preexisting life in heaven with God, or 3) in an earlier life on earth. As sinning in the womb or sinning in heaven seem to me rather unlikely scenarios, we are left with a belief in a *karma*-dominated life on earth as the most reasonable basis for the disciples' question. (Given that the Gospel of John was not written until the second century C.E., very little of the material attributed to Jesus by its author is likely to have originated with Jesus. It is more likely the case that it reveals a second century re-writing of the Jesus story in terms of the prevailing second century theology. A belief in *karma* and reincarnation had apparently continued into the new century.)

The Apostle Paul writes: "...he chose us in Christ *before the foundation of the world*, to be holy and blameless before him in Love." (Ephesians 1:4, NRSV) Origen believed this passage to be proof of pre-existence. The Apostle Paul also wrote of Adam as: "...a type of the one who was to come [Jesus]." (Romans 5:14, NRSV).

And to the Corinthian church he wrote, "The first Adam became a living being; the last Adam [Jesus] became a life-giving spirit. But it is not the spiritual that is first, but the physical and then the spiritual." (1 Corinthians 15:45-46) Paul continues, "...flesh and blood cannot inherit the kingdom of God, nor does the perishable inherit the imperishable. Listen, I will tell you a mystery! We will not all die, but we will all be changed... When this perishable body puts on imperishability and this mortal body puts on immortality, then the saying which is written will be fulfilled: 'Death has been swallowed up in victory.'" (I Corinthians 15:50-54, NRSV) Call it immortality, or call it reincarnation—life goes on.

The early Judeo-Christian group known as the Ebionites taught that the Spirit had come as Adam and later reincarnated as Jesus. The Clementine Homilies, an early Christian document, also taught that there were many incarnations of Jesus. Another possible incarnation of Christ is the Old Testament figure known as Melchizedek, the High Priest and King of Salem, who: "...without father, without mother, without genealogy, having neither beginning of days nor end of life, but resembling the Son of God, he remains a priest forever." (Hebrews 7:3, NRSV)

The Biblical picture is this: In God's Spirit, we experience life both before and following this earthly sojourn, and that we do this repeatedly, perhaps many times. The Hindus call this phenomenon reincarnation, adding to it the doctrine of *karma*. But it is simply the God-ordained pattern of human existence, and has nothing to do with hell or punishment. I envision it as the mechanism of our personal evolving, along with the rest of creation. Since our soul is eternal, meaning "not subject to death," and since *soul is that-which-is-of-God-in-us*, it is reasonable to assume that our soul is that essence of our being which transitions at the point of death to wherever and whatever God is. I anticipate that it will be a time of envelopment in Light and Love and Life and Beauty; a time of soul-replenishment before receiving our new Sacred Contracts and our next marching orders.

In this scenario the church doctrine of sin and redemption is no longer relevant. Each journey back to God is simply the opportunity to refuel for the next leg of the journey. If Jesus knows God to be "Abba," colloquially translated "Daddy," then God cannot be the tyrannical, vengeful despot some religionists have made him out to be. If, as suggested by the biblical text, Jesus has made this trip many times, then I figure he ought to know what God is like. *If* Jesus saves us from hell then it is a hell of our own making right here and now in this earthly sojourn. Jesus did not come to save us, but to show us who we are—*divine beings beloved of God.* (See p. 110-112: "Original Blessing, Not Fall and Redemption" for a fuller discussion of this understanding.)

Historically, Hinduism predates Christianity by about 2,000 years. "In the Hindu view, spirit no more depends on the body it inhabits than the body depends on the clothes it wears or the house it lives in. When we outgrow a suit or find our house too cramped we exchange these for roomier ones that offer our bodies freer play. Souls do the same." (Huston Smith, cited by Joseph Head and S. L. Cranston, 1977, p. 14) The final transformation is actually a continuous process in that, "There is nothing in my body that was with me seven years ago. In the course of my lifetime, my mind and personality have undergone changes that are just as radical. Yet through all these revisions I have remained, on some level, the same person." (op. cit., p.14) Death is just the continuing process of change.

In the Apostle Paul's second letter to the church in Corinth, he describes this ongoing process as one similar to the metamorphosis of a caterpillar to a butterfly. "Now the Lord is the Spirit, and where the Spirit of the Lord is, there is freedom. And all of us, with unveiled faces, seeing the glory of the Lord as though reflected in a mirror, *are being transformed [metamorphosed] into the same image from one degree of glory [manifest presence] to another*, even as by the Spirit of the Lord." (II Corinthians 3:18, NRSV) Reincarnation is consistent with what we observe happening all around us every day. The cycle of death and rebirth is a prominent feature of the created order. There is no reason to believe that as embodied human spirits we are an exception to the spiritual law of transmigration.

Given the track record of the whole of God's incredible creative activity, it is impossible to conceive of God failing, even partially.

However dire we think the world's prospects are, however remiss we have been as stewards of her creation, the Creator of Gaia and its inhabitants is not without options. Gaia's problems are not intractable, though we may or may not be the ones designated to solve them. The generations behind us are already showing more promise and more will in their earth-saving capabilities. Consequently, this is a time for hope rather than despair. We may also be underestimating the capability of the earth itself for self-healing. Our role may be simply to listen and respond to the ever-present voice of God. She *is* still speaking and, in spite of our frequent failures, there is *no indication that She has ever failed in Her creative efforts!*

Reconciling Gaia and God

The term *Gaia*[16] has been adopted by biologists to refer to their thesis that the earth is a living system, behaving as a unified living organism. Is it our pretensions to superiority that blind us to the essential living viability of other forms of intelligent life, including that of our planet? When individual electrons can be shown to make choices, and when plants and microbes have demonstrated the ability to self-organize and transcend themselves for the common good, and when myriads of species have successfully evolved out of the primordial ooze of ages past, who are we to claim superiority? Different, yes. But as moral and responsible human beings, severely or altogether lacking in many of the strengths of our earthly companions, we do not have much of which to boast.

It is a self-evident truism that *Homo sapiens* has been given the intelligence and the responsibility to be the stewards, but not the dominators, of creation. We may even be the personal emissaries, appointed by our Original Source in these later stages of evolution, to bring the Creation to full fruition. That comparatively few of our species have accepted this responsibility is evidenced by the earth's deteriorating condition. Much of the work to make up for our lack

---

16 Gaia is the theory that the earth itself is a living entity that functions as a single, self-regulating organism.

of diligent stewardship will fall to the generations not yet born. Let us hope that they will do what we should have already done.

Saint Augustine, 4th and 5th century theologian and bishop, observed, "Thou hast made us for thyself, O Lord, and our hearts are restless until they find their rest in thee." It may not be just our human hearts that are restless, but the heart of creation as well. Diarmuid O'Murchu notes that "a 'will for meaning' surfaces in the oft noted perception that, in a strange and mysterious way, evolution generated the conditions in which life could emerge on earth. It also underpins concepts like autopoiesis (self- organization) and the Gaia theory..." (O'Murchu 2002, p. 21) The conditions required for life to develop on earth were so precisely calibrated that the burden of proof logically falls on those who dispute the evidence of a living and intelligent Originating Source of life—human and otherwise. To claim that the creation of life was happenstance belies the overwhelming evidence that it was (and continues to be) a precisely planned and executed will for meaning.

Jesuit priest, Pierre Teilhard de Chardin, writing in the 1950's, conceived the idea of a succession of evolutionary spheres leading to the Omega Point, which is the maximum level of complexity and consciousness towards which he believed the universe was evolving. In this conceptualization, Teilhard named the last of these human evolutionary spheres the "noosphere." This is a composite of two Greek words, νοῦς, *nous*, (meaning "mind") and σφαῖρα, *sphaira* (meaning sphere). *Nous*, for example was the word used by the Apostle Paul when he wrote to the Corinthians: "For who has known the mind [*nous*] of the Lord so as to instruct him?' But we have the mind [*nous*] of Christ [the Lord]." (I Corinthians 2:16, NRSV) For Teilhard the human mind at this stage of evolutionary development is a conscious intelligence comparable to that of the "Lord," actively and knowingly participating in the Lord's work of evolutionary creation. (See Chapter 3, above) We are the agents of God for both our own evolution and that of the *cosmos*. Our will for meaning and Gaia's will for meaning coincide in the noosphere.

Teilhard believed that he could see the advent of the noosphere on the horizon when he adopted the term in the 1950's. The movement from the age of technology into the information (mind) age is the expression of the noosphere, leading all of creation into the Omega Point, *that point at which the work of creation will arrive at total unity with the Creator.* An increasing number of people are consciously participating in evolutionary processes, drawn from the future of promise when "we shall know fully even as we have been fully known." (adapted from I Corinthians 13:12, NRSV)

Reconciling Gaia and God will not be easily accomplished. Past wrongs will have to be righted. Social inequities will have to be corrected. Corrupt systems need to be changed. Violence and the conditions that breed it will have to end. Wars must cease. Economic justice within nations and between nations must be addressed. Degrading environmental practices must end. A compassionate, informed, and humble mind of God will have to become the norm in our and creation's evolutionary development.

Entelechy: Reconciling Essence and Illusion

Homo sapiens, as the reconciling agent of the Creator, has been equipped with the mental capacity to accomplish the continuing work of creation. This is our salvation as a species. We do not have many of the advantages of other species. We cannot fly as do the birds, or even as our mammalian relatives, the bats. We cannot swim as the fish or our aquatic relatives, otters and whales. We have not the sight of eagles, nor the olfactory capabilities of our canine friends.

What we do have is brain power, including the technological savvy to devise ways of competing with birds and bats with flight technology. And though we will never swim like fish, otters or whales, we have developed the technology to far outpace these creatures both on top of water and underwater. With magnification we can see what eagles cannot. (Unfortunately, we do not yet have readily available technology to compete with canines in sniffing out our quarry.) But we do have the intelligence to reflect upon ourselves and to evaluate our actions and thoughts, and thus to *know* ourselves and our evolutionary and moral options. This intelligence makes *all* the difference, enabling us to fulfill our responsibilities to our furry and feathered and scaled neighbors.

But for all our intelligence, we are also masters of self-deception. Our limited sensory capacities have misled us so completely that we have substituted our limited discernment for reality. One of our illusions is that we are made of matter, when the reality is that we are made of Light, photons—energy. Another is that we are independent, autonomous beings separated from others and the rest of creation, when the reality is that we are all connected to everybody and everything else. We think of ourselves as self-made, when the truth is we are God-made. We argue whether life begins with conception or birth, when the reality is that we have always been and will always be. We have the illusion that we know who we are, when the reality is that most of us have not the faintest idea who we are either individually or collectively.

The essence of our being, our entelechy (derived from the Greek term *entelecheia,* meaning actuality and completion) is that we are eternal divine beings who have always been and always will be. In the Apostle Paul's terminology, we are the "demonstrated presence of the Lord." In this present physical manifestation we are charged with the responsibility of discerning who we are and then acting out of that knowledge for the benefit of all creation. It is also becoming increasingly clear that this "all creation" responsibility includes, not just each other, and not just the earth, but the whole universe. What are now only tentative investigative probes of other planets will become the opportunity for mind-stretching interplanetary interactions for the eventual healing of the cosmos. This will be the "job description" for both the scientists and the spiritual visionaries of the future, as together we increasingly own our true identities as the children of God.

We already have the languages of science and spirituality to claim our future. What we need now is the courage to speak the continuing evolution of ourselves and the universe into existence, into essence, and into the completed and foreordained entelechy of our kind.

Chapter 7

THE SOUL IS THAT OF GOD WITHIN US

Men go forth to wonder at the heights of mountains,
the huge waves of the sea,
the broad flow of the rivers, the vast compass of the ocean,
the courses of the stars;
and they pass by themselves without wondering.

—St. Augustine, *Confessions,* Book X, Chapter 8

Om Namah Shivaya
(I honor the divinity that resides within me.)

—Sanskrit mantra

I do believe every soul has a tendency towards God. .

--Dorothy Day

A Little Less than God?

"When I look at your heavens, the work of your fingers, the moon and the stars which you have established, what are human beings that you are mindful of them, mortals that you care for them? Yet you have made them a little *less*[17] than God[18] and crowned them with glory and honor. You have given them dominion over the work of your hands; you have put all things under their feet, all sheep and oxen, and also the beasts of the field, the birds of the air, and the fish of the sea, whatever passes along the paths of the sea." (Psalm 8:3-8, NRSV)

There is a scientific principle which has been increasingly observed, particularly in modern physics, that *"the whole is in each of its parts."* This understanding has been around for a long time and has been seen in such phenomena as the entirety of an oak tree residing in an acorn and the adult human being in the human embryo. Everything needed by the mature tree and the mature human is already encoded into the DNA of the seed at birth. The material reality is already present. This principle has been observed again in the application of modern holograph technology. To project the whole image of an object, a laser need only be focused on a part of the object—any part—and because each and every part contains the whole, it is the whole object which is projected.

The same principle applies to spirituality. We have been created a little less than God, according to the psalmist, but that "less" reveals the whole. It is not merely poetic license to say that to see God we have only to open our eyes and look around. She is everywhere, and nowhere more apparent than in ourselves. A little less—yes, in terms of our comprehension—but the whole of God is present in every part of Her creation. We have called "that-which-is-of-God-in-us" our soul.

---

17 The original Hebrew text uses the term chacer (הסל pronounced khaw-sare). It may be translated either "lower" (as in the NRSV) or "less" (as in the RSV). It is a primary root meaning "to lack." My substitution of "less" for "lower" in this NRSV translation better reflects the primary root meaning.

18 Hebrew, *Elohim,* correctly translated here and elsewhere, "God", but, in the King James Version, inexplicably translated "angels."

This may also be what the author of the Gospel of John was alluding to when he put this prayer in the mouth of Jesus: "...As you, Father, are in me and I am in you, may they also be in us, so that they may believe that you have sent me. The glory that you have given me, I have given them, so that they may be one as we are one, I in them and you in me, that they may become completely one...." (John 17:21-23, NRSV) The author was wrestling, trying to put into words, the truth he had experienced through his association with the community of believers, the truth that Jesus' union with God was the same as our own union with God, a belief that may well have been enunciated in so many words by Jesus, but in this case reflective of the community's subsequent firsthand spiritual experience.

The Struggle to Define Soul

It was my original intent to trace the progression of the concept, or awareness, of soul from prehistory to the current day. I quickly realized, however, that, until the last few decades, there has been a steady retrogression rather than a progression in our definition of "soul," particularly since the time of Augustine (354–430 CE).

The Theologies of the Soul

Yoga (origin about 2,000 BCE)

Perhaps as early as 2000 BCE, Yoga appeared on the scene in the Indus River Valley—a river which flows north, then southwest through China, Pakistan, and India. But some scholars believe Yoga absorbed elements of Stone Age shamanism, which dates back at least to 25,000 B.C., and probably earlier. Shamanism is the sacred art of changing one's awareness to enter extraordinary realms of being and reality. The word *shaman* refers to a seasoned traveler in the spirit realm. (Knott 1998, cited on the web site, RandomHistory.com.) While yoga probably did not grow directly from shamanism, it absorbed some of its elements, such as transcendence, asceticism, and illumination (Feuerstein 1997, cited on RandomHistory.com). Whenever in the time frame of 25,000 BCE to 3,000 BCE the concept of divinity, of a Creator God, appeared, we can safely conclude that Yoga, which developed within the context of Hinduism, was the oldest spiritual discipline on earth to discern the presence of divinity within humanity.

Yoga, a Sanskrit word, can be translated as "union." It comes from the root word *"yuj,"* which means "to yoke." The intent of Yoga is to experience union with that of God within us, however we may conceive of the deity—Aten, Allah, Brahma, Elohim, Creator, Original Source, Primal Cause, Ra, Yahweh, and others. Brahma would have been the earliest.

"Yogis... say that human discontentment is a simple case of mistaken identity. We're miserable because we think we are mere individuals, alone with our fears and flaws and resentments and mortality. We wrongly believe that our limited little egos constitute our whole entire nature. We have failed to recognize our deeper divine character. We don't realize that, somewhere within us all, there does exist a supreme Self who is eternally at peace. That supreme Self is our true identity, universal and divine." (Gilbert 2006, p. 122)

In ancient Egyptian religion, the earliest evidences we have of an awareness of at least some aspects of soul, as defined here, are the burials of the Egyptian pharaohs. Archeological investigations of ancient Egypt reveal that as early as the forth millennium BCE (or earlier) there was worship of the Creator God, Ra. By the time of the pharaohs and their burial in the Valley of the Kings in the 16th to 11th centuries BCE, a belief in life after death (at least for nobility) was evidenced by the preparations in their tombs for an extended (eternal?) life. Buried with the pharaohs were foods, eating utensils, chariots, furniture, and many of the other comforts of their previous life, in order to insure their continued happiness in their next life. For the ancient Egyptians, life went on—presumably forever—just as their sun God, Ra, arose every morning without fail—and had done so for as long as humanity's collective memory.

Judaism (origin c. 2,000 BCE)

"Throughout the history of Jewish thought and its antecedent Israelite religion, there has been a theological tension between transcendent and immanent images of God as the source of ultimate reality, with ongoing attempts to determine how to bridge the gap between God and humanity." (Marc A. Krell[19] on Patheos.com)

The belief that the soul continues its existence after the dissolution of the body is a matter of philosophical or theological speculation rather than of simple faith, according to JewishEncyclopedia.com, and is accordingly nowhere expressly taught in the Jewish Scripture. As long as the soul was conceived to be merely a breath (*nefesh*; *neshamah*), and inseparably connected, if not identified, with the life-blood (Leviticus 17:11), no real substance could be ascribed to it. As soon as the spirit or breath of God (*nishmat* or *ruaḥ ḥayyim*), which was believed to keep body and soul together (Genesis 2:7, & 6:17; Job 27:2-4) is taken away (Psalm 146:4) or returns to God (Ecclesiastes 12:7-8; Job 34:14-15), the soul goes down to Sheol or Hades, there to lead a shadowy existence without life and consciousness (Psalm 6:5; Isaiah 38:18; Ecclesiastes 9:5, 10). The preponderance of Jewish scriptural testimony is that there is no eternal soul, and no soul at all in the sense of an inner reality and manifestation of God. Thus when Christianity centuries later teaches that Jesus is resurrected from death, that is anathema to the Jews for whom death is the final exit for both body and soul.

Buddhism (origin about 563 BCE)

According to Buddhism, ultimate reality is *samsara,* endless existence, but it is also impermanent, ever in flux, ever changing. It is empty, yet full. That is, form is always a temporary state of being. Some forms last for millennia, like mountains and oceans, and some are as brief as a lightning bolt. Elements come together to create a particular form, but eventually those elements will break apart again

---

19 Marc Krell, a contributor to Patheos Library, has a Ph.D. in Cultural and Historical Studies of Religions.

and the object will cease to exist. This is true of every created thing in the universe.

"When Buddhism first began, there were no gods who were recognized as existing outside the realm of rebirth, or to whom one could appeal as saviors. Buddha taught that the gods are not exempt from death and rebirth, and while their lives may last for eons, they do eventually die, and are almost inevitably reborn in a lower realm because the life of a god is too great a distraction from the work that is necessary to achieve enlightenment. The Buddha taught that he was an ordinary man, and he said that those seeking salvation should look within themselves. According to the early texts, his final words were, 'All the constituents of being are transitory; work out your salvation with diligence.' Paradoxically, the Buddha himself became the first 'god' of Buddhism. Building on a notion from the early texts that the Buddha had an 'emanation body' that could perform miraculous deeds, he is portrayed in some Mahayana Sutras as a god only pretending to be a man in order to inspire humanity." (Julia M. Hardy on www.Patheos.com)

Zen Buddhism (origin 650 CE)

Satori is a Japanese Buddhist term for awakening, comprehension or understanding. In the Zen Buddhist tradition, *satori* refers to the experience of *kenshō*, "seeing into one's true nature." Zen Buddhists believe, for example, "...that an oak tree is brought into creation by two forces at the same time. Obviously, there is the acorn from which it all begins, the seed which holds all the promise and potential, which grows into the tree. Everybody can see that. But only a few can recognize that there is another force operating here as well—the future tree itself, which wants so badly to exist that it pulls the acorn into being, drawing the seedling forth with longing out of the void, guiding the evolution from nothingness to maturity. In this respect, say the Zenists, it is the oak tree that creates the very acorn from which it was born." (Gilbert 2002, p. 329) What is this force pulling us from the future? My observations: 1) It must be an energy that is not itself bound by the constraints of time; 2) it must have vast energy; 3) it must have an innate wisdom coupled with an indomitable will to accomplish, on virtually endless fronts, the sustained effort essential to guiding countless evolutionary journeys to maturity; and 4) it must be a compassionate force that takes into account the myriad weaknesses of its evolutionary subjects. Or in briefer terms, this force pulling us to maturity must be eternal, omnipotent, omniscient, and unfailingly compassionate. Or still more briefly—God!

Christianity (origin about 30 CE)

The Psalmist said that, "He [God] restores my soul." (Psalm 23:3, NRSV) which is to say, God restores *that-which-is-of-God in me*. Centuries later, Jesus, quoting the Old Testament, indicated that the first commandment is "Hear, O Israel: The Lord our God, the Lord is one: you shall love the Lord your God with all your heart, and with all your *soul* and with all your mind, and with all your strength." (Mark 12:29-30, NRSV). "Soul," it would appear, is different from, but on a par with heart and mind. Further, it is *soul* in us which enables us to "love one another deeply from the heart." (I Peter 1:22, NRSV) It is *agapaic* Love of which the Apostle Peter speaks here.

It is, indeed, the clear teaching of the Apostle Paul that we are holy people, people set apart *to* God, rather than *from* God. "Paul, called to be an apostle of Christ Jesus by the will of God,... to the church of God that is in Corinth, to those sanctified in Christ Jesus, *called to be saints [holy people],* together with all those everywhere who call on the name of our Lord Jesus Christ, both their Lord and ours" (I Corinthians 1:1-2 (NRSV). And the author of the Letter to the Ephesians wrote, "And I pray that you, being rooted and established in Love, may have power, together with all the Lord's people, to grasp how wide and long and high and deep is the Love of Christ, and to know this Love that surpasses knowledge—that *you may be filled to the measure of all the fullness of God.* " (Ephesians 3:17-19, Today's New International Version) This fullness of God is the same as that fullness of God in Jesus of which the Apostle Paul wrote to the Colossians, "For God was pleased to have *all his fullness* dwell in him [Jesus]." (Colossians 1:19, Today's New International Version)

Greek and Roman Philosophers and Theologians:
Plato (born 348/347 BCE), Plotinus (204–270 CE),
Augustine (354-430 CE), & Thomas Aquinas (1225-1274 CE)

Plato was a philosopher in classical Greece. He was a student of Socrates, prolific author, and founder of the Academy in Athens, the first institution of higher learning in the Western world. (A. N. Whitehead, *Process and Reality,* p. 39). Plato's influence on philosophy was widespread during the later Roman Empire, the time in which Augustine lived. Plato taught that the physical world is changeable, perishable, and imperfect; in contrast with a world of ideas or Forms, which is constant, perfect, and everlasting. Because the physical world is marked by change and corruption, he taught that it is impossible to fully know it.

Plotinus (c. 204-270 CE), a Greek philosopher and follower of Plato, identifies human beings with their higher soul, reason. Plotinus drew on Plato's distinction between the world of physical, tangible things and a world of intangible ideas or Forms. The soul, being essentially a part of the intangible realm, is distinct from the body and survives it. It has a counterpart in Intellect, which Plotinus sometimes describes as the real human being and real self. As a result of communion with the body, and through it with the sensible world, we may also identify ourselves with the body and the sensible. Thus, human beings stand on the border between two worlds, the sensible and the intelligible, and may incline towards and identify themselves with either one. True knowledge can be achieved only by thinking about the intangible, eternal and perfect forms, of which the tangible world is only a copy, just as art is only an imitation of something real.

Augustine of Hippo (354–430 CE), a Father of the Church, was certainly not a follower of Plotinus, though he was clearly quite familiar with his writings. Plotinus' philosophy, rather, served as a foil against which Augustine constructed his own theological understandings. For starters, Augustine did not buy into the idea of a distinction between a physical realm of tangible things as distinct from an intangible realm of the soul. His idea of God was of a

Divine *being,* separate from humankind, bringing enlightenment to our minds from the outside rather than from within, either by supplying us with information or by leading us to a realization of truth from other sources. This understanding of the "being-ness" of God became the cornerstone of Western theology, departing not only from the spiritual teachings of the East, but also from some of the biblical teachings of the Christian canon. Throughout his long literary career, Augustine stressed the role of divine illumination in human thought. Truth is not in us, but above us, and is dispensed by God (who apparently is also above us) throughout our lives as we have need of it. For Augustine, it was inconceivable that morally destitute human beings could be vessels for truth. Consider this famous passage from the *Confessions*: "If we both see that what you say is true, and we both see that what I say is true, then where do we see that? Not I in you, nor you in me, but both of us in that unalterable truth that is above our minds." (XII.xxv.35)

Augustine's position would remain ascendant among Christian philosophers for most of the Middle Ages, and has continued to have a large following, particularly among the fundamentalist and evangelical branches of the Christian Church.

Thomas Aquinas

Thomas Aquinas (1225-1274 CE), a Latin theologian and member of the Dominican order, is credited with putting an end to Augustine's theory of divine illumination. Aquinas does reject certain conceptions of divine illumination. He denies that human beings in this life have the divine ideas as an *object* of cognition. He also denies that divine illumination is sufficient on its own, without the senses. Neither of these claims was controversial. What Aquinas further *denies*, and what was controversial, was the claim that there is a special ongoing divine influence, constantly required for the intellect's operation. Aquinas instead argues that human beings possess a sufficient capacity for thought on their own, without the need for any "new illumination added onto their natural illumination". (*Summa Theologica* 1a2ae 109.1c) He quotes Psalm 4: "Many say, 'Who shows us good things?' To this the Psalmist replies, 'The light of your face, Lord, is imprinted upon us.' This is as if to say, through that seal of the divine light on us, all things are shown to us." (*Summa Theologica* 1a 84.5c) Aquinas sees God as the First Cause. In the beginning, God imparted all knowledge to his human agents. We are thus born with the capacity to recognize the truth whenever we are confronted with it. Insight into truth was something we were given. Is not this agency, capacity, and insight into truth, Soul? Or *that-which-is-of-God-in-us*?

The Science of the Soul

An Egyptian medical textbook, the Edwin Smith papyrus, (c. 1600 BCE), may be the first document to apply what we now call the scientific method. It discusses examination, diagnosis, treatment, and prognosis as disciplines essential in the treatment of disease, thus enunciating a standard applied subsequently to scientific investigation in general.

By about 500 BCE, in Mesopotamia, astronomy had evolved into what could be called a scientific methodology, as according to the historian Asger Aaboe[20] it was, "the first and highly successful attempt at giving a refined mathematical description of astronomical phenomena. All subsequent varieties of scientific astronomy, in the Hellenistic world, in India, in Islam, and in the West—if not indeed all subsequent endeavors in the exact sciences—depend upon Babylonian astronomy in decisive and fundamental ways."

The ancient Greeks introduced theoretical science, beginning with the Archaic Period (650 to 480 BCE). Greek philosopher Thales of Miletus was the *first to refuse to accept supernatural, religious or mythological explanations for natural phenomena*, proclaiming that every event had a natural cause.

Aristotle (384-322 BCE), building on the work of the pre-Socratic school, further developed what may be called the parameters of

---

[20] Asger Aaboe, "Mesopotamian Mathematics, Astronomy, and Astrology" in *The Cambridge Ancient History* (2nd ed.), Vol. III, pt. 2, ch. 28b.

scientific methodology. For Aristotle, universal truths can be known from particular things through induction, thereby reconciling abstract thought with observation. He did not accept that knowledge acquired by induction could rightly be counted as scientific knowledge. Nevertheless, induction was a necessary reasoning process leading up to the primary premise of scientific enquiry by providing grounds required for repeatable scientific demonstrations.

The Quantum Soul

The advent of quantum physics in the last half of the twentieth century has confronted the scientific community with many conundrums. Scientists of virtually all the various disciplines have been forced to acknowledge that much of what they accepted as settled views of reality is wrong. Physics is the branch of science that has experienced the greatest impact, inasmuch as Newtonian physics, the standard for determining the laws which explain how the world operates, has been conclusively demonstrated *not* to work on the sub-atomic level. Newtonian physics was thought to have broad application across the entire spectrum of reality, large and small, a conclusion that was justified by careful observation and experimentation. However, that conclusion was made before the development of instruments, such as electron microscopes and billion dollar super-colliders, which enabled observations of the sub-atomic, otherwise invisible, interactions between and within atoms. Their findings at this level, for example, demonstrate such unimaginable phenomena as time moving backwards and the elimination of "matter" altogether, replacing it with infinitesimally small packets of light energy (or quanta of photons). Investigators have had to come up with new terminology to describe what had never been known to exist, occasionally even resorting to theological language (such as "God particles") to describe what they were observing.

Quantum theory has also impacted the fields of chemistry, biology, and cosmology, redefining much of macro reality as well as micro reality. Chaos theory, parallel universes, string theory, quantum electrodynamics, four-dimensional space-time, and quantum gravity—all of these have the potential for upsetting the cosmological apple cart. Since the microscopic level is foundational for all levels of reality, quantum physics has conclusively shown that much of what we have thought to be real is actually an illusion. Our perceptions of reality have been seriously skewed by our limited sensory capabilities. In every respect our senses have proved to be inadequate for discerning the real on *every* level—not just the sub-atomic level. Now that our senses have been substantially extended by instrumentation, we are discovering a reality quite different from what any of us—scientists and non-scientists alike—believed to be true.

One casualty of the new physics is confidence in the adequacy of the scientific method to describe all truth. One benefactor of the new physics is a new appreciation of intuitive and mystical truth. After all, if science has been so wrong for so long about so much, what else may it have missed? It has been forced to concede that such phenomena as soul and God and spirit may also be true, though not accessible to scientific confirmation. To be sure, not all scientists have gotten on board with quantum theory. They either do not understand it or find it too radical. There are still colleges, East and West, which teach Newtonian physics and refuse to acknowledge the existence of quantum physics. Their days are numbered. In the meantime there is a growing rapprochement between science and religion, quantum theory and spirituality. Scientists and mystics are discovering a new respect for one another. Collaboration instead of competition is the new evolutionary paradigm.

The Collective Consciousness

One further discipline deserves special attention. Psychology is one of the newer scientific disciplines to appear on the scene. As a branch of science it has had more difficulty than other scientific endeavors, inasmuch as its object of study is largely subjective. People are not objects, and they are consequently very hard to pin down. Being multidimensional and, at the same time, evolving, people have resisted easy categorization. Also, from the beginning psychology has had an identity problem. The word "psychology" literally means "soul study," but soul has been like an elephant in the room. Psychology either had to redefine what soul means, since as a spiritual entity soul was not amenable to the scientific method, or, failing redefinition, resign itself to being a bogus science. It tried mightily to redefine soul. One of the early psychology pioneers, Austrian neurologist Sigmund Freud (1856-1939) simply rejected the idea of soul, denying its existence. On the other hand, Freud's contemporary, Swiss psychotherapist Carl Jung (1875-1961) chose to redefine "soul" to mean the collective unconscious, which he described as follows: "...in addition to our immediate consciousness, which is of a thoroughly personal nature and which we believe to be the only empirical psyche [soul] (even if we tack on the personal unconscious as an appendix), there exists a second psychic system of a collective, universal, and impersonal nature which is identical in all individuals. This collective unconscious does not develop individually but is inherited. It consists of pre-existent forms, the archetypes, which can only become conscious secondarily and which give definite form to certain psychic contents." (Jung, 1996, p. 43)

But there was (and is) a problem. "Jung consistently failed to carefully differentiate the archetypes into their prepersonal, personal, and transpersonal components, and since all three of those are collectively inherited, then there is a constant confusing of *collective* (and archetypal) with *transpersonal* and spiritual and mystical." (Wilber 2000, p.196) Wilber identifies four archetypes (pre-existent forms or original patterns) as "Light of which all lesser lights are pale shadows," and "Bliss of which all lesser joys are anemic reflections," and "Consciousness of which all lesser cognitions are mere reflections," and "a primordial Sound of which all lesser sounds are thin echoes. Those are the real archetypes." (ibid., p.197)

Light, Bliss, Consciousness, Sound—these four appear to me to be a fairly succinct descriptions of some of the characteristics of *Soul— That-which-is-of-God-in-us!*
The Only Definition that Works

Given the options of defining soul as "spirit" or "consciousness" or "brain" or "mind"—or "*God*," I submit that since:

1. Soul is the only option favored by the mystics, both East and West; and since
2. Soul is the only option which takes into account the Soul's eternal quality; and since
3. Soul is consistent with the finding of quantum physics that we are beings of Light; and since
4. Soul is the only option consistent with our role as agents of reconciliation; and since
5. Soul is the only option consistent with our role as conveyors of *agapaic* Love; and since
6. Soul is the only option that acknowledges that *Homo sapiens* was made in God's image; and since
7. Soul is consistent with our role as co-creators with God of Her continuing creation; and since
8. Soul is the only option consistent with our human role as caretakers of God's creation; and since
9. Soul is the only option requiring the intelligence and self-reflection of the human species; and since
10. Soul is the capacity to recognize the truth whenever we are confronted with it; and since
11. Soul is consistent with God's designation of *Homo sapiens* as *hágioi*, Holy Ones; and since
12. Soul is the only option big enough to cover all the above bases collectively;

Then soul is *that-which-is-of-God-in-us*. *We are divine Beings with Divine abilities and responsibilities.*

"...it is a joy to God to have poured out the divine nature and being completely into us who are divine images." (*Meister Eckhart*)

The Twenty-first Century Awakening

Another word for change is evolution. There are those who believe that the long awaited next evolutionary leap for humankind is in fact happening right now. For all the reasons enumerated at the end of Chapter 1, I share this belief. I share my reasons here in summary fashion:

1. A growing restlessness, particularly among Western Christians, Jews, and Muslims, and others who are no longer willing to settle for faiths that have been tried and found wanting;

2. A genuine and wide-spread alarm that the world is not the friendly environment we once thought it to be;

3. The growing realization that if the planet does not kill us all first, then our technology may;

4. A refreshing and courageous honesty in the writings of many contemporary authors, including many Christian theologians, who have begun to have new insights on who we are and what we are about;

5. An abundance of age-old prophecies that appear to be converging on the present days—prophecies heralding great changes bringing either doom or a fresh start;

6. The increasing success that peace and justice activism has experienced in curbing the violence which has so characterized the last two thousand years;

7. People—particularly young people—who are smarter today than were previous generations. IQs are rising and educational programs are becoming more effective and available;

8. A budding rapprochement between science and religion;

9. Evidence that we are in the midst of a global mind change;

10. A growing recognition that we are not self-sufficient entities who have no responsibility for others.

One may add to the above evidence of an awakening humanity the observation that it has happened before, that evolution does, in fact, occur not so much as a steady progression, but rather in leaps forward, as it were, from one plateau to another. It can also be shown that the "leaps" are occurring more often and the plateaus are shorter, as in *revolution.* Beginning in antiquity, there was the agricultural revolution (from 12,000 BCE to 607 CE); in the lifetimes of a few people living today, there have been the final stages of the industrial revolution (mid sixteenth century to the early twentieth century).

The communications revolution can be said to have begun in the United States in 1775, with the establishment of the U.S. Postal Service, and the revolution continued with the telegraph (Samuel Morse, 1835) and the telephone (Alexander Bell, 1876); but it wasn't until 1971 that Raymond Tomlinson invented email, which soon made virtually instantaneous communications available globally to virtually every human being. The global technology revolution began about 1947 with the development of the ENIAC computer and is continuing today; the information era began in the 1970s and is ongoing; the digital revolution, in which we saw the conversion from analog to digital data processing, began in the 1980s and is ongoing. Today even a person living in the remotest of regions, who does not own a computer or smart phone, is still likely to have one available in the village. Global usage is still growing.

Further, the communications revolution has enabled social revolutions throughout the world, as have been witnessed in North Africa and the Middle East and East Asia. In past centuries a few mystics knew we were all spiritually connected. Now we are connected globally and universally, in ways equally mysterious to some of us, digitally and wirelessly. *Most of these revolutions are still going on* as we *Homo sapiens* wrestles with trying to maintain our equilibrium in an era of rapidly increasing change. The future has already arrived—yesterday!

Along with the various technological revolutions, however, there is a much slower and more subtle, but no less significant, revolution going on. A spiritual revolution is well underway and has been for perhaps several decades. Intimations of it were apparent in the mid 1960s, as is documented by Robert G. Middleton, American Baptist and United Church of Christ (UCC) pastor, in his 1969 book, *Privilege and Burden.* It is still seen today, in the decline of institutional religion and the simultaneous growth of more personal and, usually, more esoteric spiritual practices. Those persons who are caught up in this ongoing spiritual revolution typically experience a hunger for personal *spiritual expression* that is not being addressed by most institutional forms of religion of which they have been a part. Many are also looking for a depth of *spiritual identity* unavailable through many of the historical formulations of churches, synagogues, mosques or temples. The institutions that will survive the current spiritual revolution will be those which are able to change with the times by implementing a shift from orthodoxy to orthopraxy, from doctrine to mission, from teaching fear to teaching hope, and from eschewing change to embracing it.

Chapter 8

THE OMEGA POINT

If anyone in seeing God conceives something in his mind,
this is not God, *but one of God's effects. "*

—St. Augustine

To love another person is to see the face of God.
—Jean Valjean in the stage adaptation of Victor Hugo's *Les Misérables*

The Universe is but one vast symbol of God.

—Thomas Carlyle

In the beginning God created the heavens and the earth.

—Genesis 1:1

The divine essence itself is love and wisdom.

—Emanuel Swedenborg

I cannot imagine how the clockwork of the universe
can exist without a clockmaker.

—Voltaire

Defining The Divine

To even try to define God appears to be an effort doomed to failure from the start. But the word "God" has a meaning—in fact, many meanings. We all have some verbal concept of what we mean when we use the term "God." I am not here proposing to somehow capture all of whatever God is in essence, but rather redirecting our thinking to some ways of conceptualizing God which more fully embody much of what we say we believe when we use the term. However inadequate our characterizations of "God" may be, our thinking about God does matter because the God *we* create will either free us to own our true identities as living embodiments of God or will confine us to the lives of "quiet desperation" of which Thoreau wrote.

So who is this God who appeared out of the midst of apparently nothing to create everything that is? What adjectives can we possibly apply that give us a clue to Who or What we are talking about? To begin with let us identify some of the characterizations of God which have led us astray. It has been said that "in the beginning, God created us in his image—and then we returned the favor". I plead guilty to having participated in this exercise, but it is very hard not to do this. Since our language does not abound with options for describing the indescribable we necessarily resort to anthropomorphic terminology. Using ourselves as models, we use words like person and personal and personal pronouns like he, him, or (as I have resorted to in this book) she or her. We call God Father or Mother and attribute to God the qualities of the ideal human fathers and mothers. Like us, God speaks and loves and, according to some of us, hates and judges and punishes. "He" loves us and condemns us to eternal damnation. Indeed, the more we say about God, the smaller "he" seems to become.

Theologians are fond of using superlative language to describe God. We use words like omniscient (all knowing), omnipotent (all powerful), eternal (everlasting), omnipresent (present in all places at the same time), alpha and omega (first and last). In each instance God is shown to be just like us, only more so. Generally speaking, comparing God to ourselves is not particularly helpful for understanding this entity who preexists being itself. All of the language we have used so far describes a *being*, albeit a spiritual *being*. *What if God is none of these*? What if the concept of *being*—spiritual or otherwise—is too limiting?

Theologians try to get around this difficulty by speaking of God as *numinous*. This is derived from the Latin *numen,* a word from Roman mythology meaning deity, particularly "an indwelling and guiding force or spirit". To thus speak of God as numinous is to speak of a force *within us,* a spiritual energy, as opposed to a separate being acting upon us from without. Could it be that collectively we have been looking in the wrong place for the wrong thing? We have been searching the heavens for a being-thing, when we should have been searching inwardly for a no-thing, an indwelling creative and indomitable spirit whose initials, YHVH (Yahweh), are inscribed on every cell of our body. In a word, the mystical, the biblical, and the scientific evidences all indicate that *the God we seek is an indwelling, guiding, and empowering force and wisdom, to be found individually and collectively within us, perhaps even is us.* The ramifications of this understanding are enormous. This is what we shall be exploring in the remainder of this book.

Separation Is an Illusion

In chapter 5, the belief that we are somehow separated from God is discussed at some length. Evangelical Christian theology is explicit that *hamartia,* which is often mistranslated *"sin,"* actually means to separate that which should not be separated. Yet that is precisely what we have done. We have tried to live as though God is somehow separate from Her creation. But the separation is an illusion. We have never been separate from God, even at our worst. The Creator and the Creation are inseparable. The fact that we often act as though God is not within us is an assumption based on false premises about the nature of God. We have imagined a God so far removed from ourselves that we think of God as "out there somewhere," perhaps hiding from us in a heaven completely removed from our own experience. Instead of being taught from our infancy on that we are at the very least God-bearers, we have been brainwashed into believing that our identity, individually and collectively, is (and has been from our birth) that of sinners, separated by our sin from God. This lamentable misconstrual by our theologies not only makes God other than us, but makes God the Chief of Sinners since we are presumably created in God's image.

Not too surprisingly, it is this corrupted image of God that we have generally imaged instead of the true, uncorrupted image which we bear deep within. This is why Matthew Fox's vision of "original blessing," as opposed to Augustine's vision of "original sin," is so important for us to understand. We conform to that in which we believe. If we believe we were born in sin, then we will inevitably commit what we believe to be "sin". If on the other hand we accept the contrary belief that we were born blessed, we will conform to the image of goodness and Love. This is both psychologically self-evident and theologically consistent with the oft expressed sentiment that God *is* Love—*agápe* Love.

The "indwelling and guiding force," that uncorrupted and, therefore imperishable, force within us, is the Divine Love—*agápe* Love. *It is through Love that we express our true nature, because it is God's true nature.* Anytime we express *agápe,* whoever the recipient, and in whatever form, we are expressing God.

How can we know God? It is not through theology, the study of God. Nor do we get to know God through faithful repetition of religious rituals or church, synagogue or mosque attendance. These can help us know about God, but they will not help us know God. The surest route to knowing God is the practice of *agápe* Love. It is through *agápe* that we begin to see the presence of God in other persons and in their reflections we begin to see God in ourselves. In the practice of *agápe* for others we begin to feel both the pain and the ecstasy of God in ourselves. When we can feel their pain and join in their joy, then we will know who God is and what makes God, God. We shall know Love, and know that God *is* Love.

In time we will come to understand more of God's attributes: infinite, wise, sustainer of life, creative, holy, powerful... somewhat like Her earthly incarnations. Who should know God better than Her own children? It does not take a mystic to know who God is, though mystics have long known what should have been plain to the rest of us, had we not been blinded by our own conceit. The mystics long ago formulated a variety of paths to union with God and each other. The key element in virtually every mystical route to God is *agápe* Love, but there are other important elements in the mystic's journey as well. The Apostle Paul, himself a mystic, listed a number of these other qualities (or gifts of the Spirit of God) which facilitate our journey. Love tops the list, but it is followed by "joy, peace, patience, kindness, goodness, faithfulness, humility, and self-control." (see Paul's letter to the Galatians, 5:22-23 KJV)

I am pleased that Paul included humility in his list, as it is the antidote to pride. It is ironic that it has been our pride that has been blinding us for at least the last two millennia. It would seem that on the whole we *Homo sapiens* have not had a lot of spiritual accomplishments to justify our pride. But in any event we have not readily engaged in the exercise of humility. The gift of humility, as well as all the other provisions for the journey, is still available for the asking. The time has come for the children of God to ask.

If we seek God within we will find Her, and She will be us. Any other formulation than this will necessarily be dualistic, reflecting the Greek philosophy of dualism, which was adopted by the early Christian community in the first century C.E. The Apostle Paul, who was trained in Greek philosophy, substituted dualism for the teaching of Jesus, which specified unity as the royal road to the kingdom of God. In the Gospel of John, Jesus is said to have prayed that humanity "may become completely one" with God the Father (Gospel of John 17:23) and again, in the Gospel of Thomas: "They said to Him: 'Shall we then, being children, enter the Kingdom?' Jesus said to them: 'When you make the two one, and when you make the inner as the outer and the outer as the inner and the above as the below, and when you make the male and female into a single one... then shall you enter [the Kingdom].'" (Gospel of Thomas 22:3-4) There is only *one* Reality, and that Reality is God.

Ours is a journey that must be characterized by *1) a radical openness in faith unconstrained by doctrine, 2) a personal trust relationship with God, and 3) personal spiritual intention.* We have substituted sterile doctrine for life-giving faith, often substituting learning about God for *knowing* God personally. The letter of the law, especially religious law, kills true faith based on *agápe* Love. We, and most people, live in a society which emphasizes the rule of law. But the ideal society would be one based on the rule of Love. When we are nurtured in Love, forgiven our faults, and encouraged to accept responsibility for each other, we will have a foretaste of paradise. How we conceive of God will not be nearly as important as the way we relate to God in each other. Whether we call our Creator Allah, Brahma, God, Yahweh, Odin, Ra, or Original Source, it is essential to develop a relationship of Love and trust with the One who is *our* eternal Source *and* Being. Further, our personal spiritual intention to submit to our Original Source is the surest way to achieve *union* with God, thereby breaking the stranglehold of ego and pride which inevitably distracts us from our primary goal of achieving that union.

The sense of separation from our Source is an illusion fostered in Western society for the past 2,500 years. It is a dualistic view of the universe that has been a scourge on humanity and human progress ever since Plato (428-348 BCE) invented it. His philosophy was then picked up by Aristotle and subsequently passed on by Christianity to virtually every Westerner, down to this day. Whether or not we individually have studied Plato's teaching, we live in a culture so saturated with it that we simply accord it the status of ultimate truth. Eastern cultures, being older and more developed in many ways, were not so influenced by Plato. Thus dualism has never become the issue for them as it has for Western civilizations. Whether or not this will remain a significant difference between the East and West remains to be seen. Western communications technology is already influencing Eastern civilizations and not likely always for the best.

There are, however, some positive developments on the horizon as well. Communications travel both ways and Westerners are also learning from the East. Let us hope that we are as good students of the Eastern philosophers as we have been of Plato, Aristotle, and

Paul. I am *not* suggesting by this that we give up our allegiance to Jesus Christ. I *am* suggesting that we re-evaluate many of the biblical teachings ascribed to Jesus which, in fact, contradict rather than elucidate his teachings.

Pantheism Versus Panentheism

"*Pantheism* is the belief that all nature and, indeed, the whole universe are synonymous with God—that "God" is just another word for nature and the universe. Pantheists are those who worship nature and the creation, rather than the Creator. *Panentheism*, on the other hand, is the belief that God may be *seen* in all of creation inasmuch as all creation is *in* God. If we believe God is an indwelling, guiding, and empowering *force* and *wisdom* individually and collectively within us, then we may already in practice be panentheists. The difference between pantheism and panentheism is critical. It is one thing to have a *panentheistic* appreciation of nature and the universe as the handiwork of God, but it is quite another to worship the universe *as God,* as in *pantheism*.

So who or what *do* we worship? If God was no-thing, having pre-existed being itself, and created everything that is out of nothing, then God is not a being in the normal sense of the word, but is rather our personification of being. We are said to have been created in the image of God, but how can no-thing have an image? We have instead created God in our own image, which means that we have created an illusion of "being-ness" for both God and ourselves. This is not to say that neither God nor we exist. It does say that what we perceive with our very limited senses is not who or what we, or God, really are.

We can describe both ourselves and God—in whose image we are made—as Spirit. We have done this quite readily as pertains to God, speaking of God as Holy Spirit, typically meaning God's unembodied presence. As such, Spirit can also mean Life or Breath—a very real phenomenon, albeit invisible. The Holy Spirit is something with which we can be filled, meaning filled with God. We can be immersed (baptized) in God as Holy Spirit and we can be led by the Spirit. Soul is often equated with Spirit, and we speak of the spirit of Life and Love and Justice. In short, to be in the Spirit is to be in God, imaging God in all Her incorporeal reality. An incorporeal God has no hands but our hands and no feet but our feet. It is possible that She also has no mind or consciousness but our minds and consciousness, depending on how far we stretch the concept of Spirit. If so, then we are ourselves also the mind and consciousness of God.

Anima Mundi

In spite of the bad rap which I give Plato (and Western civilization) because of his philosophy of dualism, he had other very significant insights which, unfortunately, have not been widely received in the West. One of these is the idea of the *Anima Mundi,* or world soul. *Anima Mundi* is the Latin term which refers to an intrinsic connection between all living things and beings on the earth. The Greek translation of the phrase, *pseuche kosmou* (ψυχή κόσμου), literally, "world soul" suggests that it is not just individuals who have Soul, *that-which-is-of-God-in-us*, but that it is a corporate reality as well. Not only are we individual manifestations of The Divine, so also is the whole of creation. The premise of *Anima Mundi* is that the earth is filled with the glory (manifest presence) of God. The Hebrew prophet Isaiah quotes the psalmist, "Holy, holy, holy is the Lord of hosts; the whole earth is full of his glory." (Isaiah 6:4, NRSV)

It is *that-which-is-of-God-in-us* that connects us as individuals with each other, and it is *that-which-is-of-God-in-us* that connects us to the earth. At our best, others can readily see the family resemblance. God, our Divine Parent, can be seen in Her divine children. We live in a participatory universe. As such it is our responsibility to nourish the universe. We cannot afford to sit on the sidelines watching this corner of the cosmos collapse before our eyes. Nor can we afford to continue the pillaging and raping of the earth's land masses and oceans. We have created a cancer in the universe which will inevitably require our destruction as sentient human beings in order that the cancer may not spread to the rest of Creation. Given our present dereliction of responsibility, the rest of the universe cannot afford our presence and will not hesitate excising that which it cannot tolerate.

God's manifest presence in the world is the ultimate motivation for all Her children, who have been designated caretakers of the family estate, to respect and protect the world. That we have chosen instead to ravage and pollute it is a clear indication that we have forgotten who we are and why we are here. Though our true identity is Saints, Holy ones, we have been failing in our God-given responsibilities and consequently making a Hell of our Heaven.

We need a renewed *vision* of who we are and what we can accomplish. The biblical writer knew this when he said, "Where there is no vision, the people perish." (Proverbs 29:18, KJV) Quantum physicists take this idea very seriously. They have found, for example, that observation on the sub-atomic level is a creative act. By the very act of observing, we affect the outcomes of the molecular activities we observe. Apparently the Creation knows when it is being watched and responds accordingly. As divine beings we have powers to act for good that we do not recognize and consequently do not use. The greatest of these powers, I believe, is the power to Love.

God had a vision. In the Biblical creation story, it is said that God spoke "and there was light"; God spoke and there was the sky; God spoke, and there were dry land and seas and vegetation including trees bearing fruit. God spoke again, and there were "lights in the dome of the sky;" God spoke yet again and there were "living creatures of every kind;" and on the last day of the week, God spoke and "created humankind in his image, in the image of God he created them, male and female he created them." (Genesis 1:1-27, NRSV) And all this was created out of the "formless void." Cosmologists say that everything was created out of nothing, and they now have pictures of it happening in one incredible fraction of a second. A second earlier and presumably there would have been nothing to photograph but deep darkness.

Have we lost our vision, and with it our ability to create? Have we lost our connections with God, each other and the world? I do not think so. There are still a few visionaries in our midst who are carrying as much of the creative load as they can bear. There are, for example, the Cistercian monks at the Monastery of the Holy Spirit in Conyers, Georgia who, speaking of their around-the-clock prayer regimen, say they are praying for the world while the world sleeps. There are thousands of others like them around the world, of Christian and many other religious persuasions, who are likewise praying for a sleeping world. Devout people in churches, mosques, temples, ashrams and tabernacles have already awakened from sleep and are donning the God-given mantles of the children of God, made in Her image and responsible for the creation. For the last four decades, at least, scientists, religious and atheists alike, have been sounding the alarms concerning the enormous perils facing this world, many of which are due to the mismanagement and greed of God's children, *Homo sapiens.* The world is waking up, but none too soon. There is, however, still ground for hope—and that ground is God.

God is Not a Person—God Is All There Is

In this inquiry into the nature of our humanity, I have tried to establish that we are *divine beings,* and have drawn on evidence ranging from our genetic makeup to the witness of a variety of disciplines, including both religious and scientific disciplines. We have considered the nature of the Creator regardless of what name we and those who have come before us have chosen for Her. We have looked at the nature of reality and the illusory character of our perceptions and explored some of the scientific, religious, and historical byways relevant to our search. We have looked at religious traditions, both East and West and given particular attention to the mystical teachings of these traditions. We have made the case for God who is essentially indecipherable, in part because our language is not adequate for the task. We simply cannot fathom any existential entity that can take nothing and from it create everything. If there was nothing but God before the universe, and future space travel not withstanding, and given the Big Bang, then perhaps there has been nothing but God *since* the Big Bang. Perhaps *God stuff is still all there is.* If this is true, then that would at least shed some light on a few of our other unanswered questions: How can God be everywhere at once? Perhaps it is because together *we* are virtually everywhere. How does God answer prayer? Perhaps it is because together *we* answer prayers. How does God spread Her *agápe* Love to everybody around the world? Perhaps it is because together we spread Her Love to everybody everywhere. Perhaps God really does do her work through our hands and feet, and minds and hearts. *God is not a person. She is all of us.*

It is a reasonable proposition that 1) if we, the most intelligent sentient beings on the planet, are made of God stuff (as indicated by both our DNA and our spiritual discernments), then we may very well have the mind of God in order to accomplish the on-going work of creation. 2) If that "God stuff" of which we are made is infinitesimally small bundles of light energy called quanta (as quantum theory indicates), then we may very well be the manifestation of God who is Light. 3) If the *agápe* Love of God is demonstrated by us, then it must be the heart of God that beats in us. I believe God is *in* the Creation (panentheism), but I am positive that God is supremely in *Homo sapiens*, Her human creations, and that our souls are really only one Soul in all of us moving across the face of the waters and climbing through us the highest mountains, and reaching into the deepest despair of Her people. I can no longer separate people from God. I wouldn't know where to draw the line even if there was one.

Would you see God? Look into the eyes of your children and your parents and your spouse. Would you see God? Look into the eyes of your neighbors and co-workers. Would you see God? Look into the eyes of strangers, the hungry, and the ill, the enemy combatant and the terrorist. If at first you do not see God, look again, for God is there. And, finally, look in the mirror—and believe. *God is all there is.*

EPILOGUE

*"Faith is the daring of the soul
To go farther than it can see."*

—William Newton Clark

*"The probability of life originating from accident is comparable to
the probability of the unabridged dictionary resulting from an
explosion in a printing shop."*

--Edwin G. Conklin

*"You shall love the Lord your God with all your heart, and with all
your soul, and with all your mind. And you shall love your neighbor
as yourself.*

--Jesus of Nazareth

So What Is the Point of It All?

We are, I believe, coming of age, and are well into the final phase of our evolution as *Homo sapiens.* This is a glorious time to be alive. We, our children, and our children's children are the generations who will lead the world out of the darkness of the most recent centuries and into the glorious light of the kingdom of God. We are the ones privileged to implement this final turning point in our evolutionary journey. This is our calling. This is that for which we were born.

Episcopal Bishop John Shelby Spong put it this way: "The ultimate purpose of human life is to love in the face of hatred, to forgive in the face of pain, to live in the face of death. In doing these things one must be free of the need for self-exaltation. That is what it means to reveal the divine in the human. It was the concept that convinced Paul that the God-presence had been experienced in Jesus. The pathway into divinity is through humanity. The pathway into eternity is through time." (Spong 2011, p. 287) Jesus was not just the way-shower. His role was not so much to tell us the way to God, as to show us who we already are—a people already created in Her image, a people with God in the beginning of time and still with God past the end of time. Eternal spirits.

As embodied spirits of God, we must continue to ask the hard questions about who we are, where we are headed, and what is the point of it all? I have addressed in this treatise these three questions. To believe that the whole of creation is happenstance is no longer credible science. To *not* believe in a Creator, an Original Source and a continuing Divine Presence defies reason. As theoretical physicist Michio Kaku has observed, "Physicists who believe in this God believe that the universe is so beautiful and simple that its ultimate laws could not have been an accident." (Kaku 2005, p.358)

Intelligent life is not an accident! There is a purpose behind all of Creation. The acknowledgment of our Source and Sustainer is the beginning of divine wisdom. To acknowledge and accept that we have a role in the unfolding of the Divine purpose is a part of that wisdom. To accept that we, as present day manifestations of divinity, are a critical aspect of the successful achievement of the Divine purpose is both humbling and terrifying. *I believe that we and our children, and our children's children, have been entrusted with the responsibility of bringing to fulfillment the Kingdom of God on earth.* I can think of no other challenge great enough to warrant the investment our Creator has already made in us, Her children. This is, I am convinced, the point of it all.

Our work is cut out for us. But beyond the work, for which we have already been endowed with the technical abilities and wisdom to complete, our Source has made us Her designated Lovers. It is by the practice of *agápe* more than anything else by which the Kingdom of God will be realized in this, the final stage of our evolution. We are transition generations, quite possibly the most critically important generations in the history of humankind. This is our destiny.

ADDENDA

Addendum I

WHAT DOES IT MEAN TO BE HUMAN?
A Collection of Biblical and Non-Canonical Texts Affirming Our
God-given Identity as Divine Beings

Psalm 8:4-5 (New Revised Standard Version)
"What are human beings that you are mindful of them, mortals that
you care for them? Yet you have made them a little lower than *God*
[*Elohim*], and crowned them with glory and honor." [Note:
"Elohim" is inaccurately translated as "angels" in the King James
Version of the Bible.]

Luke 17:21 (New Revised Standard Version)
"...the Kingdom of God is *within* you." [Note: This verse has
parallels in the **Gospel of Thomas 3:3**—"The (Father's) imperial
rule is within you and it is outside of you." And in the **Gospel of
Mary 4:5** "...the seed of true humanity exists within you."]

John 3:16 (New Revised Standard Version)
"For God so loved the world that he gave his only Son, so that
everyone who believes in [into] him may not perish, but have eternal
life." [Note: The Greek term "eis," here translated "in" actually
means "into" and only "into." In Greek usage, as in English, "en" is
often substituted for "eis," but not the other way around]

John 6:53 (New Revised Standard Version)
Jesus said to them, "Very truly I tell you, unless you eat the flesh of
the Son of Man and drink his blood, you have no life in you." [Note:
Jesus is speaking metaphorically here. He was not speaking of the
Lord's Supper observance, which did not exist at that time.]

John 9:5 (New Revised Standard Version)
"As long as I am in the world, I am the light of the world." and

Matthew 5:14 (New Revised Standard Version)
"You are the light of the world. A city built on a hill cannot be hid."

John 14:13-14 (New Revised Standard Version)
"I will do whatever you ask in my name, so that the Father may be glorified in the Son. If in my name you ask me for anything, I will do it."

John 15:1-5 (New Revised Standard Version)
"I am the true vine, and my Father is the vinegrower. He removes every branch in me that bears no fruit. Every branch that bears fruit he prunes to make it bear more fruit. You have already been cleaned by the word I have spoken to you. Abide in me, as I abide in you. Just as the branch cannot bear fruit by itself, neither can you unless you abide in me. *I am the vine; you are the branches. Those who abide in me and I in them, bear much fruit;* because apart from me you can do nothing."

John 17:21-23 (New Revised Standard Version)
Jesus is praying for his followers: "...that they all may be one. As you, Father, are in me and I am in you, may they also be in us so that the world may believe that you have sent me. The glory that you have given me, I have given them, so that they may be one, as we are one—*I in them and you in me, that they may become completely one,* so that the world may know that you sent me and have loved them even as you have loved me."

Romans 8:14-15 (Today's New International Version)
"For those who are led by the Spirit of God *are the children of God.* The Spirit you received does not make you slaves, so that you live in fear again; rather, the Spirit you received brought about your adoption to sonship. And by him we cry, *"Abba,* Father." [Note: The Greek word for adoption to sonship is a term referring to the full legal standing of an adopted male heir in Roman culture.]

1 Corinthians 1:1-2 (New Revised Standard Version)
"Paul, called to be an apostle of Christ Jesus by the will of God, …to the church of God that is in Corinth, to those sanctified in Christ Jesus, *called to be saints [holy people],* together with all those everywhere who call on the name of our Lord Jesus Christ, both their Lord and ours."

1 Corinthians 2:16 (New Revised Standard Version)
"'For who has known the mind of the Lord so as to instruct him?' But we have the mind *[nous]* of Christ."

2 Corinthians 3:17-18 (New Revised Standard Version)
"Now the Lord is the Spirit, and where the Spirit of the Lord is, there is freedom. And all of us, with unveiled faces, seeing the glory of the Lord as though reflected in a mirror, *are being transformed [metamorphosed] into the same image from one degree of glory [manifest presence] to another*, even as by the Spirit of the Lord."

Colossians 1:19 (New Revised Standard Version)
"For in him [Jesus] all the fullness of God was pleased to dwell." and...

Ephesians 3:17-19 (Today's New International Version)
The biblical writer is praying for the church in Ephesus: "And I pray that you, being rooted and established in love, may have power, together with all the Lord's people, to grasp how wide and long and high and deep is the love of Christ, and to know this love that surpasses knowledge—that *you may be filled to the measure of all the fullness of God.*"

Philippians 2:5-6 (New Revised Standard Version)
"Let the same mind *[essence, nature]* be in you that was in Christ Jesus, who, though he was in the form of God, did not regard equality with God as something to be exploited..."

Colossians 1:2 (Today's New International Version)
"To them God has chosen to make known among the Gentiles the glorious riches of this mystery, which is *Christ in you, the hope of glory* [the hope of God's manifest presence]. "

2 Peter 1:3-4 (Today's New International Version)
"His divine power has given us everything we need for a godly life through our knowledge of him who called us by his own glory and goodness. Through these he has given us his very great and precious promises, *so that through them you may participate in the divine nature,* having escaped the corruption in the world caused by evil desires."

Gospel of Philip 63:35
"And the companion of the [...] Mary Magdalene [...loved] her more than [all] the disciples [and used to] kiss her [often] on her [...]. The rest of [the disciples...] They said to him 'Why do you love her more than the rest of us?' (James M Robinson, ed., *The Nag Hammadi Library,* revised edition, Harper & Row, 1978)

Addendum II

How to Remember Your Dreams

As a divine human being, you already have some capabilities of which you may not be aware. Some of these may have to do with the manipulation of your dream state and the functions of your mind. Do you have difficulty remembering your dreams? Here are some recommendations:

First, just before you turn out the light and settle in for a night's sleep, tell yourself that you are going to remember your dreams, particularly those coming from your soul. Your subconscious will hear you and respond accordingly. Also, turn off the alarm on your clock. Clock alarms have erased more dreams than I can imagine. If you need to awaken at a particular time, set your mental alarm instead. Simply tell your subconscious mind that you are going to awaken at the exact time you name. When that time arrives your eyes will open without destroying your dream.

Second, keep a writing pad and pen within easy reach next to your bed. If you awaken in the middle of the night with a dream, do not wait until morning to record it.

Third, do not open your eyes immediately upon awakening. Review the dream with your eyes shut until you have it firmly in mind.

Fourth, write down everything you remember as quickly as you can, employing abbreviations and shorthand where possible—this is your first draft of your dream report. You can come back later to fill in gaps and correct grammar.

Fifth, continue to think about your dream as you go about your day, adding to your report as additional snippets of the dream come to mind. Also write down your first impressions of what the dream means.

Sixth, if, in spite of all the above there are still holes in your dream by your next bedtime, or if you just do not understand it, ask your subconscious for another dream to clarify the previous one, and repeat the same process again.

Addendum III

My Personal Co-evolutionary Creed

I have adopted and adapted Diarmuid O'Murchu's "emerging evolutionary creed." (O'Murchu 2002, p.3) Here is my emerging *co*-evolutionary creed. *(The italicized portions of the creed are my additions to O'Murchu's creed.)*

I believe in the divine creative energy, "erupting with unimaginable exuberance," *and still transforming the primordial chaos into a universe of incredible beauty and complexity.*

I believe in the divine imprint as it manifests itself in swirling vortexes and particle formations, birthing forth atoms and galaxies.

I believe in the providential outburst of supernovas and in the absorbing potential of black holes.

I believe in the gift of agelessness, those billions of formative æons in which the paradox of creation and destruction unfolds into the shapes and patterns of the observable universe.

I believe in the divine energy that begot material form and biological life in ancient bacterial forms and in the amazing array of living creatures.

I believe in the incarnation of The Divine in the Homo sapiens' soul, a special creation evolving parallel to, but not descended from, other species.

I believe in the gift of God's Spirit, indwelling and enabling human beings to procreate other divine beings, all in God's image, perpetuating the unending work of creation.

I believe in the divine Creator, the "I am" who will be, the creative Word spoken from the very beginning and still speaking "incessantly throughout the whole of creation and begetting possibilities that the human mind can *now* only vaguely imagine."

I believe in the embodiment of The Divine in the Creation, heralding the birth of a new age of peace, radical freedom and spiritual development of humankind as we acknowledge our collective and individual identity as co-creators in the continually unfolding and unending plan of our Creator.

I believe in the eventual triumph of good over evil, as we human beings evolve spiritually, ethically, and morally, using that freedom essential to our divine identities to imagine and then create a world of peace and harmony, goodness and light, understanding and forgiveness, where truth is self evident and agápe love transcends all.

Addendum IV

WORLD CITIZENSHIP CREED

As a citizen of the world...

I BELIEVE in the dignity of all humanity, that each person is a being of supreme worth.

I BELIEVE in the wholeness of the human race, undivided by economic, cultural, racial, sexual or national differences.

I BELIEVE in the stewardship of life and resources to the end that all may mutually benefit from the earth's bounty... that no person may have to go without food or shelter.

I BELIEVE in the primacy of human relationships, as a person committed and responsible to other persons, regardless of their economic status, race, creed or nationality.

I BELIEVE in the global community, interdependent and mutually responsible for our physical and social environments.

I BELIEVE that we are One World and affirm that I am a citizen of this world. My allegiance to it and its people, my brothers and sisters, is primary over all other political entities.

I AM, therefore committed to the promotion and care of the whole of humanity without partiality or prejudice and with such resources as I have at my command, both within and without.

I HEREWITH AFFIRM that I wish, as much as I possibly can, to base my actions on my beliefs and thus contribute to a world where justice and compassion rule and greed and hatred are diminished.

The World Citizenship Creed is at least one effort to put into words a belief that, if acted upon by a significant number of the world's citizens, will transform the world.

As author of the World Citizenship Creed, I have committed myself to world citizenship and to this creed, and I invite others to join me in owning it for themselves. These are my beliefs, my inner mandate for action, my guide to how I want to relate to the world and all its peoples. We will see a global change of mind for good, as first one and then another and then another— one person at a time—recognizes the need for a change of mind and commits himself or herself to *world* citizenship.

Do you share these dreams of a new earth?

If so, you are invited to join a worldwide network of like-minded dreamers by signing the World Citizenship Pledge on the last two pages of this book. Please keep one copy and send the other copy of your signed pledge to **World Citizenship Institute, 204 Busbee Road, Knoxville, Tennessee, 37920, USA.** Please include your contact information so we can send you your citizenship card and occasional updates. Also, please share with us a written copy of your dreams and visions for a new earth so we may share them with others.

We currently have the World Citizenship Creed in English, French, Korean, and Spanish. Please write to WCI at the above address for copies of the Creed in one of these languages.

If you would be interested in volunteering to translate the Creed from English into yet other languages please let us know. Your help will enable the further spread of the Creed, making it truly a **world citizenship creed** in every sense of the word.

BIBLIOGRAPHY

Primary Sources: (Sources specifically cited or referenced in *Holy Humanity*)

Aaboe, Asger, "Mesopotamian Mathematics, Astronomy, and Astrology"; Ch. 28B, *The Cambridge Ancient History,* 2nd ed., Vol. III, Pt. 2. Cambridge, England: Cambridge University Press, 1992.

Adams, Abigail & John; L. H. Butterfield, ed. *Book of Abigail and John: Selected Letters of the Adams Family, 1762-1784.* Evanston, IL: Northeastern University Press, 2002.

Adams, Jean and Drew. "Martin's Dream". Nashville: General Board of Discipleship of the United Methodist Church, 1989.

Alexander, Eben. *Proof of Heaven: A Neurosurgeon's Journey into the Afterlife.* New York: Simon & Schuster, 2012.

Barks, Coleman. *Rumi: Bridge to the Soul: Journeys into the Music and Silence of the Heart.* New York: HarperCollins, 2007.

Bartlett, Anthony W. *Virtually Christian: How Christ Changes Human Meaning and Makes Creation New.* Winchester, UK: O Books, 2011.

Bettenson, Henry. *Documents of the Christian Church,* 2nd ed. New York: Oxford University Press, 1963.

Collins, Gary R. *The Soul Search: A Spiritual Journey to Authentic Intimacy with God.* Nashville: Thomas Nelson, 1998.

Braden, Gregg. *The God Code: The Secret of Our Past, the Promise of Our Future.* Carlsbad, CA.: Hay House, Inc., 2004.

Cross, F. L. & E. A. Livingstone. *The Oxford Dictionary of the Christian* Church, 3rd ed. New York: Oxford University Press, 1997.

Crossan, John Dominic. *The Power of Parable.* New York: HarperOne, 2012.

Ferris, Timothy. *The Mind's Sky: Human Intelligence in a Cosmic Context.* New York: Bantam, 1992.

Foster, James L. *Loving with the Love of Jesus.* Unpublished manuscript.

196

Fox, Matthew. *Creativity: Where the Divine and the Human Meet.* New York: Jeremy P. Tarcher, 2002.

_____. *One River, Many Wells: Wisdom Springing from Global Faiths.* New York: Jeremy P. Tarcher/Penguin, 2000.

_____. *Original Blessing.* Santa Fe, NM: Bear & Company, 1983.

Fox, Matthew and Rupert Sheldrake. *Natural Grace: Dialogues on Creation, Darkness, and the Soul in Spirituality and Science.* New York: Doubleday, 1996.

Gawain, Shakti. *Creative Visualization.* New York: Bantam, 1978.

Gilbert, Elizabeth. *Eat Pray Love: One Woman's Search for Everything Across Italy, India and Indonesia.* New York: Penguin Books, 2006.

Gould, Stephen J. *The Mismeasure of* Man, 2nd ed. New York: W. W. Norton, 1981.

Greene, Brian. *The Hidden Reality: Parallel Universes and the Deep Laws of the Cosmos.* New York: Knopf, 2011.

Harman, Willis. *Global Mind Change: The Promise of the 21st Century,* 2nd ed. San Francisco, CA: Berrett-Koehler, 1998.

Haught, John F. *God after Darwin: A Theology of Evolution.* Boulder: Westview Press, 2003.

Head, Joseph & S. L. Cranston, eds. *Reincarnation: The Phoenix Fire Mystery.* New York: Crown, 1977.

Hillman, James. *The Soul's Code: In Search of Character and Calling.* New York: Random House, 1996.

Hubbard, Elbert. *Elbert Hubbard's Scrapbook.* (New York: W. M. Wise & Company, 1923.

Irwin, Alexander C. *Eros Toward the World: Paul Tillich and the Theology of the Erotic.* Minneapolis: Fortress Press, 1991.

Jung, Carl G. *The Archetypes and the Collective Unconscious.* London: s.n., 1969.

Jung, Carl G.; R.F.C. Hull, trans. *Four Archetypes: Mother/Rebirth/Spirit/Trickster.* Princeton, Princeton University Press, 1969.

_____. *The Undiscovered Self.* New York: Penguin Books, 1958.

Kaku, Michio. *Parallel Worlds: A Journey* Through *Creation, Higher Dimensions, and the Future of the Cosmos.* New York: Random House/Doubleday, 2004.

Keirsey, David & Marilyn Bates. *Please Understand Me: An Essay on Temperament Styles.* Del Mar, Calif: Prometheus Nemesis Books, 1978.

Koestler, Arthur. *The Ghost in the Machine.* New York: Penguin Books reprint, 1990.

Mack, Burton L. *The Lost Gospel: The Book of Q & Christian Origins.* New York: HarperCollins, 1993.

Marion, Jim. *Putting on the Mind of Christ: The Inner Work of Christian Spirituality.* Charlottesville: Hampton Roads Publishing, 2000.

Middleton, Robert G. *Privilege & Burden.* Valley Forge, PA: Judson Press, 1969.

Moody, Raymond A, Jr. *Life After Life: The Investigation of a Phenomenon—Survival of Bodily Death.* Harrisburg: Stackpole Books, 1976.

Myss, Caroline. *Entering the Castle: An Inner Path to God and Your Soul.* New York: Free Press, 2007.

_____. *Sacred Contracts. Awakening Your Divine Potential.* New York: Random House, 2001.

Nelson, James B. & Sandra P. Longfellow, eds. *Sexuality and the Sacred: Sources for Theological Reflection.* Louisville: Westminster/John Knox Press, 1993.

O'Donohue, John. *Anam Cara: A Book of Celtic Wisdom.* New York: Harper Collins, 1997.

O'Murchu, Diarmuid. *Ancestral Grace: Meeting God in Our Human Story.* Maryknoll, NY: Orbis Books, 2008.

198

_____. *Evolutionary Faith: Rediscovering God in Our Great Story.* Maryknoll, NY: Orbis Books, 2002.

_____. *Quantum Theology.* New York: Crossroad Publishing, 1997.

Pagels, Heinz R. *The Cosmic Code: Quantum Physics as the Language of Nature.* New York: Bantam, 1983.

Rahner, Karl & Herbert Vorgrimler. *Dictionary of Theology*, 2nd ed. New York: Crossroad Publishing, 1981.

Ring, Kenneth. *Life at Death: A Scientific Investigation of the Near-Death Experience.* (New York: Coward, Geoghegan, 1980.

Robinson, James M., ed. *The Nag Hammadi Library in English*, rev.ed. New York: Harper & Row, 1988.

Schweitzer, Albert. *The Quest of the Historical Jesus.* New York: Macmillan, 1956.

Sams, Jamie. *Dancing the Dream: The Seven Sacred Paths of Human Transformation.* New York: Harper Collins, 1998.

Sheldrake, Rupert. *The Presence of the Past: Morphic Resonance and the Habits of Nature.* New York: Random House, 1989.

Singer, June. *Love's Energies.* Boston: Sigo Press, 1990.

Storr, Anthony, ed. *The Essential Jung.* Princeton NJ: Princeton University Press, 1983.

Swimme, Brian and Thomas Berry. *The Universe Story: From the Primordial Flaring Forth to the Ecozoic Era—A Celebration of the Unfolding of the Cosmos.* New York: HarperCollins, 1992.

Teilhard de Chardin, Pierre. *The Future of Man.* New York: Harper & Row, 1964.

_____. *The Phenomenon of Man.* New York: Harper & Row, 1959.

Teresa of Avila; Kieran Kavanaugh & Otilio Rodriguez, trans. *Teresa of Avila: The Interior Castle.* New York: Paulist Press, 1979.

Thiering, Barbara. *Jesus and the Riddle of the Dead Sea Scrolls: Unlocking the Secrets of His Life Story.* New York: HarperCollins, 1992.

Thoreau, David Henry. *Walden.* New York: Peebles Press International, 1967.

Vaughan-Lee, Llewellyn. *Traveling the Path of Love: Sayings of Sufi Masters.* Inverness, CA.: The Golden Sufi Center, 1995.

Whitman, Walt; Malcolm Cowley, ed. *Leaves of Grass: The First (1855) Edition.* New York: Penguin Books, 1976.

Wilber, Ken. *A Brief History of* Everything, 2nd ed. Boston: Shambhala Publications, 2000.

_____. *The Marriage of Sense and Soul: Integrating Science and Religion.* New York: Broadway Books, 1999.

Young, Al. *Bodies and Soul.* Berkeley: Creative Arts Book Company, 1981.

Secondary Sources: (Pertinent background material on topics addressed in *Holy Humanity*)

Abram, David. *The Spell of the Sensuous: Perception and Language in a More-Than-Human World.* New York: Random House, 1996.

Abraham, Ralph H. *Chaos. Gaia. Eros: A Chaos Pioneer Uncovers the Three Great Streams of History.* New York: HarperCollins, 1994.

Aczel, Amir D. *Entanglement: The Unlikely Story of How Scientists, Mathematicians, and Philosophers Proved Einstein's Spookiest Theory.* London, England: Plume Books, 2002.

"All About the Human Genome Project (HGP)." *All About the Human Genome Project (HGP).* N.p., n.d. Web. 30 Aug. 2013.

Allen, Ronald B. *The Majesty of Man: The Dignity of Being Human.* Grand Rapids: Kregel Publications, 1999.

Armstrong, Karen. *A History of God: The 4,000-Year Quest of Judaism, Christianity, and Islam.* New York: Alfred A. Knopf, 1994.

Barrow, John D. *The Artful Universe.* Oxford: Clarendon Press, 1995.

Barrow, John D. & Joseph Silk. *The Left Hand of Creation: The Origin and Evolution of the Expanding Universe.* New York: Basic Books, 1983.

Berry, Thomas. *The Christian Future and the Fate of the Earth.* Maryknoll, NY: Orbis Books, 2009.

_____. *The Dream of the Earth.* San Francisco: Sierra Club Books, 1988.

Bondi, Roberta C. *Memories of God: Theological Reflections on a Life.* Nashville: Abingdon Press, 1995.

Bonheim, Jalaja. *The Hunger for Ecstasy: Fulfilling the Soul's Need for Passion and Intimacy.* Daybreak/Rodale Books: s.l., 2001.

Borg, Marcus J. *The Heart of Christianity: Rediscovering a Life of Faith.* New York: HarperCollins, 2003.

Bosley, Harold A. *The Mind of Christ: A Personal Pilgrimage of Discovery with the Disciples.* Nashville: Abingdon Press, 1966.

Bronowski, J. *The Ascent of Man.* Boston: Little, Brown, 1974.

Brussat, Frederic and Mary Ann. *Spiritual Literacy: Reading the Sacred in Everyday Life.* New York: Scribner, 1996.

Buber, Martin; Ronald G. Smith, trans. *I and Thou*, 2nd ed. New York: Scribner's, 1958.

Buber, Martin; Maurice Friedman and Ronald G. Smith, trans. *The Knowledge of Man: A Philosophy of the Interhuman.* New York: Harper & Row, 1965.

Calvin, William H. & George A. Ojemann. *Conversations with Neil's Brain: The Neural Nature of Thought and Language.* Reading, MA: Perseus Books, 1994.

Carmody, Denise Lardner & John Tully Carmody. *Mysticism: Holiness East and West.* New York: Oxford University Press, 1996.

Chopra, Deepak. *The Path to Love: Renewing the Power of Spirit in Your Life.* New York: Random House, 1997.

Church, F. Forrester. *The Essential Tillich: An Anthology of the Writings of Paul Tillich.* New York: Macmillan, 1988.

Cohen, Jack & Ian Stewart. *The Collapse of Chaos: Discovering Simplicity in a Complex World.* New York: Penguin Books, 1994.

Comfort, Philip W. & Jason Driesbach. *The Many Gospels of Jesus: Sorting Out the Story of the Life of Jesus.* Carol Spring, Ill.: Tyndale House, 2007.

Cousineau, Phil. *Soul, An Archaeology: Readings from Socrates to Ray Charles.* New York: HarperCollins, 1994.

Cranfield, C. E. B. *A Critical and Exegetical Commentary on the Epistle to the Romans, Vols. I & II.* Edinburgh: Clark, 1975.

Cremo, Michael A. and Richard L. Thompson. *Forbidden Archeology: The Hidden History of the Human Race.* London: Routledge, 1998.

Crick, Francis. *The Astonishing Hypothesis: The Scientific Search for the Soul.* New York: Simon & Schuster, 1993.

Crossan, John Dominic. *The Historical Jesus: The Life of a Mediterranean Jewish Peasant.* San Francisco: HarperCollins, 1991.

Darwin, Charles. *The Origin of Species by Means of Natural Selection.* New York: New American Library, ©1958.

Davies, Paul. *About Time: Einstein's Unfinished Revolution.* Simon & Schuster, 1995.

_____. *The 5th Miracle: The Search for the Origin and Meaning of Life.* New York: Simon & Schuster, 1999.

_____. *God & the New Physics.* New York: Simon & Schuster, 1983.

_____. *The Mind of God: The Scientific Basis for a Rational World.* New York: Simon & Schuster, 1992.

Davis, Roy E. *Yoga: Essential Teachings and Practices.* Lakemont, GA: Center for Spiritual Awareness, 1992.

Dawes, Gregory W. *The Historical Jesus Question: The Challenge of History to Religious Authority.* Louisville: Westminster John Knox Press, 2001.

Devereux, Paul, John Steele, & David Kubrin. *Earthmind: A Modern Adventure in Ancient Wisdom.* New York: Harper & Row, 1989.

Dominion, Jack. *One Like Us: A Psychological Interpretation of Jesus.* London: Darton, Longman & Todd, 1998.

Dorrien, Gary. *Soul in Society: The Making and Renewal of Social Christianity.* Minneapolis: Augsburg Fortress, 1995.

Dossey, Larry. *Recovering the Soul: A Scientific and Spiritual Search.* New York: Bantam, 1989.

Dutton, Denis. *The Art Instinct: Beauty, Pleasure, and Human Evolution.* New York: Bloomsbury Press, 2009.

Dyson, Freeman. *From Eros to Gaia.* London: Penguin Books, 1993.

_____. *Infinite in All Directions.* New York: Harper & Row, 1988.

Ebert, David. *Twilight of the Clockwork God: Conversations on Science and Spirituality at the End of an Age.* Tulsa: Council Oak Books, 1999.

203

Eckhart, Meister; Raymond B Blakney, trans. *Meister Eckhart: A Modern Translation.* New York: Harper & Row, 1941.

Eckhart, Meister; Bernard McGinn, ed. *Meister Eckhart: Teacher and Preacher.* New York: Paulist Press, 1986.

Eckhart, Meister; Reiner Schurmann, trans. *Wandering Joy: Meister Eckhart's Mystical Philosophy.* Great Barrington, MA: Lindisfarne Books, 2001.

Einstein, Albert. *Relativity: The Special and the General Theory.* New York: Crown Publishers, 1959.

Eldridge, Niles. *The Pattern of Evolution.* New York: W.H. Freeman, 1998.

Elgin, Duane. *Promise Ahead: A Vision of Hope and Action for Humanity's Future.* New York: HarperCollins, 2000.

Eliade, Mircea. *Shamanism: Archaic Techniques of Ecstasy.* Princeton, NJ: Princeton University Press, 1964.

Elliot, Willis. *Flow of Flesh, Reach of Spirit: Thinksheets of a Contrarian Christian.* Grand Rapids: Eerdmans, 1995.

Fair, Charles M. *The Dying Self.* Garden City, NY: Doubleday, 1970.

Feuerstein, Georg. *The Deeper Dimension of Yoga: Theory and Practice.* Boston: Shambhala Books, 2003.

_____. *The Shambhala Encyclopedia of Yoga.* Boston: Shambhala Publications, 1997.

_____. *Wholeness or Transcendence? Ancient Lessons for the Emerging Global Civilization.* Burdett, NY: Paul Brunton Philosophic Foundation, 1992.

Feynman, Richard P. *The Meaning of It All: Thoughts of a Citizen-Scientist.* Reading, MA: Perseus Books, 1998.

Fox, Matthew. *The Coming of the Cosmic Christ: The Healing of Mother Earth and the Birth of a Global Renaissance.* New York: HarperCollins, 1988.

_____. *Creation Spirituality: Liberating Gifts for the Peoples of the Earth.* New York: HarperCollins, 1990.

_____. *Meditations with Meister Eckhart.* Santa Fe, NM: Bear & Company, 1983.

_____. *Passion for Creation: The Earth-Honoring Spirituality of Meister Eckhart.* Rochester, VT: Inner Traditions International, 2000.

Fromm, Erich. *You Shall Be as Gods: A Radical Interpretation of the Old Testament and Its Tradition;* Chapter 3, "The Concept of Man". New York: Holt, Rinehart and Winston, 1966.

Frykenberg, Robert Eric. *History and Belief: The Foundations of Historical Understanding.* Grand Rapids: Eerdmans, 1996.

Funk, Robert W. & Roy W. Hoover & The Jesus Seminar. *The Five Gospels: The Search for the Authentic Words of Jesus.* Polebridge Press, 1993.

"Gaia Hypothesis." *Wikipedia.* Wikimedia Foundation, 29 Aug. 2013. Web. 30 Aug. 2013.

Gingerich, Owen, et. al. *Cosmology + 1: Readings from Scientific American.* San Francisco, W.H. Freeman, 1977.

Gittelsohn, Roland B. *Little Lower Than the Angels.* New York: Union of American Hebrew Congregations, 1955.

Goldfield, Eugene C. *Emergent Forms: Origins and Early Development of Human Action and Perception.* New York: Oxford University Press, 1995.

Gould, Stephen, J. *Full House: The Spread of Excellence from Plato to Darwin.* New York: Crown Publishers, 1996.

Grant, W. Harold, Magdala Thompson, & Thomas E. Clarke. *From Image to Likeness: A Jungian Path in the Gospel Journey.* New York: Paulist Press, 1983.

Green, Vivian. *A New History of Christianity.* New York: Continuum, 2000.

Griffin, David Ray. *Archetypal Process: Self and Divine in Whitehead, Jung, and Hillman.* Evanston, IL: Northwestern University Press, 1989.

The Guideposts Parallel Bible: The King James Version, the New International Version, the Living Bible, the Revised Standard Version. Carmel, NY: Guideposts, 1981.

Guy, Henry. *Saving the World: The Spiritualization of Matter.* Arlington, TX: Vox Sophia Publishing, 2002.

Hagerty, Barbara Bradley. *Fingerprints of God: The Search for the Science of Spirituality.* New York: Riverhead Books, 2009.

Halpern, Paul. *The Great Beyond: Higher Dimensions, Parallel Universes, and the Extraordinary Search for a Theory of Everything.* Hoboken, NJ: J. Wiley, 2004.

Harned, David Baily. *Grace and Common Life.* Charlottesville, VA: University Press of Virginia, 1970.

Harner, Michael. *The Way of the* Shaman, 3rd ed. New York: Harper & Row, 1990.

Head, Joseph & S. L. Cranston editors. *Reincarnation in World Thought: A Living Study of Reincarnation in All Ages; Including Selections from the World's Religions, Philosophies and Sciences, and Great Thinkers of the Past and Present.* New York: Julian Press, 1967.

Heisenberg, Werner; A. J. Pomerans, trans. *Physics and Beyond.* New York: Harper & Row, 1971.

Heeren, Fred. *Show Me God: What the Message from Space Is Telling Us about* God rev.ed. Wheeling, IL: Day Star Publications, 1998.

Heyward, Carter. *Touching Our Strength: The Erotic as Power and the Love of God.* San Francisco: Harper & Row, 1989.

Hoeller, Stephan A. *Jung and the Lost Gospels: Insights into the Dead Sea Scrolls and the Nag Hammadi Library.* Wheaton, IL: Theosophical Publishing House, 1989.

The Holy Bible: Containing the Old and New Testaments. Nashville: Thomas Nelson Publishers, 1989.

Jäger, Willigis. *Search for the Meaning of Life: Essays and Reflections on the Mystical Experience.* Liguori, MO: Triumph Books, 1995.

Jones, Alan. *Soul Making: The Desert Way of Spirituality.* New York: Harper & Row, 1985.

Joseph, Lawrence E. *Gaia: The Growth of an Idea.* New York: St. Martin's Press, 1991.

Jung, Carl G. *Modern Man in Search of a Soul.* New York: Harcourt, Brace & World, 1933.

_____. *Memories, Dreams, Reflections.* New York: Random House, 1963.

"Judaism 101: Hebrew Alphabet." *Judaism 101: Hebrew Alphabet.* N.p., n.d. Web.

Jung, C. G.; J. Jacobi, ed. & trans; Hull, R.F.C., trans. *C. G. Jung: Psychological Reflections, a New Anthology of His Writings, 1905-1961.* Princeton, NJ: Princeton University Press, 2012.

Kaku, Michio & Jennifer Thompson. *Beyond Einstein: The Cosmic Quest for the Theory of the Universe*, revised edition. New York: Doubleday, 1995.

Kaplan-Williams, Strephon. *The Jungian-Senoi Dreamwork Manual: A Step-by Step Introduction to Working with Dreams.* Novato, CA: Journey Press, 1988.

Keen, Sam. *In the Absence of God: Dwelling in the Presence of the Sacred.* New York: Random House, 2010.

Kelsey, Morton T. *God, Dreams and Revelation: A Christian Interpretation of Dreams.* Minneapolis: Augsburg Publishing House, 1974.

King, Karen L. *What Is Gnosticism?* Cambridge, MA: Harvard University Press, 2003.

Knott, Kim. *Hinduism: A Very Short Introduction.* New York: Oxford University Press, 1998.

Kornfield, Jack. *Teachings of the Buddha.* Boston: Shambhala, 1996.

Kroeger, Otto & Janet M. Thuesen. *Type Talk: The 16 Personality Types that Determine How We Live, Love, and Work.* New York: Dell Publishing, 1988.

Kung, Hans; Edward Quinn, trans. *Eternal Life? Life After Death as a Medical, Philosophical, and Theological Problem.* Garden City, NY: Doubleday, 1984.

Lao, Tzu, and Victor H. Mair. *Tao Te Ching: The Classic Book of Integrity and the Way.* New York: Bantam Books, 1990.

Latourette, Kenneth Scott. *A History of Christianity.* New York: Harper, 1953.

Lavine, Shaughan. *Understanding the Infinite.* Cambridge, MA: Harvard University Press, 1994.

Leakey, L. S. B. *Adam's Ancestors: The Evolution of Man and His Culture*, 4th edition revised. New York: Harper & Row, 1953.

Leakey, L. S. B., Arthur T. Hopwood, & Hans Reck. "Age of the Oldoway Bone Beds, Tanganyika Territory." *Nature.* 128.3234 (1931): 724-724.

Leakey, Richard, & Roger Lewin. *Origins Reconsidered: In Search of What Makes Us Human.* New York: Anchor, 1992.

Lederman, Leon with Dick Teresi. *The God Particle: If the Universe is the Answer, What Is the Question?* Boston: Houghton Mifflin, 1993.

LeShan, Lawrence & Henry Margenau. *Einstein's Space & Van Gogh's Sky: Physical Reality and Beyond.* New York: Macmillan, 1982.

Lesser, Elizabeth. *The Seeker's Guide: Making Your Life a Spiritual Adventure.* New York: Random House, 1999.

Loomis, William F. *Life as it Is: Biology for the Public Sphere.* Berkeley: University of California Press, 2008.

Lovelock, James. *The Ages of Gaia: A Biography of Our Living Earth.* New York: Bantam Books, 1990.

Lowen, Alexander. *The Spirituality of the Body: Bioenergetics for Grace and Harmony.* New York: Macmillan, 1990.

Machuga, Ric. *In Defense of the Soul: What It Means to Be Human.* Grand Rapids: Baker, 2002.

208

Magill, Frank N. & Ian P. McGreal, eds. *Christian Spirituality: The Essential Guide to the Most Influential Spiritual Writings of the Christian Tradition.* New York: Harper & Row, 1988.

Mahbubani, Kishore. *The Great Convergence: Asia, the West, and the Logic of One World.* New York: Public Affairs Books, 2013.

Martin, Calvin Luther. *The Way of Being Human.* New Haven: Yale University Press, 1999.

Martin, Meredith. *Born in Africa: The Quest for the Origins of Human Life.* New York: Public Affairs Books, 2011.

McHugh, Heather. *Hinge and Sign: Poems, 1968-1993.* Middletown, Conn: Wesleyan University Press, 1994.

McManners, John, ed. *The Oxford Illustrated History of Christianity.* Oxford: Oxford University Press, 1990.

McNiff, Shaun. *Earth Angels: Engaging the Sacred in Everyday Things.* Boston: Shambhala, 1995.

Meier, Paul and Robert Wise. *Windows of the Soul: A Look at Dreams and Their Meanings.* Nashville: Thomas Nelson, 1995.

Moltmann-Wendel, Elisabeth & Jürgen Moltmann. *Humanity in God.* Cleveland, OH: Pilgrim Press, 1983.

Moody, Raymond A. *Reflections on Life After Life.* New York: Bantam, 1977.

Moore, John. *Sexuality and Spirituality: The Interplay of Masculine and Feminine in Human Development.* New York: Harper & Row, 1980.

Moore, Robert L. *Carl Jung and Christian Spirituality.* New York: Paulist Press, 1988.

Moore, Thomas. *The Soul of Sex: Cultivating Life as an Act of Love.* New York: HarperCollins, 1998.

Morgenau, Henry. *The Miracle of Existence.* Woodbridge, CT: Ox Bow Press, 1984.

Morrison, Clinton. *An Analytical Concordance to the Revised Standard Version of the New Testament.* Philadelphia: Westminster Press, 1979.

Murchie, Guy. *The Seven Mysteries of Life: An Exploration of Science and Philosophy.* New York: Houghton Mifflin, 1978.

Myers, Isabel Briggs, & Peter B. Myers. *Gifts Differing.* Palo Alto: Consulting Psychologists Press, 1980.

Nacpil, Emerito P. & Douglas J. Elwood. *The Human and the Holy: Asian Perspectives in Christian Theology.* Maryknoll, NY: Orbis Books, 1977.

Needleman, Jacob. *The Indestructible Question: Essays on Nature, Spirit and the Human Paradox.* London: Penguin Books, 1982.

O'Connor, Peter. *Dreams and the Search for Meaning.* New York: Paulist Press, 1987.

O'Donohue, John. *Beauty: The Invisible Embrace.* New York: HarperCollins, 2004.

Otto, Rudolf. *The Idea of the Holy.* New York: Oxford University Press, 1958.

Nadeau, Robert & Menas Kafatos. *The Non-Local Universe: The New Physics and Matters of the Mind.* New York: Oxford University Press, 1999.

Ovchinnikov, IV, A Götherström, GP Romanova, VM Kharitonov, K Lidén, and W Goodwin. "Molecular Analysis of Neanderthal DNA from the Northern Caucasus." *Nature.* 404.6777 (2000): 490-3.

Peacock, James L. & A. Thomas Kirsch. *The Human Direction: An Evolutionary Approach to Social and Cultural Anthropology.* New York: Appleton-Century-Crofts, 1970.

Pickover, Clifford A. *Surfing through Hyperspace: Understanding Higher Universes in Six Easy Lessons.* New York: Oxford University Press, 1999.

Pinker, Steven. *The Blank Slate: The Modern Denial of Human Nature.* New York: Viking, 2002.

Rahner, Karl. *Hominisation: The Evolutionary Origin of Man as a Theological Problem.* New York: Herder and Herder, 1965.

Raymo, Chet. *The Soul of the Night: An Astronomical Pilgrimage.* (Englewood Cliffs, NJ: Prentice Hall, Inc., 1985.

Reanney, Darryl. *After Death: A New Future for Human Consciousness.* New York: Avon Books, 1995.

Redfield, James, Michael Murphy, and Sylvia Timbers. *God and the Evolving Universe: The Next Step in Personal Evolution.* New York: Jeremy P. Tarcher/Putnam, 2001.

Ruether, Rosemary R. *Gaia & God: An Ecofeminist Theology of Earth Healing.* New York: HarperCollins, 1992.

Ridley, Matt. *Genome: The Autobiography of a Species in 23 Chapters.* New York: Perennial Library, 2000.

Ring, Kenneth. *Life at Death: A Scientific Investigation of the Near-Death Experience.* New York: Coward, McCann & Geoghegan, 1980.

Roberts, David E. *The Grandeur and Misery of Man.* New York: Oxford University Press, 1955.

Rucker, Rudy B. *The Fourth Dimension: Toward a Geometry of Higher Reality.* Boston: Houghton Mifflin, 1984.

Sagan, Carl. *Billions and Billions: Thoughts on Life and Death at the Brink of the Millennium.* New York: Ballantine Books, 1998.

_____. *Pale Blue Dot: A Vision of the Human Future in Space.* New York: Random House, 1994.

Sagan, Carl, and Ann Druyan. *Shadows of Forgotten Ancestors: A Search for Who We Are.* New York: Ballantine Books, 1993.

Sanford, John A. *Mystical Christianity: A Psychological Commentary on the Gospel of John.* New York: Crossroad, 1993.

Sanford, John A. *Soul Journey: A Jungian Analyst Looks at Reincarnation.* New York: Crossroad, 1991.

Saucy, Mark. *The Kingdom of God in the Teaching of Jesus: In 20th Century Theology.* Dallas, Tex: Word Publishing, 1997.

Savary, Louis M, Patricia H. Berne, and Strephon K. Williams. *Dreams and Spiritual Growth: A Judeo-Christian Way of Dreamwork: with More Than 35 Dreamwork Techniques.* Mahwah, NJ: Paulist Press, 1984.

211

Schrödinger, Erwin, and Erwin Schrödinger. *What Is Life?: The Physical Aspect of the Living Cell ; & Mind and Matter*. Cambridge: University Press, 1967.

Segaller, Stephen, and Merrill Berger. *The Wisdom of the Dream: The World of C.G. Jung*. Boston: Shambhala, 1989.

Sellner, Edward C. *Soul-making: The Telling of a Spiritual Journey*. Mystic, Conn: Twenty-Third Publications, 1991.

Shlain, Leonard. *Art & Physics: Parallel Visions in Space, Time, and Light*. New York: HarperCollins, 1993.

Shroder, Tom. *Old Souls: The Scientific Evidence for Past Lives*. New York: Simon & Schuster, 1999.

Singer, June. *Boundaries of the Soul: The Practice of Jung's Psychology*. Garden City, N.Y: Doubleday, 1972.

_____. *Seeing Through the Visible World: Jung, Gnosis, and Chaos*. San Francisco: Harper & Row, 1990.

Slusser, Gerald H. *From Jung to Jesus: Myth and Consciousness in the New Testament*. Atlanta, Ga: J. Knox Press, 1986.

Smith, Chadwick C, Rennard Strickland, and Benny Smith. *Building One Fire: Art + World View in Cherokee Life*. Tahlequah, Okla: Cherokee Nation, 2010.

Smith, Greg. *God's Art*. Mesa, Ariz: Grand Canyon Publishing, 2006.

Smith, Huston. *The Religions of Man*. New York: HarperCollins, 1986.

Snyder, Ross. *On Becoming Human: Discovering Yourself and Your Life World]*. Nashville, Tenn. [etc.]: Abingdon Press, 1967.

Spong, John Shelby. *Eternal Life: A New Vision*. New York: HarperCollins Publishers, 2009

_____. *Re-claiming the Bible for a Non-Religious World*. New York, NY: HarperCollins, 2011.

_____. *Why Christianity Must Change or Die: A Bishop Speaks to Believers in Exile: A New Reformation of the Church's Faith and Practice*. New York: HarperCollins, 1998.

Spretnak, Charlene. *States of Grace: The Recovery of Meaning in the Postmodern Age.* New York: HarperCollins, 1991.

Stock, Gregory. *Redesigning Humans: Our Inevitable Genetic Future.* Boston: Houghton Mifflin, 2002.

Strickland, Glenn G. *Genesis Revisited: A Revolutionary New Solution to the Mystery of Man's Origins.* New York: Dial Press, 1979.

Talbot, Michael. *Mysticism and the New Physics.* New York: Penguin Books, 1993.

Taylor, Brian C. *Becoming Christ: Transformation Through Contemplation.* Cambridge, Mass: Cowley Publications, 2002.

Teilhard de Chardin, Pierre *Christianity and Evolution.* London: Collins, 1969.

_____. *The Divine Milieu.* New York: Harper & Row, 1968.

_____. *Toward the Future.* New York: Harcourt Brace Jovanovich, 1975.

Thomas, Lewis. *The Fragile Species.* New York: Scribner's, 1992.

Thompson, William I. *Gaia, a Way of Knowing: Political Implications of the New Biology.* Great Barrington, MA: Lindisfarne Press, 1987.

_____. *The Time Falling Bodies Take to Light: Mythology, Sexuality, and the Origins of Culture.* New York: St. Martin's Press, 1981.

Thoreau, Henry D, and Bradley P. Dean. *Faith in a Seed: The Dispersion of Seeds, and Other Late Natural History Writings.* Washington, D.C: Island Press, 1993.

Trinh, Xuan T. *Chaos and Harmony: Perspectives on Scientific Revolutions of the Twentieth Century.* Oxford: Oxford University Press, 2001.

Tillich, Paul. *Systematic Theology.* Chicago: University of Chicago Press, 1967.

213

Tillich, Paul, and F. Forrester Church. *The Essential Tillich: An Anthology of the Writings of Paul Tillich*. New York: Collier Books, 1988.

Tipler, Frank J. *The Physics of Immortality: Modern Cosmology, God, and the Resurrection of the Dead*. New York: Doubleday, 1995.

Torrance, E. P. *The Search for Satori & Creativity*. Buffalo, N.Y: Creative Education Foundation, 1979.

Trible, Phyllis. *God and the Rhetoric of Sexuality*. Philadelphia: Fortress Press, 1978.

Trueblood, Elton. *The Essence of Spiritual Religion*. New York: Harper & Row, 1936.

Ulanov, Ann B. *The Wisdom of the Psyche*. Cambridge, Mass: Cowley Publications, 1988.

Underhill, Evelyn. *Mysticism; a Study in the Nature and Development of Man's Spiritual Consciousness*. New York: Dutton & Co, 1961.

Van, de C. R. L. *Our Dreaming Mind*. New York: Ballantine Books, 1994.

Vardey, Lucinda. *God in All Worlds: An Anthology of Contemporary Spiritual Writing*. New York: Vintage Books, 1996.

Vedral, Vlatko. *Decoding Reality: The Universe As Quantum Information*. Oxford, England: Oxford University Press, 2010.

Waldrop, M M. *Complexity: The Emerging Science at the Edge of Order and Chaos*. New York: Simon & Schuster, 1992.

Walter, Katya M. C. *Tao of Chaos: Merging East and West*. Shaftesbury, England: Element, 1996.

Watts, Alan W. *Nature, Man and Woman*. New York: Random House, 1991.

_____. *The Spirit of Zen: A Way of Life, Work and Art in the Far East*. New York: Grove Press, 1960.

_____. *The Way of Zen*. New York: Random House, 1957.

Weinberg, Steven. *Dreams of a Final Theory: The Scientist's Search for the Ultimate Laws of Nature.* New York: Random House, 1992.

Westcott, W. W. *Sepher Yetzirah: The Book of Creation.* N.p., n.d. Web.

Whitehead, James D. & Evelyn Eaton Whitehead. *Holy Eros: Pathways to a Passionate God.* Maryknoll, NY: Orbis Books, 2009.

Wilber, Ken. *Quantum Questions: Mystical Writings of the World's Great Physicists.* Boulder, Colo: Shambhala, 1984.

_____. *Sex, Ecology, Spirituality: The Spirit of Evolution.* Boston: Shambhala, 1995.

_____. *A Theory of Everything: An Integral Vision for Business, Politics, Science, and Spirituality.* Boston: Shambhala, 2001.

_____. *Up from Eden: A Transpersonal View of Human Evolution.* Garden City, N.Y: Anchor Press/Doubleday, 1996.

Wilber, Ken, and Mark Palmer, ed. *The Simple Feeling of Being: Embracing Your True Nature.* Boston: Shambhala, 2004.

Wilken, Robert L. *The Christians As the Romans Saw Them.* New Haven: Yale University Press, 1984.

Williams, Charles, Alice M. Hadfield, ed. *Outlines of Romantic Theology; with Which Is Reprinted, Religion and Love in Dante: The Theology of Romantic Love.* Grand Rapids: W. B. Eerdmans, 1990.

Wink, Walter. *Engaging the Powers: Discernment and Resistance in a World of Domination.* Minneapolis: Fortress Press, 1992.

_____. *The Human Being: Jesus and the Enigma of the Son of the Man.* Minneapolis: Fortress Press, 2002.

Wolf, Fred A. *The Dreaming Universe: A Mind-Expanding Journey into the Realm Where Psyche and Physics Meet.* New York: Simon & Schuster, 1994.

_____. *The Spiritual Universe: How Quantum Physics Proves the Existence of the Soul.* New York: Simon & Schuster, 1996.

_____. *Taking the Quantum Leap: The New Physics for Non-Scientists.* New York: Harper & Row, 1989.

Zimmer, Carl. *Soul Made Flesh: The Discovery of the Brain and How It Changed the World.* New York: Simon & Schuster, 2004.

Zohar, Danah, and I. N. Marshall. *The Quantum Self: Human Nature and Consciousness Defined by the New Physics.* New York: Morrow, 1990.

Zukav, Gary. *The Seat of the Soul.* New York: Simon and Schuster, 1989.

216

INDEX OF SCRIPTURAL CITATIONS

<u>Hebrew Scriptures</u>

Christian New Testament

Non-Canonical Texts

TOPICAL INDEX

WORLD CITIZENSHIP CREED

As a citizen of the world...

I BELIEVE in the dignity of all humanity, that each person is a being of supreme worth.

I BELIEVE in the wholeness of the human race, undivided by economic, cultural, racial, sexual or national differences.

I BELIEVE in the stewardship of life and resources to the end that all may mutually benefit from the earth's bounty... that no person may have to go without food or shelter.

I BELIEVE in the primacy of human relationships, as a person committed and responsible to other persons, regardless of their economic status, race, creed or nationality.

I BELIEVE in the global community, interdependent and mutually responsible for our physical and social environments.

I BELIEVE that we are One World and affirm that I am a citizen of this world. My allegiance to it and its people, my brothers and sisters, is primary over all other political entities.

I AM, therefore committed to the promotion and care of the whole of humanity without partiality or prejudice and with such resources as I have at my command, both within and without.

I HEREWITH AFFIRM that I wish, as much as I possibly can, to base my actions on my beliefs and thus contribute to a world where justice and compassion rule and greed and hatred are diminished.

Signed_____

Date_____
(Keep this copy for your records)

Please keep one copy and mail the other copy of your signed pledge to:

World Citizenship Institute
204 Busbee Road
Knoxville, Tennessee, 37920, USA.

Please include your contact information so we can send you your world citizenship card and occasional updates. Also, please share with us a written copy of your dreams and visions for a new earth so we may to share them with others.

WORLD CITIZENSHIP CREED

As a citizen of the world...

I BELIEVE in the dignity of all humanity, that each person is a being of supreme worth.

I BELIEVE in the wholeness of the human race, undivided by economic, cultural, racial, sexual or national differences.

I BELIEVE in the stewardship of life and resources to the end that all may mutually benefit from the earth's bounty... that no person may have to go without food or shelter.

I BELIEVE in the primacy of human relationships, as a person committed and responsible to other persons, regardless of their economic status, race, creed or nationality.

I BELIEVE in the global community, interdependent and mutually responsible for our physical and social environments.

I BELIEVE that we are One World and affirm that I am a citizen of this world. My allegiance to it and its people, my brothers and sisters, is primary over all other political entities.

I AM, therefore committed to the promotion and care of the whole of humanity without partiality or prejudice and with such resources as I have at my command, both within and without.

I HEREWITH AFFIRM that I wish, as much as I possibly can, to base my actions on my beliefs and thus contribute to a world where justice and compassion rule and greed and hatred are diminished.

Signed_____

Date_____